7

THE COUNTER TENOR

Also by Peter Giles:
A Monster Unto Many

THE COUNTER TENOR

PETER GILES

with additional material by
David Mallinder

FREDERICK MULLER LIMITED
LONDON

First published in Great Britain 1982
by Frederick Muller Limited, Dataday House,
London, SW19 7JU

Copyright © Peter Giles 1982

British Library Cataloguing in Publication Data
Giles, Peter
   The counter tenor.
   1. Vocal music—History and criticism
   I. Title
   784   ML1400
   ISBN 0-584-10474-x

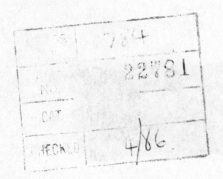

Photoset in VIP Bembo by
D. P. Media Limited, Hitchin, Hertfordshire,
and printed in Great Britain by Biddles Ltd,
Guildford.

CONTENTS

Dedication

Alfred Deller, in memoriam

FOREWORD

I really feel that this book should be subtitled 'Everything you ever wanted to know about counter tenors, but were afraid to ask'. Those incessant, but perfectly justified questions like 'How did you discover that you were a counter tenor?' or 'What IS the difference between a male alto and a counter tenor?' now have their answer, backed up by an impressive amount of historical and musicological information. Although we counter tenors are now hopefully an integral part of the musical scene, there was still a great need for a sensible, factual study which didn't read as an apology or as an excuse. The fact that we sing at a higher pitch than the other adult male voices does not instantly make us a peculiar breed apart – distant relatives of the castrati. There is no 'mystique'. We are just singers who, for one reason or another, have preferred to develop the upper reaches of our voices, and this has become a natural means of vocal expression.

It is only right that this book should be dedicated to the late Alfred Deller; we are all in his debt.

JAMES BOWMAN
London, March 1981

ACKNOWLEDGEMENTS

Although this book was conceived and most of the research was carried out several years ago, it was written between August 1980 and January 1981. Pressure from other creative commitments was such that I asked my vocal pupil and friend David Mallinder to act as a semi-independent amanuensis for the first six pages of Chapter 3, to write out a succinct description of the basic workings of the normal human larynx in Chapter 4, following our valuable discussions with Alan Ardouin, the laryngologist; and to contribute most of the appendix, 'The Counter Tenor and the Parish Choir'.

For these and general help in the present work, I warmly thank him.

I gratefully acknowledge and thank all others who helped in the preparation of this book. First, Alan Ardouin, F.R.C.S., D.L.O., for his expert help concerning the physiological section; then John Wheeler for his photographic generosity and advice; my wife Elizabeth for endless patience and practical assistance; the Dean and Chapter of Canterbury Cathedral for allowing me the run of the cathedral library and extending to me their very generous permission to use any material I needed. I thank them too for allowing John Wheeler to photograph during a service and a choir rehearsal. I extend my thanks to Dr Allan Wicks, Organist of Canterbury Cathedral, and the choristers, lay clerks and choral scholars of the choir for being patient during the flashing of bulbs.

I am especially grateful to James Bowman for his foreword and for reading the manuscript, also to John Whitworth, Martin Renshaw and Alan Ridout for reading it too and for various invaluable help and advice. I thank Mrs Peggy Deller and Mark Deller for their assistance in the provision of photographs of Alfred Deller and for the additional information and insight they were able to provide about his life and work. My thanks also to Anthony West and Wil and Dymmy Barten for help in additional research.

Acknowledgements and in most cases thanks for their generosity are due to the following for their permission to reproduce illustrations and music in this book: *Chatham News*, the Dean and Chapter of Canterbury Cathedral, the Department of the Environment, the Guildhall Library, *Kent Messenger*, James Bowman, John Whitworth, Mrs Pamela Bridger, Mrs Peggy Deller, Novello & Co. Ltd., Paul Esswood, The Royal College of Music, The Victoria and Albert Museum and Sydney Spence.

Acknowledgements are similarly due to those who allowed quotations to be made from other copyright material: Collins Ltd. – *Collins Encyclopaedia of Music*; David Higham Associates – *Music in Medieval*

Britain, by Frank Harrison; David Wulstan for 'The Alto or Counter Tenor Voice', from *Vocal Pitch in 16th Century Polyphony*; the Dean and Chapter of Canterbury for various works in the Cathedral library; Dobson Books Ltd. for *Bel Canto* by Elster Kay; Duckworth Ltd. for *The Grand Tradition* by J. B. Steane; Ernest Benn Ltd. for *A History of British Music* by Percy M. Young; Faber Ltd. for musical examples originating in *Masterpieces of Music before 1750*; Harvard University Press for an entry from *Harvard Dictionary of Music* by Willi Apel; Joseph Patelson Music House for *The Free Voice* by Cornelius L. Reid; Julian Gardiner for *A Guide to Good Singing and Speech*; Methuen Ltd. for *English Cathedral Music* by E. H. Fellowes; Michael and Mollie Hardwick for *Alfred Deller: A Singularity of Voice*; Novello and Co. Ltd. publishers of *The Musical Times*; *Opera* Magazine for material in the *Wexford Festival Review* by Rodney Milnes; Oxford University Press for *English Madrigal Composers* by E. H. Fellowes and various musical excerpts from *Medieval Music*, *The Church Anthem Book* and sheet music; Penguin Books Ltd. for 'The Raw Materials of Music' by Brian Trowell, from *The Pelican History of Music*; Peters Editions for 'Nachthelle' by Schubert; Princeton University Press for the selected list of music for men's voices; by J. Merrill Knapp; Royal School of Church Music for *English Church Music*, 1965; Robert Hale Ltd. for *The Voice of the Mind* by E. Herbert Caesari; Stainer and Bell Ltd. for *A Manual of Voice Training* (Galliard) by E. Davidson Palmer.

Apologies are due to the Executors of the late A. K. Holland whom I have failed to trace, for a quotation from *Henry Purcell – The English Musical Tradition*, and Anthony Frisell and his publishers Bruce Humphries of Boston, U.S.A. (three letters have been returned marked unknown) for a quotation from *The Tenor Voice*.

My thanks are also due to my editor, Katie Cohen of Frederick Muller Ltd., for her patience with a no-doubt infuriating Creative.

PETER GILES
Canterbury, March 1981

Introduction

COUNTER TENOR – THE MYTHICAL VOICE?

FOR YEARS NOW I have awaited the publication of a full length book on the counter tenor. Strangely, none has appeared. Why? The subject is a fascinating one.

I myself encountered a record of Alfred Deller when I was twelve or thirteen and I still remember the impact that he made. As adolescence progressed there was never any question but that I must myself sing counter tenor eventually if my voice continued the way it seemed to be heading. Indeed, my vocal change seemed to occur ambiguously. I was singing in a full range treble, progressively more piercing and powerful, until, aged sixteen and a half, I moved into the back stalls to sing alto, whereupon the top notes faded and I acquired a new, stronger bottom! From then on I read everything I could on voice; consulted eagerly every encyclopaedia of music, ancient and modern, to see how each defined alto and counter tenor. I searched through works on voice production by the cognoscenti of past and present. This is something I still do, and although it has brought me more dismay than joy, the balance *is* shifting.

In the 1950s there were very few articles of length available on the counter tenor/alto question and I soon exhausted these. Clearly the most useful was the famous paper by John Hough, *The Historical Significance of the Counter Tenor*, given to the Royal Musical Association in 1937. It was, and still is, a good springboard for the student. Nothing weightier existed. The few books on early music were helpful on the historical side, but not one suggested that the solo counter tenor existed any more, despite the living proof of Alfred Deller, and later, John Whitworth, of whom I soon began to hear. I could not understand why so few modern writers seemed to notice them, but just went on trotting out the same old information which could be summed up as follows: 'Falsetto singing, that peculiarly

English Cathedral Choir aberration, is weak, unnatural and unmanly. No singer worth the name indulges in it. Especially before the eighteenth century, much music was written for a legendary male alto called counter tenor. That voice is now extinct. Cathedral altos are at best a feeble, hooty bunch, useless for solo work.'

I began to wonder, if so few *appreciated* the counter tenor, or even admitted its modern existence, how likely it was to take its rightful place permanently. Looking back from 1980, it appears I need not have worried. Superb counter tenors abound. All seems well.

More written material on the subject, often contradictory, has appeared since the 1950s, and there have been a few broadcast talks. Yet there has been no comprehensive work, no long, serious book which combines musicological facts and considered opinion; appropriate musical history; something of the physiological background; psychological and sociological matter appertaining to the subject; and including discussion of the developments we might expect in the future and the possible dangers discernible in certain modern trends. Such a book would be a weighty encyclopaedia in itself, and I am not sure any single writer could attempt it. Until one does, the present volume is intended to fill the gap.

Here in Canterbury where the counter-tenor renaissance started, I am acutely aware of the late, great Alfred Deller looking over my shoulder. This present book was half complete when his biography, *A Singularity of Voice* by Michael and Mollie Hardwick (Proteus, 1980), was published in an enlarged edition on Deller's death. Apart from purely personal, fascinating material, it includes some succinct discussion of the counter-tenor question. I recommend it highly for obvious reasons, though I disagree slightly with some of its statements concerning the eighteenth century.

I hope that the following chapters will prove a help to fellow counter tenors, music students, the musically interested public, choir directors, and those singers who like myself are wearied by the eternal question: What is the difference between alto and counter tenor?

I originally titled the book *Counter tenor – the Mythical Voice?* because amidst the argument and debate one has often been *tempted* to cry let altos be called altos, tenors remain tenors and forget you ever heard the term counter tenor!

So I present here a mixture of fact, some personal opinion, and one counter tenor's twenty years' experience of a variety of solo and ensemble work, in England and in the United States, Canada and Europe, plus thirty-two years, boy and man respectively, in church and cathedral music.

This book is the brainchild not of a musicologist but of a working singer, one who has been deeply concerned for his subject over many years. Each chapter could clearly be in more detail to satisfy the specialist, but I make no apology for the general nature of some information given. This, the first book of its kind, is intended for a wide audience. Those desirous of further reading should refer to the bibliography.

This book is a greatly expanded version of lectures delivered in the United States, Canada and Britain, to audiences of university, college or high school students; musical societies and the general public. I am indebted to my associate, David Mallinder, for his suggestions and valuable extra research.

Great efforts have been made to obtain truly useful relevant illustrations. I have spent much time and thought on the matter; so many books of this type are either bland or the pictorial matter seems under-considered. It is therefore a great disappointment that I have been unable to find a print of the Chapel Royal, Whitehall Palace which Purcell and Blow knew, in which the King's four and twenty strings played so bravely, and which heard so much important music for counter tenor.

Some of my views may appear to contradict dearly loved traditionalist ones. A few learned vocal teachers may pick at my conclusions, even violently disagree; which vocal teacher does not disagree with the next? But for most I hope that this book, to use J. B. Phillips's admirable phrase, has *The Ring of Truth*. That is surely an appropriate way to refer to the sound of the counter-tenor voice.

Chapter 1

PREJUDICE AND THE STATUS QUO

ONLY RELATIVELY few years ago, to see the four soloists emerge onto the concert platform for a performance of Mendelssohn's *Elijah* was to encounter a status quo. Soprano, contralto, tenor and bass stood before us confidently as if put there by God. As it Was in the Beginning is Now and Ever Shall Be, World Without End, Amen. Yet it was *not* from the beginning at all, only since the mid-nineteenth century.

There were of course certain permitted variations, known as mezzo-soprano, baritone, and bass baritone; but they, then and even now, are often billed either soprano, contralto, or bass, respectively, because those words occur on the title page of some particular musical work. This status quo, indeed the characteristics of the oratorio *Elijah* itself, originated in an age of unyielding order and strait-laced establishment which were challenged only at great risk. Even the subject matter of *Elijah*, the rebellion but eventual return of the people of God to Him and His true way, could be said to epitomise the thinking of Victoria's age. The scandals and improprieties of the eighteenth century were past and best forgotten. There was a tremendous confidence in the way forward. The tenor soloist speaks for nineteenth-century hopes and ideals when, near the end of *Elijah*, he sings in the sumptuous key of A flat major: 'Then shall the righteous shine forth as the sun in their heav'nly Father's realm.'

At the height of its long popularity, Mendelssohn's great oratorio rivalled and challenged the pre-eminent place Handel's *Messiah* held and still holds in England.

Of course our society is very different from that which produced Mendelssohn. Victorian thinking has long been overturned in most human spheres of activity, and mainly for the good, but its influence is still strong in the conservative world of serious music.

'You're crazy,' someone will protest; 'think of the Promenaders at

I

the last night of the Proms – how informal can you get? And there's André Previn conducting in roll neck sweater or other casuals – he's a live wire. It's all nowhere near so *stuffy* as it was!'

However, think of the archetypal stern-faced chamber recital seemingly alive and well (surely Mozart wasn't meant to appear funereal; and certainly in England there was no such thing as a purely instrumental chamber recital in the eighteenth century). More to the point, what of the larger choral societies continuing to roar out *Messiah*, two or three hundred strong sometimes, despite Watkins Shaw and the fact that Handel intended the work for a small band and a choir of perhaps thirty-five? And how often do we hear Handel's alternative versions of various arias? Think of the Baroque and classical works, especially Bach,. with his high alto arias, still performed a tone or semitone higher because the modern instruments – i.e. mostly late nineteenth-century pattern – are not at the original pitch of the music.

The excuse is made that transposition is not uniformly possible. This leaves many masterpieces just outside the range of most counter tenors. There has been very little effort from the non-specialist orchestras to play earlier music on the authentic instruments. Of course, it is a complex problem for large orchestras, but authentic instruments are being produced in reasonable numbers. It is questionable whether all colleges of music have moved wholeheartedly on these matters when planning their student tuition. Either way, little evidence of it has reached general public performance yet, except for small specialist orchestras and ensembles playing in large cities to the esoteric interest, and of course the controlled world of the gramophone record industry with its hidden resources and infinite possibilities.

Thurston Dart in his *The Interpretation of Music* reminds us of the effect that authentic pitch would have on our favourite masterpieces:

> Thus Bach's *Mass in B minor* ought properly to be performed in B flat minor or even A minor; the opening movement of *Messiah* should be in D sharp minor; Beethoven's *Ninth Symphony* should be in D flat minor or even in C (which would make the solo and chorus parts much less of a strain to sing). Obviously transpositions of this kind will sometimes be quite impossible to carry out, since they make certain passages quite unplayable on instruments using today's standard tuning.

Even if they were playable, some purists would object to such transpositions, maintaining that the modern instruments lack more than merely the correct early pitch for pre-nineteenth century works, but tone, timbre, delicacy, and so on. They are right of course, but it does seem unnecessarily hard on certain voices, notably the counter tenor, to be denied participation in works which are so suitable, and often in their original fine repertoire. Thurston Dart certainly was of the opinion that some transposition attempt should be made: 'Many highly publicised attempts at producing authentic versions of this or that piece of early music have quite ignored the question of restoring it to its proper pitch, though there seems little doubt that when such transpositions are possible they should be carried out.'

On we go, however, still held by the obstinate nineteenth-century attitudes to custom and pitch, despite recent advances. Our modern B minor is not Bach's B minor. Even in the 1980s, and despite, perhaps almost because of the contemporary world of 'pop' music in which flauntingly untrained voices of young men and women swap places amongst electronic gadgetry and decibels, the strait-jacket of the nineteenth century will not quite disappear in serious or 'art' music.

And so, despite the growing number of counter tenors, despite the existence in performing editions of a wealth of literature for this particular voice, there is a sense of 'thus far and no further'. In fact there is almost a counter tenor recession. Contraltos, called alto, and high tenors have begun to reappear in specialist early music in place of counter tenors. We seem to have reached an invisible barrier made of three elements. One is either a dissatisfaction with the performance of counter tenors or the beginning of a fashion swing. Another is still a certain reluctance in some 'conventional' musical circles to accept the counter tenors on truly *equal* terms. The third is to do with *general public* taste and prejudice.

The whole world of serious music is itself the subject of incredible prejudice. It is ignored good-naturedly, or scornfully dismissed as irrelevant by a now sizeable and growing proportion of the general public, who know nothing of any tradition before Elvis Presley and care less. J. B. Steane, in *The Grand Tradition*, 1974, puts it all so well. For 'opera' read 'serious' or 'trained':

Perhaps consignment to the museum is the inevitable fate both of grand opera and the tradition of singing associated with it. Perhaps for the majority of people, the average television-viewer, the fate has already overtaken; an evening's opera on the television, or the appearance of some celebrated (in other words, unheard-of) opera singer is an obvious occasion for switching over to the other channel. More powerful than the modern composer is modern pop-culture, and that has now taken hold long enough for 'singing' to mean something quite different. To the average youngster, the sound of the operatic soprano voice on records or television is now quite actively unpleasant: it sounds unnatural, being so high above the speaking voice, it sounds assertive, unfriendly and uncomfortably loud in its power, and its quality carries a mental image that is somewhat comical. The male operatic voice is easier to take, and most will see, in a theoretical kind of way, that there is 'something in it'. But 'singing' means something else: it may be deafeningly loud coming over the amplifiers, or it may be the merest breathing into the microphone, but its purpose is to express a lifestyle which is in utter opposition to all that grand opera and its traditions seem to them to stand for. Grandeur is implied in the whole nature of opera: its theatres, its formalities, the size and complexity of its resources, its social history, its principal subjects, its kind of singing. There is nothing more remote from the pop-world, and this utter remoteness from popular culture is something new. Only thirty or forty years ago, popular singing had something in common with operatic singing . . . These links with the singing-style of grand opera have largely disappeared. Sometimes a pop-singer will show that he has a voice: he will sing high A's and B flats without apparent difficulty and the sound could obviously be trained to good effect. There may be a strong personality, and some musical feeling: a generation or two ago this pop-star would have found his voice, would have warbled 'Because' or 'Santa Lucia' until he heard a record of Caruso, would decide that that was the life for him and would set out on a career which in those days could have a glamour beyond that of rival attractions. The tradition has in fact depended very much on recruitment from unsophisticated people, whose voices were an asset they learnt to try out in fields, churches, private and public houses, and who would bring both respect and vitality to the art they were to serve. And what they took up, though involving formidable disciplines, was not absolutely foreign to what they already knew. 'Two lovely black eyes' or 'La paloma' or 'Old folks at home' were fairly and squarely diatonic and regular in rhythm; so were the Toreador's Song or any of the roles in *Il Trovatore*. But to move from the world of T. Rex to *The Knot Garden* involves the sort of inter-planetary travel that the wonders of our age can do little to facilitate. The grand tradition is caught up in a complex of cultural change.

(By kind permission of Duckworth Ltd.)

So we have a fascinating situation: on the one hand a tradition legitimate and honoured, successor to the Romantic, Classical and Baroque, going back to Renaissance and Medieval times, but hidebound in many matters. Next to it, another tradition, recent and clearly illegitimate, artificial, of mammon, in many ways barbaric, all too prey to the whim of the moment and the wave of the manipulator's chequebook; but at least utterly free to go where it will within its limited abilities and 'cultural' boundaries. The first is the undoubted arena for, surely, the ultimate in vocal and instrumental technique, for mankind's most profound musical experiences and statements. The second, for the most part and with the exception of the art form 'jazz' and certain musicianly groups like 'Sky', comprises ephemera perhaps more of interest to the sociologist than the true artist musician.

The highest male voice has been re-accepted half-heartedly by the legitimate tradition, but only half-heartedly. For example, imagine putting on a 'popular' performance of Handel's *Messiah* for Christmas in your local town hall. The local choral society is perhaps to be joined by the local operatic society (which in England invariably means operetta). The four soloists alone are engaged from outside. How many organisers of such a venture would even consider using a counter tenor and not a comfortable contralto?

Comparatively little new music is composed for solo counter tenor, yet in what we will call the illegitimate tradition, the influence of the Beatles and their wilder descendants (with more than a glance at the Afro-American tradition), has made use of the falsetto commonplace. This at least might make the situation look brighter. Yet even this is not certain. For despite the Promenade Concerts, most though admittedly not all, the same young folk who listen happily to untrained, strained falsettos shrieking would, as J. B. Steane has pointed out, run a mile from any seriously trained voice, including counter tenor, performing quality music of almost any period, including the avant-garde compositions of the present day.

It may be justly claimed that the King's Singers are highly trained academic musicians, and they could not be more popular. They sing only the lightest material on television, however, and seldom are the counter tenors heard *alone*. The smoothness and blend of the group is all. Anyway, this popular side of the King's Singers does *not* appeal to real pop culturists, but to 'light' music enthusiasts.

While the real pop world has undeniably welcomed the male falsetto, it is, in my opinion, for the wrong reasons! True, we should rejoice that youngsters seem no longer 'hung up' on the *sexuality* of vocal pitch. But surely what they are celebrating, even flaunting, is sexual *ambiguity* for its own purposes.

There is a real worry that, far from helping the course of the counter tenor, pop just may be damaging it. For to many serious musicians, and other people who refuse to pay even lip-service to 'pop' (our modern emperor with no clothes), the degeneracy they see in beat music will include the sexually ambiguous and that could to them include the falsettists. So there is a chance that the situation could relapse, that the pop world, far from helping the counter tenor, might actually cause the pendulum to swing back to square one. It might even in the end *reinforce* the nineteenth-century status quo in art music.

It is of course theoretically possible that the pop world one day might prove to have played a creative part in the wearing down of musico-sexual prejudices and hang-ups. Perhaps we may be able to discern that the acceptance of counter tenors, not as novelties smiled on patronisingly or endured in the name of authenticity, but accepted on *equal* terms with other voices, owed much to the excesses of pop culture.

It is my opinion that the majority of adults still retain the primitive notion that the serious singing voice *must* express sex in the most obvious way of all: pitch. So this prejudice now stands in the way of art. Perhaps for prejudice we should read custom: custom that a woman's singing voice must always sound higher than a man's merely because speaking voices usually do.

There have been improvements. We have seen how the King's Singers, sporting two counter tenors, are regularly seen on television. How different it was even fourteen years ago. In 1966, twenty-three years after Deller's debut, I was teaching full time in a small town grammar school, and taking part in a concert given by several musical staff members before a large audience of parents. I was to sing a Scarlatti solo alto cantata and I felt slightly self-conscious, singing for the first time in the school, but it went well, and was followed by applause. At the social gathering afterwards a few compliments came my way (I had been the only 'professional' in the concert). Yet it was the head of classics, a friendly man of about fifty, who came up confidentially and whispered with an extremely embarrassed expression: 'That voice – it's only normally a *church* voice, isn't it – you wouldn't *normally* sing in *public* with it would you?'

I tried to explain in a few sentences. He listened. Then, as if he had not heard, said: 'Yes, but you wouldn't *normally* sing in public like that, surely?'

It was useless. I dropped the subject and he never mentioned it again. I felt betrayed, for he was an *educated* man, a man of Greek philosophy, ancient wisdom, history and language, a man who knew of the music of the spheres. Yet it was he, and not some upstart chemistry master who was shocked! I knew what the Psalmist meant when he mourned: 'But it was even thou my companion, my guide and mine own familiar friend!'

Yes, we have progressed since 1966, but there is still much misunderstanding of the high male voice when connected not with variety turns but serious music. Much of it stems from the legendary castrati and the monumental backlash which followed in the

6

nineteenth century. Perhaps nineteenth-century opera is responsible for the following 'traditional' static vocal system, traditional for 175 years anyway:

SOPRANO: Heroine.
CONTRALTO: Heroine's friend, queen or mother-earth figure.
TENOR: Hero, or light relief.
BASS: Villain, trusty old friend, or father.

(This simplistic list is merely an indication. Clearly there are more characters in most operas.)

Jonathan Miller, writing in 1980 in the *Radio Times* about a forth-coming programme of his, describes beautifully what has happened to opera: 'Opera is encrusted with barnacles and seaweed and the accumulated mess of virtually 100 years of often very thoughtless productions. I think it's often necessary to scrape that off in order to get back to the clean lines of its original artificiality.' We surely may assume that included in the 'scraping off' operation of which he speaks is the careful examination of voice allocation in pre-nineteenth-century opera and the opening up, in new works, of the static vocal system listed above.

Most people are surprised to learn that like the oratorio 'big four' this system, this *operatic* status quo, was not always so. For example, the eighteenth-century castrati were not just tolerated. Their fine voices and incredible technique earned them idolisation and follow-ings similar to present-day pop stars. A very big man singing the hero's part but at soprano pitch would startle many of today's average operatic-selection lovers. Yet high voices have always fascinated peo-ple. *The Times* music critic, writing at the very end of the 1950s, said:

> . . . The long held top notes of an Italian soprano are sometimes hardly distinguishable from a scream and are therefore at once repellent and delightful. Heroic parts are always given to tenors – only Verdi admitted baritones to respectability. The angelic choir-boy is admired for his high notes. Folk singers regularly pitch their songs as high as their voices can manage. The eighteenth century liked the loud, strong, and high sounds of the castrato . . . So does taste dictate to nature. Perhaps it is this very versatility of the larynx that assures its permanent pre-eminence among instruments of music.

So it should become obvious why the counter tenor had appealed so much for centuries. But it is necessary to shake off an inheritance of purely nineteenth-century notions in order to understand. As we begin our investigation it would be as well to ignore the vexed alto versus counter tenor argument until later discussion.

The present book mostly confines itself to European culture, the chief influence for obvious reasons on North American white culture at its beginning. But though they require a separate study, there must be a sideways glance at other rich traditions – Negro, Aboriginal and Asian – which relate to our subject.

Chapter 2

THE COUNTER TENOR IN HISTORY

WE MUST ACKNOWLEDGE that the nomenclature of voices was centuries in settling. The word 'tenor' occurs first. Ignore its modern meaning as a medium or high male voice. It started, the way all terms started, as a part to be sung or played. Tinctoris, the Flemish theorist and composer, wrote in 1487: 'In loud music a tenor part is played on a bombard, a low contratenor (and indeed often any contratenor) on a trombone.' To take a later example, Anthony Wood of Oxford, speaking of the year 1657, said: 'Gentlemen in private meeting played three, four and five parts with viols – as treble viol, tenor, counter tenor and bass . . .'

We still talk in similar language of instrumental parts or harmony paperwork on occasion. This does not mean that the instrument is, for example, an actual human voice. But there is no doubt that the human voice has always led musical development. In a later chapter we discuss details of physical voice production, but shall now examine the development of the sung parts as harmony which led to the term counter tenor.

Although harmony existed in various forms and cultures centuries before Gregorian chant, it is to unison plainsong we must first turn, for it is the basis of modern Western harmony. The following historical sequence is of course much simplified. Notice how other parts clearly to be sung by voices of counter tenor (alto) range often occur other than on that line labelled contra or counter tenor, when it appears. Remember that because the counter tenor was a part, appropriate voices sang it at whatever pitch it appeared.

As primitive harmony and counter point began their slow development, the plainsong melody remained the main tune (the vox principalis or tenor, not consistent in range, sometimes pitched high as for a modern tenor voice, sometimes more baritone in character; sometimes even pitched as high as a modern counter tenor line). This

9

'tenor' was added to by first one part then another over many years of experiment.

We are so accustomed to regard developments in any art as a logical creative progression that we often forget that steps forward can come as a result of an observed accident. In music, I would venture that the first known harmony, called organum, probably happened because a tone-deaf monk or dozy cleric droned unknowingly above or below his brethren in Quire. And lo, there hath come something new! Or perhaps it was caused by the frustration experienced by someone whose instincts drove him to create a counter melody.

Mode 4 (Hypophrygian)

[Solo]

Laus_____ De___ o____ Pa - tri pa - ri____ li - que____ Pro - li,

et ti - bi___ San___cte stu - di - o per____ en___ ni___ Spi___ ri____ tus,

no - stro____ re____ so - net ab____ o____ re om____ ne per____ ae - vum.

Example 1 *Antiphon,* Laus Deo Patri. *Psalm 113,* Laudate pueri.
(By permission of Faber and Faber Ltd.)

The first exposition of the nature of strict organum occurs as early as the ninth century in *Musica Enchiriadis*. The added part (vox organalis, later descant) was at first beneath, then subsequently either above or below the plainsong tenor, or even both, doubled in octaves, note for note. The result is known as parallel organum. (Depending on the set pitch of the tenor, this could produce alternatively or simultaneously an accidental, temporary 'bass' and accidental, temporary 'alto'. The latter could well have been a falsetto part.)

If boys were present in Quire, they would be likely to sing discant where it was in their range – almost certainly with only their low chest register at first – to join with the higher men's voices.

From about 1100, the vox organalis began to be placed only above the vox principalis. This important move created what came to be the standard relationship between a plainsong and one additional voice.

By the mid-twelfth century, free organum had been developed. It was no longer note for note, and it often moved in contrary motion. In the following example, the plainsong tenor is interrupted by *tropes* (two basic freely-composed non-plainsong parts). It is worth remembering that ordinary unison plainsong continued as 'bread-and-butter' chanting throughout the development of organum. Harmonised pas-

Example 2 *Parallel organum (9th century) sequence,* Rex caeli, Domine.
(By permission of Faber and Faber Ltd.)

sages did not displace, but were added to unison plain-chant, and these were mostly sung either by soloists or perhaps a smaller group. Notice that in the example the trope voices are equal, pitched about our modern tenor range, crossing each other freely. The harmonic intervals are octaves, fifths, fourths and unisons – consonances – and a few thirds, regarded at this date as dissonances.

The older, note-for-note organum became known as discantus style (it remained very popular); the newer was simply termed organum style.

Example 3 *Free organum (12th century) trope,* Agnus Dei.
(By permission of Faber and Faber Ltd.)

In the twelfth and thirteenth centuries, melismatic organum continued the development of independent counterpoint. The plainsong tenor moves slowly in the example given, while the upper organal part moves freely, utterly independent of the lower part.

The great Parisian school of Notre Dame produced the important composers Léonin (*c.* 1170) and Pérotin (*c.* 1200), from whom the last organum example comes. It is in mixed form. The plainsong tenor is now combined with two upper parts which dance freely across each

Example 4 *Melismatic organum. School of St Martial,* Benedicamus
Domino.
(By permission of Faber and Faber Ltd.)

other in dotted rhythm and phrases of different lengths. We may
assume that these parts were sung by voices resembling our modern
counter tenor or tenor.

The terms vox principalis and vox organalis had begun to be
superseded by the terms tenor (tenere – to hold) and duplum, second
part, sometimes labelled motetus (with text) and triplum, third part
(seemingly the ancestor of treble). Pérotin sometimes even added a
quadruplum, fourth part. We should remember these parts were sung
by any voices able to sustain them. There was no labelling yet of the
human voice itself in any way. This would have been difficult in any
case. (See Aelred of Rievaulx and John of Salisbury.)

There is still disagreement over which preceded which – contra-
tenor or the part triplum. What must be remembered is that while
triplum simply means a third added part, contra-tenor describes not
just a part but a *device*, see p.14.

Once polyphonic music began to develop in earnest, there were
difficulties arising from the inevitable experiments being made.
Aelred of Rievaulx (*c.* 1109–1166) issued a commination against what
he disliked in the church music he witnessed. There is much in it of
interest. First, the picture it gives of the *nature* of the sound made;
second, the ambiguous uses of musical terms – i.e. a man singing
treble – and third, a reminder that the voices were seldom unaccompanied, but coloured with various instruments. Also remember that
the translator, Prynne, was acquainted with Stuart technical terms.

Whence hath the Church so many organs and musicall instruments?
To what purpose, I pray you, is that terrible blowing of belloes,
expressing rather the crashes of thunder than the sweetnesse of a

Example 5 *Pérotin (12th century) organum,* Alleluya (Nativitas).
(By permission of Faber and Faber Ltd.)

voyce? To what purpose serves that contraction and inflection of the voyce? This man sings a base, that a small meane, another a treble, a fourth divides, and cuts asunder, as it were, certain middle notes: and while the voyce is strained, anon it is remitted, now it is dashed and then again it is enlarged with a lowder sound. Sometimes, which is a shame so to speake, it is enforced into a horse's neighing: sometimes the masculine vigour being laid aside it is sharpened with the shrillnesse of a woman's voyce: now and then it is writhed and retorted into a certaine artificial circumvolution. Sometimes thou may'st see a man with an open mouth, not to sing, but to breathe out his last gaspe by shutting in his breath, and by a certain ridiculous interception of his voyce as it were to threaten silence . . . In the meantime the common people standing by, trembling and astonished, admire the sound of the organ, the noyse of the cymballs and musicall instruments, the harmony of the pipes and cornets.

(Speculum Charitatis, 1123)

Aelred also suggests particular vocal effects like nasal tremolando and vibrato that were a particular characteristic of the Paris Notre Dame School. It is clear that he was used to four part singing, which was quite common by the start of the thirteenth century. John of Salisbury (d. 1180) was also worried by much of what he heard:

> The very service of the Church is defiled, in that before the face of the Lord, in the very sanctuary of sanctuaries, they, showing off as it were, strive with the effeminate dalliance of wanton tones and musical phrasing to astound, enervate, and dwarf simple souls. When one hears the excessively caressing melodies of voices beginning, chiming in, carrying the air, dying away, rising again, and dominating, he may well believe that it is the song of the Sirens and not the sound of men's voices; he may marvel at the flexibility of tone which neither the nightingale, the parrot, or any bird with greater range than these can rival. Such indeed is the ease of running up or down the scale, such the dividing or doubling of the notes and the repetitions of the phrases and their incorporation one by one; the high and the very high notes are so tempered with the low or somewhat low that one's very ears lose the ability to discriminate, and the mind, soothed by such sweetness, no longer has power to pass judgement upon what it hears. When this type of music is carried to the extreme it is more likely to stir lascivious sensations in the loins than devotion in the heart. But if it is kept within reasonable limits it frees the mind from care, banishes worry about things temporal, and by imparting joy and peace and by inspiring a deep love for God draws souls to association with the angels.
>
> (*Frivolities of Courtiers and Footprints of Philosophers*,
> a translation of Policraticus by John of Salisbury, ed. Pike, 1938)

During the twelfth century, in France, non-plainsong tenors began to appear, called conductus, free melodies which were later harmonised like the plainsong tenors, but in simpler rhythmic structures, and similar in all parts. The parts used the same terms as the organum compositions. Composers rather lost interest in this conductus form to concentrate on the development of the motet. A medieval theorist, describing the procedure for composing conductus, gives us a valuable contemporary account of method. 'First choose the loveliest melody you can think of, then write a descant to it in the manner shown. If you wish to add a third part, look carefully at the melody and the descant, so that the third part will not be discordant with them both together.'

During the late thirteenth century another part was added, contra-tenor, or sometimes simply concordans, lower than discantus but 'against' the tenor, i.e. straddling or crossing it freely, much as the trope voices of the free organum example did with each other.

The contra-tenor sometimes achieved intervals strange for the time – occasionally a major seventh may be seen. Bear in mind also that motetus and triplum are obviously falsetto parts.

Example 6 *Isorhythmic motet. Anonymous (English early 14th century).*
(By kind permission of O.U.P.)

Guillaume de Machaut (*c.* 1300–1377) is a brilliant figure and leader
of Ars Nova, the New Art. He composed the first fully polyphonic
Mass. At least, *Messe de Notre Dame* is the earliest extant complete
polyphonic setting. The next example demonstrates not only how
low the contra-tenor part could be, as it fulfilled the duties of both the
modern bass and (in this case) the modern tenor, but that it was
probably an *instrumental* part in this particular instance.

There is no text set for it in the original; it may have been played on
the organ. Interestingly, the motetus part here corresponds to our
modern alto part in range. We are still far from a settled nomenclature.

In the written form of the originally improvisatory technique eventually known as English discant or descant, a plainsong was 'harmonised' usually as the middle voice of three. The three parts moved
largely in note by note fashion. Discant or descant had remained a
favourite device, and in England it was to take the development of
harmony a large step forward with its amazing thirds and sixths. In

Example 7 *Guillaume de Machaut (c. 1300–c. 1377) Agnus Dei (1) from*
Mass VIII.
(By permission of Faber and Faber Ltd.)

fact, the almost peculiarly English fondness for descants, i.e. an added
melody high above a hymn or song, is still noticeable today.

English conservatism proved to be both a strength and the way
forward in the fifteenth century. John Dunstable, who died in 1435,
was of great importance in the development of European music. He
was hailed in the 1470s by Tinctoris as the leading English composer
of the earlier English School, and the father of a new age in music.
Dunstable's origins led him to be in true English style at once conservative and adventurous, experimenting more fully with the older
forms. Among them were the further possibilities of discant.

Dunstable treated the top part increasingly as a harmonised tune in
the modern manner. English faburden is thus closely related to discant. Example 8 is part of an antiphon in faburden style, *Ave
Regina Coelorum*. The Marian plainsong tune (developed with additions) is mostly in the top part (discant); the faburden part proper is the

second line down (contra-tenor), and it is this part which supplies the characteristic sweetness of the English style. (The main harmonies are all $\frac{6}{3}$ and $\frac{5}{8}$ chords, disregarding the ornamental additions). What is nicely called the migrant cantus firmus – the occasional placing of the plainsong in another part for the odd phrase – is an English invention. It is interesting to note in both examples 8 and 9 that the discant part seems to be our modern high or first counter tenor voice. Example 8 has contra-tenor as either a low counter tenor or a modern tenor, the tenor part as a modern second tenor or baritone.

Example 8 *Antiphon* Ave Regina Coelorum, *John Dunstable.*
(By kind permission of Penguin Books Ltd.)

Example 9 by Lionel Power (*c.* 1370–1445) also demonstrates the English manner of the harmonised tune. Note that the lowest voice is labelled 'counter' – an early Anglicising of contra-tenor – and is of baritone range. It is an early contra-tenor bassus, while like the Dunstable, the discant part is the vocal equivalent of contra-tenor altus and is clearly an alto part. Discant and superius seem interchangeable labels, as is often the case.

Example 9 *Votive antiphon in English discant style. Lionel Power*
(c.1370–1445).
(By kind permission of O.U.P.)

Boys' voices were used more and more over the course of years.
The choral range spread both upwards and downwards. Eventually,
the contra-tenor became permanently split into two distinct parts, at
first labelled contra-tenor and contra-tenor secundus, then contra-
tenor altus and contra-tenor bassus. Losing their unique involvement
with the tenor, thereafter they remain each side of it except for special
effects. These two separate parts eventually discarded their contra-
tenor prefix, first the lower then the higher; but the latter, the altus,
always kept contra-tenor as its alternative title.

There was continued indecision as to what the lower part should be
called. Although the simple term bassus eventually won the day,

manuscripts are full of a variety of names for the new bass part. Subcontra, baritonans, baricanor, baripsaltes, basis, basistenor, and theumatenor are just a few other examples.

The split in the contra-tenor occurred in the mid-fifteenth century, and two composers associated with the resulting establishment of the modern four part choir are Johannes Ockegham (1425–95) and Jacob Obrecht (1430–1505). The previously tight-knit medieval voice parts have now become carefully spaced strata in which the new four voices had definitive territory in which to move (see example 10). The tenor now tended to remain a slightly higher part in the texture as a result of the new bassus permanently below. The contra-tenor altus had risen correspondingly. Example 11, part of an English Mass, demonstrates this well.

The range of early *mean* parts suggests that counter tenors might well have sung them either alone or with boys using chest register. Later of course the mean range became a higher part and was surely sung exclusively by boys. The modern treble part is a fusion of the early high treble and mean parts.

These early male choirs were both the product of, and catalyst to, the development of European harmony. Thus all European choral music has the monastic or collegiate choir as its ancestor. We know of course that plainsong was also sung by nuns. They may have sung some organum an octave higher, but it seems unlikely that they were the innovators. Had they been, basic vocal pitch would surely have been situated above middle C.

Gilbert of Sempringham, concerned at the spread of improper music in convents, said: 'We do not permit our nuns to sing. We absolutely forbid it, preferring with the Blessed Virgin to hymn indirectly in a spirit of humility rather than with Herod's notorious daughter to pervert the minds of the weak with lascivious strains.' By improper he merely meant the sinful voluptuousness of harmony. Gilbert followed in the footsteps of St Paul, who had said in his letter to Timothy: 'Let the women learn in silence, with all subjection, but I suffer not a woman to teach, not to usurp authority over men, but be in silence.'

Presumably this could hardly be appropriate in a convent, except in relation to visiting priests; but while smirking at Paul's male chauvinism, we should remember that because the early church took his instruction literally, mixed choirs were never even a remote possibility. This more than almost anything else was responsible for the development of the high male voice: falsetto, castrato and tenor altino. Women must have sung in some medieval secular music, but this activity would have been restricted, and probably confined to domestic music-making.

Example 10 *Johannes Ockegham (c.1425–1495). Sanctus (first section) from the* Missa prolationum.

So, because the male choir had the benefit of the full range of voices from lowest to highest, all important vocal developments took place in and as a result of these choirs. The boy trebles in a monastic or collegiate choir were educated at a school run by the foundation, either expressly to supply boy choristers, or because educating the young formed part of the function of most abbeys or minsters of any size. Sometimes one suspects it was a shrewd mixture of both.

Example 11. *Movement from cyclic mass. Cousin (mid 15th century).*
(By kind permission of O.U.P.)

As Frank L. Harrison says in *Medieval Music in Britain*:

The size and balance of the choirs of collegiate churches and colleges in the later Middle Ages, as well as what the statutes reveal about the qualifications and training of their members, show that the performance of polyphonic music was an essential part of their function. In their establishment of similar choirs the monasteries followed in the footsteps of the secular institutions, and at the same time took advantage of the presence of a qualified master for their stipendiary singers to employ him for some of their own services. The institution and development of balanced groups of singers was the most significant feature of the musical history of the later Middle Ages, and was comparable in importance to the rise of the orchestra in the eighteenth and nineteenth centuries. It was closely related to the origin and growth of choral polyphony, as distinct from the polyphony of soloists practised in the larger secular and monastic choirs in earlier centuries.

(By permission of David Higham & Associates)

Such an important situation requires a closer look. Percy M. Young explains that at least in England, cathedral and collegiate foundations were likely to be ahead of monastic choirs in the use of boys' voices. We know that in the last years of Edward I's reign, the Chapel Royal was brought into line with the cathedrals by the new employment of boy choristers.

In his *A History of British Music* Mr Young talks of the Sarum Customary, 1210:

Under the general direction of the Precentor of a cathedral vicars-choral and singing-boys performed the music of the Liturgy. The boys were housed in clergy residences and prepared for junior church appointments or for a higher education, leading to eventual promotion to the superior ranks of the clergy. The vicars-choral gradually formed themselves into separate corporations and throughout the Middle Ages occupied a position of some independence of and considerable importance in the development of church music. Subordinate to the vicars-choral there were in due course professional singing-men of lower ecclesiastical rank than that of deacon. These were the lay-clerks. In monastic foundations the whole community formed the choir which, as in a secular cathedral, was directed by the Precentor, to whom the Succentor acted as assistant. Instruction in plainsong was part of the education of every novice. That monks were sometimes inclined to protest against the imposition on them of a musical education is demonstrated by two monks, of the reign of Henry II, possibly from Norwich, who complained of the difficulties of learning church music in the poem 'Un-comly in Cloystre'. It was not until the fourteenth century that singing-boys were employed in the performance of liturgical music in monastic foundations; and only then outside the monks' choir. Until the fifteenth century larger groups of singers in church were concerned only with unison plainsong. Polyphony, as it developed, was for solo singers and players.

(By kind permission of Ernest Benn Ltd.)

This could suggest that extensive, higher counter tenor singing might well have developed earlier in England in monastic choirs than secular foundations with boys for the top line.

On the Continent, boys seem to have been employed regularly much earlier to sing liturgical music in monasteries. Odo of Saint-Maur (who studied at Cluny) wrote a musical handbook in the eleventh century, setting out a method of teaching boys to attain perfect sight reading in less than a week. The choirboys' lot was not easy: 'At Nocturns, if the boys commit any fault in the psalmody or other singing, either by sleeping or such like transgressions, let there be no sort of delay, but let them be stripped forthwith of frock and cowl and beaten in their shirts only, with pliant and smooth osia rods provided for that special purpose.'

In the Cluniac Monastary of Saint Benigne at Dijon (later the cathedral), and after Winchester's famed scriptorium had finished the Troper, Guido of Arezzo wrote in his antiphoner, explaining his system: 'Should anyone doubt that I'm telling the truth, let him come, make a trial, and hear what small boys can do under our direction, boys who have until now been beaten for their gross ignorance of the psalms.'

So boys were clearly used for the upper part at least in some monasteries and it seems strange that English monastic practice differed. If boys were present in monastic schools – as they certainly were at Canterbury, for example – then they could surely have sung the treble line in quire on occasion before the fourteenth century. The problem is that even late medieval manuscripts do not include details of specific voices or instruments to be used. All the indications are that they were often interchangeable.

Although monastic, cathedral and collegiate foundations varied in size (and some communities, full muster, were extremely large at the height of the monastic period, filling a large quire like Canterbury), choirs, i.e. specialist singers, were not big. We are all familiar with the small choral group in fifteenth-century art for example, standing round the same lectern singing from the same huge choir book. The average group is about ten – not that the artist would have been concerned normally to depict accurate numbers as some writers have suggested. A larger choir would have sung from part-books which began to be used from the mid-fifteenth century.

However large the singing community – the unison plainsong choir – these harmony 'semi-choruses' continued modest in size, the ancestors of our modern English cathedral and collegiate choirs which now average eighteen boys and eight men. From the last thirty years or so of the fifteenth century, contemporary illustrations show two large choir books which suggests that by this time both sides of the choir sang in harmony, and that the specialist singers were divided in the midst of the community. This Decani and Cantoris system survives today. (Dean's side and Precentor's side respectively.)

In 1347, the Chapel Royal of St Stephen, in the Palace of Westminster, numbered thirteen vicars, four clerks, and six boys. St George's Chapel, Windsor Castle, was similar. Cambrai Cathedral kept ten vicars and six boys in 1386, but things were more sparse in Italy. Mentions of reasonable numbers are rare, and in Milan Cathedral in 1407 only one singer was in employment. Later three men are mentioned by voice: soprano, tenor, and counter tenor, giving a clear idea of three part performance. The counter tenor was supposedly a counter tenor bassus. The word soprano is presumably used to mean falsettist. There are no records of castrati as early as this in church.

There were thirty singers in 1451–2 at the Chapel Royal, Westminster Palace, excluding boys. (There were later reductions under Edward IV and the early Tudors.) When the King travelled abroad he took with him about twenty men singers and a few boys.

The Papal choir numbered only nine in 1436, but increased to twenty-four by 1500. Ockegham joined the choir of Our Lady in Antwerp in 1443. There were on the Cantoris side twenty-five skilled singers; and twenty-six opposite, presumably to cope with plainsong in unison.

There are many written details of the sizes of the various establishments. Our chief interest in these records is the implied presence and proportional numbers of counter tenor singers. Of the skilled singers, at least one third must have been high counter tenor, i.e. alti, perhaps more as the voice grew ever more popular.

In York Minster in 1507, the vicars had to undertake to study polyphonic singing before proper admission. Each new vicar was required to take an oath to learn pricksong and faburden if he had a tenor voice, or descant, pricksong and faburden if his voice was not a tenor. This suggests that all non-tenors were expected to be able to supply both the highest and the lowest parts, in other words they were reckoned to be a collection of contra-tenori; some bassus, some altus. The implication is that the tenors stood apart as a vocal type.

We know that after William Cornyshe died in 1523, the Chapel Royal Choir was enlarged from ten to twelve boys. In Leckingfield Castle, Yorkshire, at about this time there existed a choral establishment rivalling the Chapel Royal. Other than Dean, Sub-Dean and a number of priests, there was a musical body of specific voices which indicates several points nicely for our purposes, among them the amount of singers per part and how the nomenclature had settled in normal parlance.

The lists are in the *Household Book* of Henry Algernon Percy, the powerful 5th Earl of Northumberland. Let us examine them well.

GENTYLLMEN *and* CHILDERYN *of the* CHAPELL.

ITEM Gentyllmen and Childryn of the Chapell xiij
Viz. Gentillmen of the Chapell viij Viz. ij Bassys – ij Tenors – and iiij Countertenors – Yoman or Grome of the Vestry j – Childeryn of the Chapell v Viz. ij Tribills and iij Meanys – xiiij.
Gentillmen of the Chapell – ix Viz. The maister of the Childre j – Tenors ij – Countertenors iiij – The Pistoler j – and oone for the Organys Childer of the Chapell – vj.
    ' The gentlemen ande childrin of my lordis chapell whiche be
' not appointid to uttend at no tyme, but oonely in exercifing of
' Goddis fervice in the chappell daily at Mattins, Lady-Mafs,
' Highe-Mafs, Even-fonge, and Complynge.

	' Gentlemen of my lordis chappell.
' Furft.	A bafs.
' Item.	A feconde bafs.
' Item.	The thirde bafs.
' Item.	A maifter of the childer, a countertenor.
' Item.	A feconde countertenour.
' Item.	A thirde countertenour.
' Item.	A iiijth countertenour.
' Item.	A ftanding tenour.
' Item.	A feconde ftanding tenour.
' Itcm.	A iijd ftandyng tenour.
' Item.	A fourth ftanding tenour.

	' Childrin of my lordis chappell.
' Item.	The fyrft child a trible.
' Item.	The ijd child a trible.

' Item.   The iijd child a trible.
' Item.   The iiijth child a fecond trible.
' Item.   The vth child a fecond trible.
' Item.   The vjth child a fecond trible.
'The noumbre of thois parfons as childrin of my lordis chap-
' pel vj.'
' The orderynge of my lordes chapell in the queare at
' mattyngis, mafs, and evynfonge. To ftonde in ordure as
' hereafter followeth, fyde for fyde daily.

' The deane fide.	' The feconde fide.
' The Deane.	' The Lady-maffe prieft.
' The fubdeane.	' The gofpeller.
' A baffe.	' A baffe.
' A tenor.	' A countertenor.
' A countertenor.	' A countertenor.
' A countertenor.	' A tenor.
' A countertenor.	' A countertenor.
	' A tenor.

' The ordurynge of my lordes chappell for the keapinge of our
' Ladyes maffe thorowte the weike.

' Sonday.	' Monday.
' Mafter of the Childer a coun- ' tertenor.	Mafter of the Childer a Coun- ' tertenor.
' A tenor.	' A countertenour.
' A tenour.	' A counter-tenour.
' A baffe.	' A tenor.
'Twifday.	' Wedynfday.
'Mafter of the childer a coun- ' tertenour.	' Mafter of the childer a coun- ' tertenor.
' A countertenour.	' A countertenour.
' A countertenour.	' A tenour.
' A tenour.	' A baffe.
' Thurfdaie	' Fryday.
' Mafter of the childer a coun- ' tertenor.	' Mafter of the childer a coun- ' tertenor.
' A countertenoure.	' A countertenour.
' A countertenoure.	' A countertenour.
' A tenoure.	' A baffe.

26

' Satturday.   ' Fryday.
' Mafter of the childer a coun-   ' And upon the faide Friday
      ' tertenor.   ' th'ool chapell, and evry day
    ' A countertenor.   ' in the weike when my lord
    ' A countertenour.   ' fhall be prefent at the faide
    ' A tenour.   ' maffe.

' The orduringe for keapinge weikly of the orgayns one after an
  ' outher as the namys of them hereafter followith weikly.

' The maifter of the childer, yf he be a player, the firft weke.
' A countertenor that is a player the ijde weke.
' A tenor that is a player the thirde weike.
' A baffe that is a player the iiijth weike.
' And every man that is a player to keep his cours weikly.'

Table 1 *The choir at Leckingfield Castle, Yorkshire in the early 16th century.*

Note that the bass coming first seems to have assumed more importance than the tenor line now. Also that in the more formal list of voice
parts the counter tenors are placed next to the basses, either in order of
prestige, or perhaps because of the shared origin of the two parts. Or
could this all merely be nothing more significant than alphabetical
order – B.,C.,T.?

The word 'standing' before tenor is interesting – possibly it is an
allusion to the traditional, but by that date largely obsolescent, role of
the tenor, to hold, to provide the 'cantus firmus', the 'vox principalis'.
(There are four tenors, presumably to allow for this historical role.)

Notice that the first counter tenor is the Master of the Children,
interesting because it underlines the obvious, that the highest male
voice is most suited to teach the boys their parts. The appointment
looks permanent. If not, surely the voice would have been listed first,
followed by the incidental post of Master. This dual role also suggests
that the origin of 'all choir-masters and organists sing alto' is an
ancient one. But as was customary at this date, the Chapel Singing
Men above took turns to play the organ.

At Chichester Cathedral in 1530, in addition to the existing foundation of vicars choral, there was added a 'foundation of four lay clerks'.
They were 'to be singers of polyphonic music, for their voices were to
blend well together and one at least should be a good natural bass,
while their combined voices should have a range of fifteen or sixteen

notes'. (See Sherborne's Donations, Sussex County Library, Chichester.) By Weelkes' time these four had been doubled to eight.

By the early sixteenth century it was clear that the 'traditional' English penchant for three part harmony was still favoured highly. Richard Cromwell, in Rome with an embassy, seems to have taken singers with him – possibly some of the Gentlemen of the Chapel Royal – and arranged to have three part songs sung to the Pope. This may have been to impress him with English musical usage. (The men's voice trio in England, as we shall see, was to survive many centuries and changes of musical styles.)

It was still required of a singer in England in the early sixteenth century that he could discant on a plainsong, or counter a popular tune, extempore. Study of *Musica Britannica*'s volume *Music at the Court of Henry the Eighth* will give a very good idea of the result expected.

It is quite clear that counter tenor altus and bassus were still thought compatible. Yet the Chichester stipulation seems to underline that *specialist* singers, in that case a 'natural bass', were required as well as those implied to be baritones with an extension into head voice. Most singers, i.e. not specialist tenors or specialist basses, were therefore required to be versatile 'enough to sing either in a true or falsetto voice', says John Stevens in *Music and Poetry in the Early Tudor Court*. He continues:

> The idea is sometimes put forward that Englishmen have a prerogative of natural, straightforward singing, and that this singing displaced the old falsetto singing. Neither the music itself or the acid comments of the Reformers, nor the general tone of courtly life (with its tendency to garnish everything) supports the idea. The popularity of the counter tenor (presumably using a falsetto when necessary) has already been suggested. At one time Northumberland's Chapel had six counter tenors to two tenors and two basses.

A letter about the appointment of John Taverner (*c.* 1495–1545) as Master of the Choir at Cardinal College, Oxford, Wolsey's foundation later to become Christchurch, specified that he must have 'both his breste' (chest plus falsetto) 'att will' plus the handling of an instrument.

It is important to remember that though the traditional sound of boys' and men's voices together, indeed all voices, may alter slightly over centuries as cultural and musical demands twist and turn, it is from this physiological and psychological ecclesiastical background that the counter tenor *singer* first came. How important this is will recur in other sections of this present work.

Let us take stock. By the early sixteenth century, we have reached the start of something very like our modern English system, at any rate in terms of the cathedral or collegiate choir. Boys, where available, extremely high voiced men if not, sing the highest part, cantus; men with very high voices the next down, altus, ex contra-tenor altus; those with highish voices the next, tenor, ex plainsong, now a free part like the others and rather higher than before; low voices were gathered on the bottom part, bassus, ex contra-tenor bassus. The choir is divided equally antiphonally and harmony is sung on both sides.

Sub-divisions are readily available and frequently written for, as they had been for many years, but the basic four part choir is as above. It is interesting that England produced less 'normal' four part polyphony than most other European countries for many years. The English high treble and lower mean boys' voices, developed in the fifteenth and still popular in the early sixteenth century, were partly responsible.

But probably the most common sub-division in England, after the mid-sixteenth century was the combination S.A.A.T.B.★ The Reformation seems to have played a large part in the fading popularity of extreme treble parts. (See Wulstan in his vocal colour article.)

Considering double counter tenor parts, we are accustomed today to think of Decani side taking the higher, and Cantoris the lower parts, and that in verse work the same principles apply. But this is a relatively modern simplification of the real situation as it affected the counter-tenor parts. In the early seventeenth century the Cantoris first counter tenor was the principal voice, and his partner, Cantoris second counter tenor, sang the same part as Decani first counter tenor, and vice versa; this was to ensure that when the choir sang antiphonally in five parts, all five would be present on each side. Also it meant that both counter tenor parts were strong throughout their range.

This practice had been in existence for most of the sixteenth century too, but as the alto parts were formerly almost always equal, crossing each other frequently, the voices were equal too. It would appear then that either the writing altered and counter tenors followed it and specialised, or less likely that the parts followed the needs and developments of the singers themselves.

By the close of the sixteenth century, the age of Victoria, Gabrieli, Marenzio, Lassus and others on the Continent; Byrd, Gibbons, Mor-

★ Compositions with two alto parts, even on occasion three, are found in abundance until the Civil War, then through Henry Purcell and even to many of Handel's English choral works. He had inherited the English tradition through Purcell. These sixteenth- and seventeenth-century almost inevitable double counter tenor parts are not of course to be confused with the mid-fifteenth-century split contra-tenor. The former is the direct result of the popularity of the high vocal register, the latter a fifteenth-century logical division to exploit the already noted possibilities of sub-tenor erritory.

ley and other giants in England, the four basic parts had settled to *cantus*, *altus*, *tenor*, *bassus*, with the option of counter tenor (thus Anglicised finally) for *altus*. Florio (1598) defines the term 'alto' as appertaining to 'a counter tenor treble in musicke'. This delightful mix of terms suggests strongly how the high alto was viewed as a counter to the treble in the same way as the original counter to the tenor had been the counter tenor.

It should be borne in mind when considering choir sizes, that they would have varied according to the importance of the foundation. Clearly, St Paul's Cathedral or the Chapel Royal for example, had a larger number of singers. But let us take Chichester, a modest provincial cathedral, where Thomas Weelkes was organist from about 1602 until 1623. At that time the choir consisted of eight boys and eight lay clerks. There were also four vicars choral, but by this date they rarely sang with the choir. Knowing the usual assignment of vocal parts in cathedral music, we may assume that of the eight lay clerks, four would be counter tenors – two per side in order to cope with the frequent and antiphonal divisions requiring two altus parts – two would be tenors and two basses.

It is important to remember always that altus denoted a high part sung by a high voice. That many of the altus parts appear only medium or even low can mislead. Quite apart from questions of pitch (see Ch. 6), do not forget that however 'low' the altus part, it is still higher overall by the early sixteenth century than the tenor, and a man singing it must be in the higher reaches of the male voice.

We have discussed male choirs, the music written for them and the sound expected, in order to establish the ancestry of first a part then a particular register. (The mixed choir has an honourable but later ancestry, and most would maintain, a more important function than the male choir in the twentieth century for a variety of reasons, not all of them musical.)

We have dwelt for some time on choral music, but solo or semi-solo music had existed for centuries. Much of it would have been sung at counter-tenor pitch where this lay naturally within reach of the performer. Folk song, Italian 'lauda'; medieval trouvere, troubadour song and virelai – all these must have been sung by the high male voice. (There is, for instance, an early example of the virtuoso high counter tenor part in the fifteenth century song in praise of Italy by Ludbicus de Armino, preserved in the Trent codices.)

The sixteenth and seventeenth centuries in England saw the most glorious opportunities for the counter tenor. Few verse anthems and settings of the canticles in cathedral music were without its almost constant use in solo, duet, trio or semi-chorus combination. The secular equivalents of these, odes, welcome songs and the like,

demonstrated the same preoccupation. There was little or no difference in musical style in many cases. There were consort songs to the
viols, both sacred and secular; less for some reason to the lute; madrigals; part-songs; early opera and stage music and early glees (gentlemen's singing and drinking club songs).

The importance attached to the counter tenor is reflected in the
continued high proportion of them at the English Chapel Royal at the
turn of the sixteenth century: eight boys, eight counter tenors, four
tenors and four basses. Parallel, in sixteenth-century France, the
haute-contre (alto) tradition flourished. In about 1585, 'Nicholas
Mauregan, Anglois' was engaged by the French Chapel Royal *pour
chanter sa partie de haute-contre au coeur et à l'aigle*. Mauregan was an
English Chapel Royal singer, but there seems no reason to suppose
that the French had to lure their counter tenors from England for lack
of their own. The voice was a European one. (More can be learnt
about Nicholas Mauregan in Michael Brenet's 'Les Musiciens de la
Sainte-Chapelle du Palais', 1910). See *Mus. Ant.* Vol iv. p. 59.

The high male voice tradition seems to have been virtually identical
on the Continent of Europe with what obtained in England. For many
years the famous school of Spanish falsettists had sent singers
throughout the Continent, notably into France, Italy and the Sistine
Chapel choir, even possibly to England. These specially trained falsettists sang the soprano part. This was not of course necessary in
England until the Restoration because of the boy treble tradition. It is
thought possible that the famous choir at Montserrat in Spain may
well owe much of its past reputation to links with the Spanish falsetto
school. It is not impossible that some of these very high Continental
falsettists came to England in 1660 to help with the musical regenera-
tion following the Restoration. (See later mention of Damascene
p. 36.)

But what of the Continental treble tradition? One wonders whether
the Europeans were dissatisfied with their boys' performances, or
perhaps the kind of vocal tone admired abroad was fiercer and
stronger than could be easily obtained by boys.

In the sixteenth century the Spanish falsettists certainly sang the
soprano part; for example, most of Palestrina's Masses and Motets
were written either for falsettists or for boys. Their ranks included
famous musicians such as Cristobal Morales (c. 1500–1553) and Tomás
Luis da Victoria (c. 1548–1611). The Sistine Chapel choir boys from
the Orphanotropia or Scholae Cantorum may well have been displaced by these more powerful falsettists. The Spanish falsetto
technique was a carefully kept secret, but was known not to involve
castration. We have some of the names of falsetti in the Papal choir. In
addition to Morales and Victoria were Bartolomeo Escobedo and

Francisco Soto (1539–1619). The last named is known to have preserved his voice to the age of eighty. The top parts of most Italian
madrigals were sung by falsettists.

Ludovico Viadana (1564–1645) advises the employment of falsetti
in his works according to the famous set of rules he set before the *Cento
Concerti* of 1602, and claims that the said voices give an improved
effect.

Dr Burney, writing in the eighteenth century, quotes from a seventeenth-century writer on the subject:

> Du Cange (1610–1688) in his *Glossarium ad scriptores mediae et infimae
> latinitatis*, derives the word 'falset' from 'Fausetum', a term used,
> during the middle ages in the same sense; and this, he supposes,
> from 'faucibus' whence the high tones of voice proceed. 'Pipeth'
> was sometimes used in a similar sense to express 'piping', or such
> high singing as imitated the sound of pipes or small flutes. These
> 'feigned voices', as we should call them, seem to have been much in
> request for the treble parts of vocal compositions, at the beginning
> of the last century, when women were not allowed to sing: as
> appears from a letter written by the celebrated traveller Pietro della
> Valle to Bapt.Doni, of which more notice will be taken here-
> after . . .
>
> Lodovico 'Falsetto', Gio. Luca 'Falsetto', Giuseppe 'Tenore', and
> Melchior 'Basso', singers mentioned in this letter, had their cogno-
> mens from their species of voice. Singing in 'falset' had very early
> admission in the Church, during times of 'Discant'.

Yet even while the falsetti reigned in Rome, there appeared omens
of the future, a small threat at first, but one which was destined to push
them from their exalted position. The decline of the counter tenor
began much earlier abroad than in England. By 1562 there is already a
mention of a castrato singing in the Papal choir. By the end of the
century there were two. Fuller discussion on the nature and character
of the castrati is included in Chapter 3, but suffice to say now that with
the advent of these brilliant artificial voices, the falsettists/counter
tenors entered into relative decline on the Continent. The last falsetto
of the Sistine Chapel, Giovanni di Sanctos, a Spaniard, died in 1625.
Decline yes, extinction no. A glance at the works of Scarlatti, Buxtehude, Viadana, Marcello, and many others reveals music clearly written for the counter tenor range, in solo and ensemble.

But it is still true to say that on the continent of Europe, by the
beginning of the seventeenth century the door was wide open for the
castrati, or everati, as they were often called, an age destined to last for
nearly two centuries and to dominate church music, opera, and what
today would be called the concert platform. Yet in England it was to

be another 107 years before castrati appeared on the opera stage, or indeed any stage. The English counter tenors flourished untroubled by events over in Italy, until twenty-seven years after the Restoration of King Charles II.

The mid-seventeenth century, excluding the Commonwealth period, proved especially beneficial for counter-tenor singers. For though choirs were disbanded, service books burnt, organs destroyed, boy choristers sent home permanently, lay clerks paid off and the glorious tradition laid waste, the situation was eventually redeemed. In any case, domestic music making and singing continued, and although no boys were trained, lay clerks were able to keep their voices in trim, no doubt privately hoping for a speedy removal of Cromwell's regime. Some went through difficult financial straits, for it was to be twenty years' wait for settled times.

Whereas before 1640, each cathedral and collegiate foundation no doubt boasted many superb boy singers, the twenty-year gap meant that at the Restoration in 1660 there were no boys whatsoever, no trained treble line. This could have been the end of the English male choir tradition, perhaps of counter tenors for centuries, even for ever; for had choirmasters filled the treble stalls with young intelligent women sopranos, it surely would not have been long before the alto part would have succumbed too.

Not many years after, Bach, in common with many choirmasters in (Protestant) Germany, was gradually introducing women into church choirs to replace castrati and falsetti singers, and as it turned out, eventually many of the boys. This could easily have happened in England, certainly under later Hanoverian influence. Or, equally, at the Restoration the castrati could have been imported or created on the Continental pattern, leaving the field open to women singers when the castrati age was fading about one hundred years on.

England, being both Catholic and Protestant, stood as usual between the extremes. England is by nature conservative. There is no record of castrati singers being created in England: this practice seems to have been considered abhorrent with regard to English boys, however much foreign solo singers of this type were admired. The castrati reigned chiefly in the high Catholic countries, but were not so popular in the Protestant lands.

So, predictably some would say, in England at the Restoration not only were the choirmasters and lay clerks recalled, organs repaired and new part books copied, but strenuous efforts were made to train new boy choristers, despite the difficulties of re-creating a singing tradition after a twenty-year vacuum.

This difficulty should not be underestimated: luckily boys are imitative, able quickly to absorb a common style or usage, be it

33

football, school boy folklore, cheeky impersonations or highly skilled singing. An American couple, recently impressed by a particularly renowned cathedral choir, asked was the Organist and Master of the Choristers the boys' 'teacher of voice'? The answer was humorous, but had the ring of truth: 'We don't teach *voice* in England, boys just step on to the tradition!' Without this stepping 'on to a tradition', this implied escalator, English boy choristers would not have the reputation they possess. After all, English larynxes can be no different from any others. The boys must have an object of imitation.

At any rate, at the Restoration in 1660, counter tenors were the answer, not normally to sing treble, though some may well have done so, but to provide a brilliant solo alternative until such time as the boys were trained to their former sophistication. This would take several years. To help support the boys, wooden cornetts were brought in. The newly written anthems and settings are notable for their short choruses and often florid, lengthy solos and trios for three men's voices, counter tenor, tenor and bass. Out of this situation grew the second golden age for the counter tenor which would last until a gradual decline towards the end of the eighteenth century.

It was once thought, quite wrongly, that the counter tenor voice was first used at the Restoration because of the weakness of the boys. This view was never very credible, and is now quite absurd.

If only tape recorders had been invented several centuries earlier! As it is, we have only *written* accounts of the voices and personalities of the past before say 1890, and of course the painting and sculpture of each period. Knowing that each person reacts differently to almost every phenomenon, we must not forget that verbal, graphic and written description is by its very nature subjective. However, it is still valuable, for it represents our only chance of a peep into the past. Thus we may but glimpse the age of the counter tenor. Let us pause to examine what has been said of the counter tenor before continuing the story to the present.

Probably the first mention of a high counter-tenor singer occurs very early and with interesting idiomatic brevity (recalling the name style of Joe 'Mr Piano' Henderson.) The Manuscript Chantilly in the Musée Condé has a collection of motets by various composers including one by 'J. de alto bosco'. He may well be the J. de Bosco who was a singer at the Papal Chapel in Avignon in 1394.

One of the earliest descriptions of the voice *seems* to occur in a letter from the Venetian ambassador to the Signory of Venice. He had just wined and dined and heard mass in Richmond Palace with Henry VIII, '. . . and after a grand procession had been made, high mass was sung by the King's choristers whose voices are more divine than human; non cantavano ma giubilavario; and as to the counter bass voices, they probably have not their equal in the world.'

By 'counter bass' he could mean counter tenor. His term could come about either because he was speaking in an unfamiliar idiom in a foreign country, or possibly by 'counter bass' he showed actually *more* erudition than seems the case at first, and meant to suggest the traditional bass–alto relationship. There is, though, just the chance that he referred not to alti but *bassi*, counter tenor being a variation of contra-tenor, and the term contrabassi being in normal usage in Italy.

One of the first definite descriptions of the voice is in a sixteenth-century poem, and it describes its *function* beautifully: 'The bass and treble are extremes, the tenor standeth sturdily, the counter tenor rangyth then me seems.'

Other than de Bosco, the first names we know to be 'falsettists' are the great Spaniard Tomás Luis de Victoria (1548–1611), and his fellow composer Cristobal Morales (1500–53), Bartolomeo Escobedo and Francisco Soto (1539–1616), who still sang aged eighty.

Sir Francis Drake, no less, is thought to have been a counter-tenor singer in addition to his professional sea-faring career.

The English lutenist composer Dowland (1563–1626) is also thought by some to have sung counter tenor, although most of his songs lie either rather high or low (depending on the octave used). Perhaps he was a particularly high range counter tenor. At any rate, anybody who has heard Alfred Deller's recording of, for example, 'In Darkness Let Me Dwell', could never doubt that Dowland would have approved. Shakespeare surely had a counter tenor in mind when he wrote: 'O stay and hear your true love's coming that can sing both high and low.'

There is a valuable account by Thomas Coryate (1577–1617), the traveller and writer, of a solemn feast at Venice and an unknown counter tenor:

> Of the singers there were three or four so excellent that I think few or none in Christendome do excell them, especially one, who had such a pureness and (as I may in a manner say) such a super-naturall voice for sweetnesse that I think there was never a better singer in all the world, insomuch that he did not only give the most pleasant contentment that could be imagined, to all the hearers but also did as it were astonish and amaze them. I alwaies thought that he was an Eunuch, which if he had beene, it had taken away some part of my admiration, because they do most commonly sing passing well; but he was not: so therefore it was much more admirable. Againe it was the more worthy of admiration because he was a middle aged man

of about forty years old. For nature doth more commonly bestow such a singularity of voice upon boyes and striplings, than upon men of such years. Besides it was farre more excellent because it was nothing forced, strained or affected, but came from him with the greatest facilitie that I ever heard. Truely I think that had a Nightingale beene in the same roome and contended with him for the superioritie, something perhaps he might excell him because God hath granted that little birde such a priviledge for the sweetnesse of his voice, as to none other: but I think he could not much. To conclude, I attribute so much to this rare fellow for his singing, that I thinke the country where he was borne, may be as proude for breeding so singular a person as Smyrna was of her flower . . .

A description of the five voices, treble, mean, alto (counter tenor), tenor and bass, appears in Charles Butler's *Principles of Musick*, 1636. Here is the counter tenor entry:

The Countertenor or Contra-tenor, is so called, because it answereth to the Tenor, though commonly in higher keys: and therefore is fittest for a man of a sweet shrill voice. Which part though it have little melody by itself; (as consisting much of monotones) yet in Harmony it hath the greatest grace: especially when it is sung with a right voice which is too rare.

The phrase 'right voice' might intrigue some. It is suggested that it refers to a cultivated, natural sounding voice as opposed to a demonstrably unsophisticated one.

The composer Henry Lawes (1596–1662) is reputed to have been a counter-tenor singer. We also know of a famous Purcellian alto, Alexander Damascene, of French origin, who settled and sang in England from 1685. According to Fétis, 'these haute-contre singers sing the part next below the treble in *operas*'. (Note the word *treble* – presumably boys still took the operatic top line at this date, or it could be a loose use of the term.)

John Abell (1650–1720) is a famous name, and one of which we know more. He was probably educated at the Chapel Royal, was outstanding in this country for his alto singing, and travelled abroad. Abell usually accompanied himself on the lute. Evelyn wrote in his diary: 'After supper came in the famous treble Mr. Abell, newly returned from Italy. I have never heard a more excellent voice, and would have sworn it was a woman's, it was so high and so well and skilfully managed . . .' (January 27th, 1681)

There are two points here, the first being the use of the word 'treble'. Nobody would claim that Abell, aged thirty-one, had a *treble* voice. Yet he was *not* a castrato. The term is surely here used loosely, meaning 'high' in the same manner as the Medievals. The second point is the allusion to a woman's voice. Unless I am utterly mistaken, and Abell sounded like some of today's young counter tenors, good but in timbre often rather effeminate, see page 187, then here again Evelyn is telling us something of the ease and skill with which Abell sang. Congreve also wrote of him in 1700: 'He certainly sings beyond all creatures on earth.'

Evelyn also commends the castrato Siface, or Grossi, for his singing in the Chapel of James II in 1687 when the Italian also sang at the house of Samuel Pepys. English falsettists were welcomed aboard too, for Evelyn says: 'I dined at Lord Sutherland's being invited to hear the celebrated Mr Pordage, newly arrived from Rome, his singing was after the Venetian recitative, as masterly as could be and with an excellent voice, both treble and bass.' This could mean that he sang in two registers, or that he sang both bass and alto songs. (Purcell himself sang bass on occasion, never as soloist, yet we know of him as a counter tenor.)

Other counter tenors associated with the Chapel Royal at this time were the composers, Michael Wise (1648–87), William Turner (1651–1739), of whom Burney said, 'his treble voice settled* to the pitch of a counter tenor – a circumstance which so seldom happens that if it be cultivated, the possessor is sure of employment', and Purcell. John Weldon, (1676–1736) is another. Michael Wise, described as 'a counter tenor from Salisbury', was admitted in the place of Raphael Courteville (composer of the hymn tune 'St James').

In 1692, Henry Purcell is reported to have sung in his own *Ode to St Cecilia's Day* of that year, taking the great ' 'Tis Nature's Voice' counter tenor solo with 'incredible graces' as a contributor to the *Gentleman's Journal*, of November, 1692, puts it: 'The following ode was admirably set to music by Mr Henry Purcell, and performed twice with universal applause, particularly the second stanza which was sung with incredible graces by Mr Purcell himself.'

Dr W. H. Cummings, writing in 1881, says of the opera *Dido and Aeneas*: 'There is a tradition that the part of Belinda (or Anna), written

---

* Perhaps the word 'immediately' inserted here helps to explain this statement. Or Burney may possibly have been thinking of the tenor altino type, for he uses the words *so seldom*. Alternatively, we may quote David Wulstan in *Vocal Pitch in English 16th Century Polyphony*. He makes an extremely valuable observation which applies:

There is yet another characteristic which the best contemporary altos share: the extremely gradual rate at which their voices broke. Singers whose voices broke more rapidly find greater difficulty in producing the typical 'counter tenor' tone. This is one of several reasons which make research into the vocal aspect of puberty overdue. As will become apparent later, this question is directly relevant to conditions in sixteenth century England. So, although an extended treatment is not at present possible, the subject of pubertal change requires at least some consideration.

for alto voice, was sung and acted by Purcell himself. In 1794, S. Harding published a portrait of "Henry Purcell, musician and *actor*", copied from the original in Dulwich College. I have made a diligent search for the portrait without success.'

At first this seems unlikely. Why would Purcell have taken a woman's role? Written as *Dido* was for a Chelsea girls' school, it seemed far more likely that he took rehearsals and during these occasionally supplied the part of Belinda in his usual alto voice. So consulting the first *printed* edition of the opera by MacFarren it is surprising to find that not only was the part of Dido listed as *treble*, but that Belinda – exclusively called Anna – was placed very low in an alto clef and had a very definite low counter-tenor range. It looks too low for a schoolgirl, even up one tone, which would take Dido up to A''. The duet between Anna and an attendant, 'Fear no Danger' (now generally sung up one octave for soprano and mezzo), is identical in style to Purcell's counter tenor/tenor duets, and including the (figured) bass resembles the familiar A.T.B. trio so much that it appears as a glee in important collections made in the early eighteenth century.* So perhaps Cummings was correct. There is perhaps also a chance that Purcell thought of 'Mopsa' in *The Fairy Queen* because of Belinda, despite one being tragedy, the other high comedy. Or perhaps it is more likely that Mopsa's real ancestry lies in medieval farce.

The original Mopsa was played by 'Mr Pate', 'in the habit of a woman'. He sang his duet with the character Corydon, taken by a bass called 'Mr Reading', in 1692, and is also recorded as having sung the song allotted to 'Summer' in the same work. W. H. Cummings wrote of 'another kind of duo' when they were both involved in a riot at the Dog Tavern in Drury Lane in 1695, dismissed from the Playhouse,† then later were reinstated. Evelyn's diary mentions him, just returned from Italy, but apparently misnames him: 'May 30th, 1698. I dined at Mr Pepys, where I heard the rare voice of Mr Pule, who was lately come from Italy, reputed the most excellent singer we had ever heard. He sung several compositions of the late Dr Purcell.'

Handwriting being what it is, 'Pule' is almost certainly 'Pate'.

Purcell composed songs in 1688 for a comedy by D'Urfey, *The Fool's Preferment*, or *The Three Dukes of Constable*. They were sung by a

---

* Since writing this I have realised that this MacFarren edition is itself corrupt. It converts the original into more of an oratorio or concert work. Alterations were made including a *bass* sorceress, a tenor sailor and first attendant in addition to translating Belinda down an octave into a counter tenor or contralto. But most of my remarks still stand. Purcell could very well have performed the part of Belinda, filling in for an indisposed young girl soloist, or indeed during rehearsals. Either could have begun both the tradition and the glee version of 'Fear No Danger'.

† A John Pate was buried in Hampstead Churchyard on January 14th, 1704. The burial register described him as 'belonging to ye old Playhouse'.

William Mountford of whom Colley Cibber says in *Apology for the Life of Colley Cibber*: 'William Mountford sang a clear counter tenor and had a melodious warbling throat.'

The presence of other favourite altos of the period is hinted at but they are not always named; unlike the four counter-tenor soloists who took part in the first performance of Purcell's *Duke of Gloucester's Birthday Ode*, 1695 (Damascene, Robert, Turner and Howell). As there are no tenor parts in the score, perhaps the chorus inner parts were completed by some of these counter tenors? Mr Howell, (d. 1714) is a great name, styled by Purcell himself as 'the high contra-tenor' who 'takes the high D with agility'. The Purcell Society tells us:

Mr John Howell, a celebrated counter tenor, took part in many performances of Purcell's works, notably the 'Cecilia Ode', 1692. He was appointed Epistler in their Majesties' Chapel Royal, by warrant from the Right Reverend the Lord Bishop of London, Dean of the Chapel on the 1st October, 1694; and by virtue of four warrants from the Dean, was sworn Gentlemen of the Chapel, in full place, in the room of Mr Boucher, December 10th, 1695. He died July 5th, 1708.

The London Gazette of December 29th, 1698 has: 'On Wednesday next will be performed at York Buildings, Mr Daniel Purcell's musick, made for last St Cecilia's Feast, for the benefit of Mr Howell and Mr Shore, with an addition of new vocal and instrumental musick.' (Shore was a famous trumpeter.) We know little of Mr Boucher (alias Bowcher, or more usually Bouchier), whose name is on Purcell's scores, and whose Chapel Royal counter-tenor place Howell took in 1695. He may well have been of French birth like Damascene. (The latter took the late greatly lamented Henry Purcell's place as a counter tenor at the Chapel in 1695.)

Because, of all counter tenors and probably of English composers, the name Henry Purcell will always be pre-eminent for obvious reasons, we print the following as companion to the illustration of his house in Bowling Alley, Westminster, when Abbey organist (plate 1). Some parts of his *birthplace* were still standing in 1881 when W. H. Cummings published his book *Henry Purcell*. A sketch of the house was made on April 15th, 1845, by R. W. Withall, and included this note:

Three ancient houses in Westminster; in the right-hand one of which the great H. Purcell was born, 1658, and passed his early life. They are now in the last state of ruin, and have long been uninhabited. The houses adjoining that of Purcell are of modern date, and

Example 12 *A trio from the Purcell anthem 'Behold I bring you glad tidings', showing how the alto part blends in with the tenor.*

project before the others, as well as encroach somewhat on Purcell's doorway, hiding one side of the door-frame. Of the old house the windows and doorways are nearly all boarded up in the roughest manner, under which however, the original panelled doors are still to be partly found. The houses are of old red brick. The first door was the back way into the public-house called the 'Bell and Fish', kept by Mr Oldsworth, who lost his licence. The second door the entrance to the skittle-ground. The third was Purcell's house.

Freeman was a favourite solo alto for whom Purcell wrote much. In Handel's time, Hughes is an important singer appearing much in connection with Handel's scores for the Chapel Royal. The celebrated Richard Elford preceded him as first high voice of the Chapel. The part of David in *Saul* was originally sung by a Mr Russell. Walter Powell (1697–1744) is another celebrated name, of which more later.

When using English (counter tenor) singers as soloists, Handel wrote that he thought them 'equal to the Italians' (castrati). Yet he continued to erode the traditional position of the counter tenors. Though it began a long period of English musical self-effacement, when *all* things foreign were considered superior, the eighteenth century operatic scene was dominated, as since, by Italy. The influence of Handel, who settled permanently in England, was, in opera, always towards the Italian. Consequently, his imported castrati took over the operatic scene as prima donnas, leaving the lower, less demanding solo work and of course all chorus work to English counter tenors. However, Handel also began to use women solo contralti. This took some time to spread, and during the gradual introduction of contralti, ambiguous mix-ups occurred. They were even engaged on occasions to sing serious male roles *and* were styled counter tenors. The eighteenth century was one both of oddity *and* reason.

Actually, sexual ambiguity on stage was not new. Long before castrati were heard in England, and during the era of the unchallenged counter tenors in the seventeenth century, women had taken male parts in *parodies* of English operas or semi-operas. The main female role was taken by a male comedian. One can easily see the relationship of the famous Corydon and Mopsa comic duet – the role of Mopsa taken by the counter tenor Mr Pate (see page 38) – to these opera parodies. Also, we glimpse the origins of English pantomime, with its principal Boy and Dame or Widow Twankey traditions. Today's 'Hinge and Bracket' and 'Dame Edna Everage' are clearly related to Mopsa.

During the eighteenth century, even at the height of the castrato period, there was seldom more than one castrato in any one English opera production: he was the star. But it is considered that Handel only ever wrote two solo parts specifically for castrati in all his oratorios.

Roger Fiske, in *English Theatre Music in the 18th Century*, is of the opinion that men began to feel reluctant to sing counter tenor because of the castrati:

> But the establishment of the castrati deprived perfectly normal men of their pleasure in singing counter tenor, for they found themselves viewed with the same amused and patronizing contempt as the castrati but without the compensation of an equally heroic and profitable voice. In our own time the renaissance of the counter-tenor soloist is still bedevilled by the unease such singing occasions in some circles, an unease born of the triumphs of Nicolini. It would scarcely have been understood before 1700.

Fiske's view would be understandable had this been so, but there is some doubt whether the fear of confusion with castrati could have affected more than a minority until the very end of the eighteenth and beginning of the nineteenth centuries. The evidence is that there were plenty of counter tenors on the scene throughout the eighteenth century, even if they were not as fashionable as before. Fiske is only too right about the modern situation of course.

So the eclipse of the solo counter tenor actually started in the most obvious way of all – a change of musical and cultural fashion. It was completed much later by prejudice.

The castrato Siface's visit to England in 1687 had had little or no effect on the English counter tenors, yet within twenty years there was an ominous sign of change to come. The eighteenth century began well enough, but in 1707 the first of a succession of castrati arrived here – Valentino Urbani – and the great Hughes, instead of taking the male lead, was now understudy to Urbani. Burney gives us useful detail:

> But before a character is given of the great foreign singers who arrived here after the Italian opera was firmly established in this country, it is justice to say something of the English singers, who were able by their performance to excite curiousity, give pleasure, and set censure at defiance, when the opera was in its infancy, and regarded by some as an idiot, and by others as a shapeless monster. Mr Hughes had been a favourite singer at concerts, and between the acts of plays. For several years he was assigned the part of first man, in the first opera that ever was performed on our stage in the Italian manner. His voice was a counter tenor, as we are told in the dramatis personae of *Thomyris*; and, indeed, as the compass of his

songs discovers. He continued to perform the first part till the arrival of Valentini, after which no further mention is made of him either in opera or concert annals.

We know that Hughes was in *Arsinoe* (1705), and *Camilla* (1706) and played Sir Henry in *Rosamund* in 1707. Then he was Valentini's understudy in the part of Orontes in *Thomyris* in December 1707. Hughes' voice was a high counter tenor. Elford was a low counter tenor, and they sang together in trios in Handel's *Utrecht Jubilate* with the bass, Gates. John Hough, in *The Historical Significance of the Counter Tenor*, has taken this to suggest that the alto duets which occur in works like Maurice Greene's *God is Our Hope and Strength* are really written for alto and high tenor – it being his view that Elford was really a very high tenor (as he terms it a true counter tenor). Though strangely, a few lines later, Hough says: 'The composers of the period still observe the distinction of "high countra-tenor" and the ordinary high tenor of the Restoration period.' (Does he not mean *low* counter tenor in this context?) At any rate, earlier, he *had* realised that the present-day sharp distinction between alto and tenor voices was almost non-existent: the 'counter tenor making use of his higher notes and blending them to his bass or baritone compass, if a falsetto alto, or the tenor using his high voice judiciously. The easy production of the alto rather points to former practice . . .'

Hough's modern-day (1937) suggestion of using a tenor if a 'true' counter tenor is not available, is based on what seems a fundamental contradiction in his paper. For having once stated the opposite he then seems to say that 'altos' do not sing over the break with any real success or even at all, and that counter tenors *have* no break. As I have said, I see no real distinction between the two voices. The terms are interchangeable. A low counter tenor of the John Whitworth type deals well with the lower parts of the Maurice Greene anthem mentioned earlier, apparently thought unsuitable for alto by Hough.

The castrato Senesino had been engaged for the specially composed part of Joad in *Athaliah* in 1733, but just before the performance he let Handel down, and Walter Powell, the English counter tenor, was substituted. (Many castrati parts can be taken untransposed by suitable counter tenors today.)

The Rev Daniel Lysons says, in his *The History of the Meetings of the Three Choirs*, 1812:

Though the memory of Mr Powell does not appear to be recorded in any musical publication, or to be known to the professional men of the present day, I find, upon inquiry, that it is not yet forgotten in the University of Oxford, where some of the senior members recollect their seniors were used to talk of the extraordinary vocal powers of Walter Powell, and to relate various anecdotes concerning him. He was a member of the choirs of Christ Church and other Colleges, was first one of the yeomen, and afterwards, one of the esquire beadles, and was the principal male oratorio singer when Handel presided at the Act, and the celebrated Strada sang there, in the month of July, 1733. On this occasion his singing was so much admired that he was immediately afterwards appointed one of the gentlemen of the Chapel Royal: the general idea is that his voice was a fine counter-tenor.

The Gloucester Journal, 1733, reports that, 'The famous Mr Powell of Oxford, did the meeting the honour of singing in the Cathedral on both days'. It was announced in the papers, in 1734, that the Steward had procured the best hands, and that, 'He had a promise of the most celebrated English voice to adorn the church music' (Lysons).

In Powell's obituary in the *Gentleman's Magazine*, in 1744, it is said that he was esteemed to have the best voice in England, and that the following lines were written by a gentleman of the University, on hearing of his death:

> Is Powell dead? Then all the earth
> Prepare to meet its fate
> To sing the everlasting birth
> The Choir of Heav'n's complete.

Rimbault says, in a footnote: 'A tradition is still extant in the University, that, on his deathbed, a short time before his decease, he sang an anthem, with the full powers of his voice, and with the most animated enthusiasm.' An English sense of humour appreciates the possibilities of the scene; perhaps Powell was using his own for the last time in this life.

The counter tenor, Russell, of whom we wrote earlier, may be the Russell in Smollett's satire, *Advice*, 1746–1747, 'a famous mimic and singer, engaged by certain ladies of quality, who engaged him to set up a puppet show in opposition to the oratorios of Handel . . .' As Hough says: 'If these men are identical, Russell must have been particularly mercenary after singing under Handel in 1739. The fickle instigators of the counter attraction deserted him, and after seeing the interior of Newgate he ended his days in Bedlam.'

The role of the Boetian prince, Athamas, in Handel's *Semele* was sung in 1744 by a Mr Sullivan; a Mr Brent originally sang the part of Hamor in *Jephtha*. The truth is that even while bringing eminent castrati from abroad for opera, and occasionally engaging the new women contralti, Handel wrote for and used his English altos continuously in solo and ensemble. Together with obvious castrati arias, all his alto parts are most suitable for men, and most modern contraltos do not sound their best in them. Perhaps Handel had found a source of eighteenth-century Kathleen Ferrier-toned contraltos.

Antonio Lotti (*c.* 1667–1740), the Venetian composer, was also an alto singer. He began as a chorister in the Doge's Chapel, and was a member of the Confraternita Musicale di Santa Cecilia by 1687. In 1689 he was appointed 'cantore di contra alto' with a salary of one hundred ducats. Note the use of the 'contra alto'. Lotti was not a castrato; he was a falsettist. At first, the phrase seems another infuriating example of seventeenth-century inconsistency; it is not unique to Lotti by any means; but in fact the use of the word 'contralto' is logical. (See page 109.)

François Couperin was writing for the French Chapel Royal in 1700, where the haute-contre (alto) tradition was still strong. Recalling the great influence all things French and music in particular had had on Charles II of England, there is an interesting parallel with what was happening in England by this date. A Mr du Four is a haute-contre (counter tenor) whose name appears in *Oeuvres complètes*, and who was evidently of some note.

One famous French counter tenor was the celebrated Pierre de Jélyotte (1713–87). He was the leading haute-contre on the French stage in his day. Marmontel, admittedly a friend of the singer, wrote that he possessed: '. . . the most outstanding voice one could hear, either by its volume and fullness or by the piercing impact of its silvery tone. He was neither handsome nor well-built, but to appear more handsome he had only to sing; one could say that he charmed the eyes at the same time as the ears.' (Translation: Carol Marcetteau.)

Like the English counter tenors, Jélyotte appeared with castrati on occasions, Farinelli and Caffarelli for example. He was in *Le Devin du Village* by J. J. Rousseau, and in revivals of works by Lully and Rameau.

Back in England, counter tenors continued to appear with success and renown. The Rev Daniel Lysons in his *The History of the Meetings of the Three Choirs*, 1812, tells us of the fine counter tenor, Price:

Price had been some years a member of the choir at Gloucester: he had a fine counter tenor voice, and was particularly remarkable for singing the air in Milton's *L'Allegro* which describes Laughter 'holding both his sides'. In this air, without losing sight of musical correctness, he worked himself up to so hearty and so natural a laugh, that few of his auditors could avoid partaking of his apparent merriment. The late Signor Rauzzini was singularly affected the first time of his hearing it at the Meeting of the Three Choirs. Dr

William Hayes, from whom it is probably that Price learnt it, was remarkable for singing this air.

Interestingly, an Italian counter tenor was singing with success in Edinburgh ten years later, thus proving once again a fallacy the idea that the castrati had pushed the falsetti into extinction in Europe. From 1770, a Signor and Signora Domenico Corri, from Rome, were favourite singers in Edinburgh, and well patronised by the nobility. Robert Burns' friend, Thomson, says that the Signor had a falsetto voice which he managed with great skill and taste. Dr Burney also reports on Domenico Corri, in a letter from Rome, September 2nd, 1770: 'The day after my arrival at his Grace, the Duke of Dorset's, I heard Signor Celestini, the principal violin here . . . He was ably seconded by Signor Corri, who is an ingenious composer and sings in very good taste.'

We must remind ourselves at this point that we have been hearing of several types of high male voice, natural and unnatural, each tailored (we will not say doctored!) to a rather different vocal function.

First, we have the tenor altino type of low counter tenor, possibly of the Richard Elford variety (assuming he was not a 'baritone' counter tenor); then the low counter tenor of the Henry Purcell type, that is with a baritone chest and developed specialist falsetto head voice which uses both registers, thereby achieving incredible range. Both types are useful in solo work, verse anthems and similar pieces, but while the tenor altino engages head voice at a higher degree in the scale and has less trouble with register changes, the 'baritone' can usually sustain a higher tessitura. The third variety is the high counter tenor, like Abell or Howell, who specialised in works of high tessitura, and seldom moved out of head register. The very highest voices of this third variety would be those like the Spanish falsettists – Morales or Victoria – who could and did maintain the soprano part. It is from the high counter tenors and these 'soprano falsettists' that we normally expect capabilities which rival the tessitura of the medium range castrati, and they can deputise for them with distinction. The fourth and last variety of high male voice is the castrato, a voice achieved only by a surgical operation.

We mention only one other specific country, though as we have said, the counter tenor was a *European* voice. It is not always realised that Germany too possessed a flourishing alto tradition, and also that the castrati were employed more there than in England, for they sang in both Lutheran and Catholic choirs as well as in opera and secular music. They seem to have displaced alti naturali rather later than in Italy, but in fact the Italian 'contralto' tenors were originally alto naturali. As the 'contralti' continued into the late nineteenth century it became clear that the alto tradition in Italy survived in all but name (see page 109).

Sanford Terry, the English authority on Bach, wrote a biography of the Master in which we find useful information on alti in eighteenth-century Germany. The Weimar Kapelle included in 1700, one Adam Emanuel Weldige or Weldig, as falsettist and Master of the Pages. He seems to have been appointed to this position on the death of Daniel Dobricht, a falsettist. Besides a tenorist and two bassists, there were two altists. John Hough reminds us that the distinction between falsettists and altists is surely significant:

In 1714 the singers comprised boys and two men on each of the three underparts, altists being stated. Late in 1715, there were six singing boys, two falsettists, one altist, two tenorists, and two bassists . . . the possibilities of these singers are seen in cantatas written for the Weimar Kapelle. For the Cothen Kapelle a descantist . . . was engaged in 1718 and in 1719, Ginacini a male descantist who received more [money] than two horn players for the first Brandenburg Concerto. Both these singers may have been sopranists from the opera houses, but the Rudolfstadt descantist may have been a good falsettist.

In a footnote, Hough states that Sanford Terry thinks Weldige took Pales in Bach's *Was Mir Behagt*, a role too high for him, unless he were a soprano falsettist.

Examining all this twice through, the reader may agree that the conclusions are ambiguous. At first one gets the distinct impression that Hough, by emphasising the difference between falsettist and altist, is about to state that here were the equivalent of English 'falsetto alto' and 'true' counter tenor; but then we begin to suspect that he is saying that the altists were often boys, not counter tenors. Does he mean then that the falsettists were either soprano singers who sang the line *above* the altists – a second treble, or mean part – leaving the alto part to be sung by 'elderly' boys, or boys with highly developed chest voices on the continental pattern; or by mature altists, the equivalent of our low counter tenor? Or is the position of falsettist a single voice engaged to teach the boys their parts? (Rather in the same way as in early sixteenth century England, in the Earl of Northumberland's household the Master of the Children was a counter tenor.) Two falsettists were mentioned in 1716 and one may have been assistant to the other.

Apparently, Bach had to call in University students to help his Leipzig boy altists during heavy works. He seems also to have arranged to stiffen his choir with a bass, tenor, and mature (falsetto) alto, plus a few instrumentalists. We may assume that the students were augmenting their meagre finances in time honoured fashion.

We may be tempted to think that the number of men and boys seems smaller in Bach's choirs than was the case in England; but the lists could be of the soloists or permanent semi-chorus, the larger, more amateur choir being anonymous. (The soloist system was taken up and still exists in the United States which culturally has always had a German musical system.)

Most Bach alto solo arias are high, even making allowance for our modern pitch pushing them up between a semi-tone and a tone further. Specialist high falsettists could have coped well at the original Bach pitch; certainly a castrato would have had no problem. These arias may of course have been meant for boys – for which most are suited – but with the evidence of the presence of high, mature male natural voices in his musical forces, we must assume that Bach and other German Kapellmeisters would surely have used them for alto solo work.

We know that Bach, and by implication other Kapellmeisters, were gradually bringing in women singers, either purposely to replace castrati or because the castrati were not easy to obtain. It is possible that women sang some of the alto arias on occasions as the century progressed. Not that Bach betrayed interest in women's voices officially in 1730. In a Leipzig memorandum, he writes, recommending for each church choir that, 'There must belong, at least, three trebles, three alti, three tenors, and as many basses . . . [as a minimum] . . . a motet may be sung with, at least, two voices to each part . . .'

By mid-century, choirs and opera choruses and soloists were a merry confusion, sexually if not musically, Protestant and Catholic. Friedrich Wilhelm Marpurg records, in *Historisch Kritische Beytrage*, Berlin, 1754:

> *Gotha, chamber and chapel:* . . . Two female singers: one male soprano, one male alto, one tenor, two basses . . .
>
> *Breslau, Bishop's Chapel:* Five male singers (including two sopranos and one alto) . . .
>
> *Paris, opera:* Eight female solo singers, four male altos, one tenor, seven baritones, chorus of seventeen women and twenty-one men . . .
>
> *1755 Paris, Concerts Spirituels:* Many of whom also belong to the opera . . . four female and four male solo singers, choir of six females and six male sopranos, six male altos, seven tenors, five high basses, eight low basses . . .
>
> *1756 Dresden, King's Chapel:* Five female, six male sopranos, one female and three male altos, three tenors, four basses . . .

Mannheim Court Chapel: Three female and three male sopranos, two male altos, three tenors, two basses.. . .

1757 Schwarzberg-Rudolfstadt Chapel: One female and one male soprano, one male alto, one tenor (the Kapellmeister), one bass . . .'

Anhalt-Zerbst Chapel: One male soprano, one male alto, one tenor . . .

Salzburg, Archbishop's Music: Solo singers, five male sopranos (three vacant), three tenors, two basses, with additions from the choir; fifteen boy singers, their prefect and their preceptor, three male altos, nine tenors, nine basses (Chorherren) and one male alto, three tenors, four basses . . .

All this should remind us that the counter tenor was not an exclusively English voice even by the eighteenth century. It would seem that the Catholic countries and England were moving in similar directions, but that the natural alto fared rather better in England than in most countries as the eighteenth century developed. The English seem to have retained an affection for this voice (see Appendix C).

For reasons easily understood, Catholic churches tended to retain alti and castrati for far longer than Protestant ones. Indeed, the last castrato of the Sistine Chapel, Professor Alessandro Moreschi, only died in 1924, almost exactly 300 years after the death of its last high falsettist. In the churches of the Reformed religion, the use of women's voices accelerated throughout the eighteenth century. It is a firm tradition now in most if not all countries that Protestant churches have mixed choirs, often of exclusively adult voices.

Charles Knyvett (1751–1822), an ex-chorister of Westminster Abbey, became a noted alto singer of his day. One of the principal alto soloists at the Handel Festival of 1784, he was a Gentleman of the Chapel Royal from 1786–1808, and from 1796 also Organist to the Chapel. He was considered 'one of the best singers of glees' and 'perhaps the best catch singer in England'.

John Hindle (1761–1796) was another celebrated counter tenor of the time. He was appointed a lay vicar of Westminster Abbey in 1785, sang before the Royal Family at the Worcester Musical Festival of 1788, and often at the London Vocal Concerts in 1791–2, appearing with Charles Knyvett. He composed many glees and songs.

In England, the end of the eighteenth century had approached with solo counter tenors in a much less happy situation than at its opening, but with no apparent real cause for utter despondency. After all, the castrati were on the wane, and in England at least, despite the rival contralti, there was still plenty of work and opportunity for the solo counter tenor. The glee clubs flourished, providing entertainment in small ensemble. Major solos and trios for men's voices were still being written in the cathedral tradition, and cathedral counter tenors still obtained important engagements on the concert stage.

The famous John Saville of Lichfield appears at Gloucester in 1790; a letter in the *Gloucester Journal* of September 19th, 1791, is relevant and its tweak in the tail has long been used as ammunition by the alto/counter tenor separate voice lobby: 'In Mr Saville's triumphant songs, "O Thou that Tellest", and "O Death Where is Thy Sting?" his voice was clear, sweet and powerful as we ever remember to have heard it, and they were given all his animated expression. His indignant scorn in "Thou Shalt Break Them in Pieces" was very fine.' This last phrase has caused many people much puzzlement, as it is a tenor aria. At first, one is tempted to wonder if perhaps the writer confused the voice of Saville with the tenor, Spreay, in his letter – presumably written later from either memory or notes. (After all, to call the duet 'O Death Where is Thy Sting' a song is incorrect.) If Saville *did* sing 'Thou Shalt Break Them' he must have had the technique to do so, and so was presumably a low counter tenor of one or other variety. For further discussion of occasions of counter tenor/tenor interchange, see page 139.

One wonders momentarily if perhaps 'Thou Shalt Break Them' was performed in a higher key by Saville especially for the occasion, but at first it seems unlikely. Though Handel himself was happy to transpose, even recompose single arias to accommodate particular singers in particular performances of *Messiah*, the practice must surely have died with him. Who would dare tamper with a masterpiece except its composer, dead thirty-one years by 1790. We do not of course count Mozart and others who *enlarged* the orchestral forces and orchestration to match.

The probable answer to the Saville question seems to be very simple and is provided by Lysons' *History of the Meetings of the Three Choirs*. He reports authoritatively that: 'The performance at Gloucester, in 1790, consisted wholly of *selections* (chiefly from Handel), except the masque of *Acis and Galatea* on the first evening . . . Mr. Saville . . . appeared at the Meeting of the Three Choirs for the first time this year, as principal counter tenor. The other principal singers were Spreay . . .'

Thus the letter writer referred not to a performance of *Messiah* at all, but to a concert at which selections were performed, probably from various Handel works. If Saville sang a tenor aria, it could quite easily have been in a transposed key for the occasion. It would make a fine declamatory aria for counter tenor and out of context there was no reason at all why Saville should not have sung it slightly transposed as a vehicle for his own voice. In fact, so high is the aria already, that it could be taken by many counter tenors in its original A minor.

Writing in 1889 in his famous *History of English Cathedral Music*, John S. Bumpus refers to the important cathedral composer, Jonathan Battishill (1738–1801):

> Battishill was one of the professionals engaged to sing at the private concerts given by those marvellous boys Charles and Samuel Wesley at the house of their father, the Rev Charles Wesley, in Chesterfield Street, Marylebone. In after years, Samuel Wesley was wont to relate that Battishill's singing was 'very engaging, energetic and commanding' and that it was 'a high treat to hear him take part in a duet of Handel's or a canzonet of Travers's, or sing any one of Purcell's songs or anthems'. His voice was a fine counter tenor.

Edward Rimbault (1816–1876) the musical historian and organist, writes of Sir John Goss's uncle, John Jeremiah Goss, that his voice was a pure *alto* of beautiful quality. He was a Gentleman of the Chapel Royal, and Vicar Choral of St Paul's and Westminster Abbey.

The word 'pure' applied to a voice may mean tonally pure, or possibly describe a purely natural sound. A 'pure' alto *could* therefore describe a typical round-voiced falsetto cathedral alto of yesterday, or indeed a 'natural' sounding voice. Or it could easily mean *both*.

Words are wretched things. We grab and grasp at them, twisting them to our own use, hoping they support our particular argument. It is therefore interesting to learn from Lysons' *History of the Meetings of the Three Choirs* that, 'Goss, a favourite *counter tenor* at the Vocal Concerts in London . . . appeared at the meeting this year for the first time [1807]'.

Here is another description of alto tone, this time at Norwich. The Minor Canons there in the early nineteenth century were a musical group and sang with the cathedral choir. An ear witness writes:

> Well do I remember the delight with which I used to listen to the service in Norwich Cathedral, when the Minor Canons, eight in number, filed off to their stalls, Precentor Millard at their head, whose admirable style and correct taste as a singer I have never heard surpassed, Browne's majestic tenor; Whittingham's *sweet* alto [our italics], and Hansell's sonorous bass; while Walker's silvery tones and admirable recitation found their way into every corner of the huge building . . .

Outside the cathedrals, cold winds began to blow for counter tenors, but Lysons' *Three Choirs* history confirms that there was no shortage of demand for and supply of counter tenors from London and elsewhere at least up to 1812.

If the Everati and eighteenth-century fashion edged the counter tenor from the centre of the secular solo stage, then it was the female contralto and the Romantic period which pushed him off it completely for about one hundred years. Yet counter tenors as secular *chorus* altos continued, (just) into the twentieth century. As Percy Scholes says in *The Oxford Companion to Music*, 1938: 'Mendelssohn gave the contralto prominence by writing solos for Madame Sainton Dolby in *Elijah* (1847), and since then solos for that voice have been a recognised feature in Oratorio composition, the alto voice falling more and more into the background, even in chorus work.' He was only too correct, and Scholes continues, Dr Charles Burney's comprehensive tome on the subject presumably open at his side: 'In the great Westminster Abbey Handel Commemoration Festival of 1784, there were in the chorus forty-five altos (called counter tenors), with not a single contralto (not from any objection to the appearance of women in the cathedral, since there were such among the sopranos).' The soprano soloists included two castrati, Signors Pacchierotti and Bartolini. In addition, three others of the principal soloists were counter tenors and together with those in the chorus made a total of forty-eight altos, small in contrast to the number of altos in the gargantuan Crystal Palace Handel Commemoration Festival Choir in 1859.

Estimates of total numbers before this last event suggested 1600 total choir strength, but 2765 apparently took part, of which 419 were altos, and 300 were contraltos! It sounds rather impressive, but there were no solo altos. The solo contralto reigned. *The Musical Times* review of the event speaks of, 'The alto voice – well defined throughout . . . large number of male voices . . . ladies not powerful enough in lower register.' It also mentions the presence of eight serpents, perhaps an appropriate instrument in the unisexual circumstances.

In 1900 there were only seventy-three, and by 1903, the altos' numbers had shrunk to twenty-three in the same choir (still presumably of comparable size overall). The fact that it was a Handel Festival suggests the possibility of instinct for the aptness of this voice, felt even in the early twentieth century.

The 1903 review, again in *The Musical Times*, said: 'The alto part, sweet in quality, might have been strengthened by a larger number of male altos, there being only twenty-three "bearded altos" as Mendelssohn called them, on the Handel orchestra.' The last phrase is a bit puzzling.

Even the Purcell Commemoration Choir, 1895, in Westminster Abbey, assembled and conducted by the staunch Purcellian, Sir Frederick Bridge, contained only eighteen altos as against forty-four contraltos. We do know however that the alto solos were taken by men, lay vicars of the Abbey Choir. The names of the four altos in the Westminster choral foundation in the late nineteenth century are known. Apparently, the Cantoris altos were a wine merchant named Birch who travelled up from Brighton each day for service, and John

Foster, who was described by Edward Pine in *The Westminster Abbey Singers*. Foster, 'as a small boy had stood on William IV's dining table to sing to the guests . . . He [Foster] was particularly fond of Tallis and Gibbons and used to say to the boys that Farrant's "If Ye Love Me" was one of the finest pieces of church music.'

It is clear that Foster was in no doubt about the most suitable repertoire which existed for his particular voice range; even in the lugubrious late nineteenth century. Foster sang in the 1902 Coronation choir of Edward VII, and it is interesting to note that his long life was concurrent with the years of the alto in decline. Pine describes the Westminster Decani altos thus: '. . . Sexton and Schartau, both possessing good voices, but not liked by the boys, who objected to their singing the solos which they regarded as their due.' Clearly, Decani was the favoured side for alto solo work of which there must have been a generous amount to judge by the boys' reaction.

'Sexton possessed black "mutton chop" whiskers and a heavy black moustache, and used to sing out of the side of his mouth. The boys considered he "looked like a tom-cat and sounded like one"; but it is doubtful whether they were very good judges.' The singing from the side of the mouth underlines the fact that even altos in the important choir of Westminster Abbey were probably self-trained, or at least had not enjoyed the comprehensive vocal training undertaken by their tenor and bass colleagues.

Cathedral music had a sheltered existence, and though the secular work had died for the alto singer, there was plenty to do in church. As we have seen earlier, chorus altos still existed in choral societies and the like, but the air was getting a bit thin there too. Back in 1883, the Leeds Festival Chorus still included forty-two altos but only seventeen contraltos.

Percy Scholes says: 'Apparently there was at this period a definite movement set on foot in favour of contraltos as against altos, for in June 1884 a protesting letter in *The Musical Times* insisted that it was a great mistake to do away with altos.'

The complete letter is interesting, but Percy Scholes quotes only part. For reasons best known to himself he decided not to include everything from the phrase 'curiously enough' onwards. It is worth including – it speaks volumes:

I . . . protest against the gradual disuse of the 'alto' voice in our leading choral societies. It is, I think, a very great mistake to do away with altos and substitute contraltos in oratorio music, at all events. Curiously enough, in one of our most celebrated choirs this is gradually being done, as I am informed, through the conductor holding the opinion of ladies' superiority, while he himself is an

Example 13 *Section of anthem 'Let us lift up our heart', S. S. Wesley (1810–1876) in the original format.*
(By kind permission of the Dean and Chapter of Canterbury.)

THOU JUDGE OF QUICK AND DEAD

CHARLES WESLEY
(1707–1788)

SAMUEL SEBASTIAN WESLEY
(1810–76)

*This may either be quietly sung by contraltos or left to the tenors and basses. [*Ed.*]

Example 14 *Section of S. S. Wesley's anthem 'Let us lift up our heart' in the 1930s format.*
(By kind permission of O.U.P.)

alto, and has had several relatives in the profession with that voice. Hoping my protest will avail to lessen this (as I conceive) injustice to a very useful and beautiful voice . . .

In the next Leeds Festival (1886) we find only sixteen altos as against fifty-seven contraltos, and in the Norwich Festival of forty years later (1924) seventy-one contraltos and not a single alto (even the altos of the cathedral not being brought into use). Percy Scholes' phrase sums it up poignantly: 'Thus in 140 years we have a swing over from oratorio choirs with not a single contralto to oratorio choirs with not a single alto.'

The 1884 letter of protest had obviously been ignored, as forty-eight years before another had also been ignored. As late as the 1830s clearly there had been counter tenors *expecting* solo secular employment. A plaintive letter appeared in the journal *Musical World*, in 1836. 'It was,' said the writer, 'to draw your attention to a situation in which myself, and others who have the misfortune of being denominated counter tenor singers, are placed by the introduction of female contraltos in most of the festivals and concerts instead of the legitimate altos. For instance, not one of us is engaged at the forthcoming festivals at the Exeter Hall . . .' We must assume that this refers to *solo* counter tenors as there were still a substantial number of chorus altos in the Handel Festival Choirs at Crystal Palace until the end of the century.

Yet at about the same date as that heartfelt letter, there was still work for the solo alto at least in the relatively sheltered world of the University. Describing the installation of a new Chancellor at the University of Cambridge in 1835, Bumpus writes: '. . . the task of composing an Ode fell upon [Thomas Attwood] Walmisley. The performance took place in the Senate House, the exponents of the solo parts being Malibran, Terrail [a favourite alto of enormous bulk], Braham, Henry Phillips, and John Parry . . .' (Was this Parry the composer of glees?) Proponents of the theory that alto and counter tenor were different voices need not be too encouraged by Bumpus. Study the letter above to *The Musical World*.

As the Romantic period gathered momentum, so the alto parts had begun to rise in pitch, especially in secular music increasingly influenced by foreign composers like Mendelssohn. Cathedral music was affected eventually, but kept at first to its own brand of Romanticism in the major form of Samuel Sebastian Wesley, deep in the English tradition. Generally he continued to write for a male choir including counter tenors.

Take the examples shown here from his anthem, *Let us Lift up Our Heart*, the section beginning 'Thou Judge of Quick and Dead'. The original 1853 version is compared to a relatively modern edition intended for *parish* choirs, and made in the 1930s. The footnote gives us another secondary point of interest. At this date, *circa* 1933, the editors obviously expected there to *be* no altos, or at least only ineffective ones available. Clearly they expected contraltos to be present.

Parish church contraltos were hardly new. Advertisements for voices in musical journals indicate quite clearly the way things were headed. An 1859 *Musical Times* contains an advertisement for sopranos and a contralto for a London church, and one for a 'contra-alto' and basso for a parish church in Manchester. Remember too, that the mid-nineteenth century was the flowering of the Oxford Movement and new or newly restored male parish choirs, of which more later. This makes the trend the more puzzling. Perhaps the Evangelical wing preferred contraltos as being nearer in spirit to Non-conformist practice? Cathedrals were unaffected. Durham wanted a counter tenor in 1858.

By the mid-nineteenth century, not only had the alto secular solo parts become the exclusive province of the female contralto but the secular chorus parts – i.e. all non-church music – were going the same way. Composers now wrote oratorio alto lines much higher on average, presupposing female voices. (Compare the chorus alto tessitura in Purcell and Handel to that in Beethoven, Mendelssohn then Brahms, for example.) The alto part was now unsuited and uncomfortable, sometimes even impossible for the 'male' alto, that strange and somehow undignified name by which the counter tenor had become known. Not that it remained known by any name much past the turn of the nineteenth century, except in church surroundings.

So the concert counter tenor became extinct. And this in a tradition-loving country which more than any other had savoured and loved the counter-tenor sound, whose native composers had honoured it for centuries with work of high rank. But the counter tenor was biding his time.

An illuminating example of probably the only secular activity open to altos – if thus it can be termed – other than glee singing, can be seen in the *Handbook of a Grand Bazaar to be held in the Athenaeum, Highbury New Park, Islington, London, 1894*, in aid of the fund for providing a vicarage for the parish of St Thomas, Finsbury Park. On the 13th of November, at eight-thirty, was the Grand Concert. A Mr Ernest Marriott, Alto (St Paul's Cathedral), Mr W. H. Stevenson, Baritone, Mr Douglas St Aubyn, Tenor (St Mary, Stoke Newington), Mr Vernon Taylor, Bass (St Paul's Cathedral) were the 'Amphion Quartet', billed as a main attraction.

Ernest Marriott and his Chapel Royal, cathedral and collegiate alto colleagues throughout England were the linear descendants at least, of Abell, Howell and Hughes; how tragic that even the best of the

LORD, I FLEE TO THEE FOR REFUGE
LASS, O HERR, MICH HÜLLE FINDEN

FELIX MENDELSSOHN-BARTHOLDY
(1809–47)

Example 15 *The 19th-century 'alto' solo, showing its high tessitura, from 'Lord I flee to Thee for refuge', Mendelssohn (1809–1847). (By kind permission of O.U.P)*

late-Victorian altos were unlikely to be engaged outside cathedral or church for anything more exciting than the Islington Bazaar! Stevenson, St Aubyn and Taylor were no doubt heavily engaged singers elsewhere. Islington, for them, was probably just a bit of fun. For poor Marriott it may well have been his only extra-cathedral outing for months.

It must be admitted that the unique timbre of the *classical* counter tenor does not suit music of the Romantic period any more than the music suits the voice. Try playing Mendelssohn on a harpsichord! This is surely the main reason for the warmer, rounder, more mellow sound that 'male' altos made by the latter nineteenth century and first part of the twentieth. Also, we must remember that the *untutored* falsetto makes that type of sound most readily. As the tone of tenors and altos gradually diversified, alto must have seemed more appropriate than counter tenor as a name for that voice which soon was the only one left employing falsetto as the teachings of the old Italian School began to disseminate.

No small wonder then that most Romantic alto voices were so unsuited for the performance of much of the earlier repertoire, and why the old name counter tenor seemed so inappropriate. Like many modern breeds of dog, the original characteristics had become blurred or had been bred out in other interests.

By about 1880, it is likely that most altos sounded unhappy in much solo work written before the nineteenth century. This only applied in cathedral or church anyway, but out in the secular sunshine the contraltos, too, struggled to make Handelian or any other counter tenor solo parts they met sound convincing. They were not necessarily much more successful in pre-Romantic ensemble either.

A contralto singing an alto part written for a counter tenor in ensemble copes physically with the notes, but the effect must be inappropriate and heavy. However beautiful the sound might be in itself, the result will press down on the tenor like a wet blanket. And regarding solo counter tenor work, as Stuart Humphry Ward has put it: 'Anyone who has heard a contralto attempting the solo counter tenor role in Purcell's *Ode to St Cecilia*, 1692, will have done their best to forget the experience.'

Alfred Deller talked in *A Singularity of Voice* of the problems encountered by contraltos. He had been asked about the Bach alto arias. Discussion had reached the Magnificat in D, performed of course at authentic pitch, down about a tone or semi-tone from modern A = 440. The duet 'Et misericordia' for alto and tenor is highish in the tenor but rather low for a contralto even at modern pitch. The result is always difficulty in matching the two tones. As Deller said, when the voices cross each other, '. . . it is not a question of whether the contralto is any good or not, but whether you can really get this intertwining of sounds and timbres between the two voices. With the counter tenor replacing the [contra] alto you can get it, because of this instrumental quality I'm speaking of.' Then he mentioned an example of the effect of the solo contralto: 'Out of the same work there's the 'Esurientes' for alto, which pipes along with two flutes. The counter tenor voice, having the same sort of fluty sound, answers the instruments ideally, while a female voice, however beautiful its quality, just does not match the quality of the instruments.'

All this is far from the nineteenth-century view of the matter, except in regard to church music. While the secular world went its way, the English church musicians quietly retained good sense. Read what J. Varley Roberts, the noted choirmaster and organist of Magdalen College, Oxford, has to say in his treatise *A Practical Method of Training Choristers* (1898, Oxford University Press). He is discussing the obtaining of altos:

Boy-altos must necessarily use almost entirely 'chest' register, which is thick and rough, and this quality of voice is most objectionable in an inner part – indeed as objectionable as contraltos (i.e. when females sing the alto part). Boys should only be resorted to when it is absolutely impossible to obtain men-altos. Many Bass singers might sing Alto; and if they would confine themselves to exclusively practising the falsetto voice, men-altos would be sufficiently numerous to supply the demand. The old Church composers always wrote for men-altos. Few things are more intolerable than to hear a boy-alto or lady-contralto sing the highest part – say, in a trio for Alto, Tenor, and Bass voices, in anthems by such Church writers as Greene, Croft, Boyce, etc. Of course, if it be quite impossible to obtain men-altos, then, as a last resource, adopt boy-altos or contraltos. For the singing of Solos, no doubt a Contralto is better than an Alto voice, but to obtain the quality of tone most desirable in Church choirs, men-altos are essential. For some years it was the experience of the writer of this treatise to have a mixed choir of women and men, several of whom were professional singers. After a certain evensong when Boyce's anthem 'O where shall wisdom be found' had been sung, an eminent musician, who happened to be in the church, subsequently remarked on the singular and disastrous effect of a 'thick' chest voice singing the highest part in the 'verse' portion of the anthem: it was, he said, 'as if a "bass-singer's" quality of tone was singing the top part.' He said the truth: nothing can replace the beautiful thin flute-like tone of the pure Alto, it brightens the entire quality of the tone of the choir.

(It is interesting to note Varley Roberts' views on *solo* contraltos. He no longer expected an alto of solo standard to be available.)

Not only were altos waiting in the wings, so to speak, in the cathedrals; they were now in parish churches too. The influence of the Oxford Movement had brought about large, male, robed choirs, however weak musically some of them may have been to begin with, in almost every parish church in the land. Altos were thus reintroduced into parish choirs, though it must have been difficult to obtain them in any number at first.

Most parish churches had enjoyed the dubious benefits for centuries of very mixed gallery choirs and ad-hoc yokel or stout-hearted citizen ensembles. (The few especially important medieval parish churches which had boasted salaried singers had mostly lost them at the Reformation.) Some notable Oxford Movement church choirs have continued with distinction to the present day, like Leeds Parish Church and St Michael's College, Tenbury. The recently late, great, much-lamented all-male choir of All Saints, Margaret Street, London was another. Alas it is no more.

In some instances the movement towards establishing a proper choral tradition actually *restored* a choir after many wretched years of musical neglect or total absence. One such foundation was the Temple Church, London, which has enjoyed a distinguished musical tradition since. Another was the Chapel Royal, Hampton Court, which by 1737 never saw its official choir – the Choir of the Chapel Royal (Whitehall until 1698 when it was burnt down: St James's Palace thereafter) because Hampton Court had ceased to be occupied by the reigning monarch. In the 1830s and 40s a new indigenous choral foundation was sought after, then finally established at Hampton Court which perhaps thereby returned to something like its ancient situation in Wolsey's day when he employed a choir of sixteen boys and sixteen singing men in a manner befitting the private chapel of a Cardinal. We may relate this foundation usefully to the Earl of Northumberland's, mentioned earlier in detail (page 25). Wolsey would not have been content merely to equal but must needs surpass the Percy household.

Except for a slight 'hiccup' in the 1960s, Hampton Court Chapel Royal Choir has continued as an all-male foundation, including counter tenors, to the present day. During the 1920s and 30s, the Gentlemen were London singers, many from the colleges of music, so we are told by an ex-chorister. But this only refers to tenors and basses. Counter tenors were in short supply and unavailable from any colleges of music, so they were either local men or ex-choristers trained as altos. (The late Thurston Dart was a chorister at Hampton

Court. Whether he ever went back as an alto we cannot say, but perhaps his subsequent musical career was noteworthy enough!)

So there was and has been no break in the cathedral and alto tradition, nor in the glee club or male quartet. There was also positive widespread renewal for the voice throughout England in churches, though only in churches. (The male quartet was not, incidentally, unique to England. 'The Comedy Harmonists', a German–Jewish ensemble of superb standard, was famous between the wars in Europe. They died tragically in concentration camps. The group included at least one counter tenor.)

The solo concert platform was a different matter. From the mid-nineteenth century until the mid 1940s, the very idea of the very high male *solo* voice was no more than a joke, formed from a Freudian folk memory of the castrati: an irritating bug-bear which refuses to die completely, even today. But in cathedral circles there were distinguished names, altos of repute who, though seldom singing solo outside through lack of opportunity, were nevertheless justly celebrated. Atherley Clarke of the Chapel Royal (St James) was one. He was active in the earlier part of this century. 'Nobby' Clark (no relation), at Ely until the late 1950s, was another.

We seem to have suggested that altos were awaiting their chance to stage a 'come-back'. This is perhaps over-simplification. A come-back was a forlorn hope until altos regained some real style, some panache, some self-respect. There had to be one man outstanding enough to take on the prejudice of at least a century.

Although cathedral choir altos had survived, the situation in parish churches by the second world war was very different for the most part. As more years had gone by and two horrific world wars had taken choir men away, many never to return, more contraltos (and sopranos) had infiltrated previously male parish choirs and the now familiar process of attrition was in hand yet again.

Percy Scholes, writing in 1938 in the *Oxford Companion to Music*, was able to say, 'The real alto being now so rare, it is becoming common to speak of contraltos as altos . . .'

Alfred Deller (1912–1979) is of course the name which will for ever represent the resurgence of a fine tradition, not just in Britain, but in North America, the rest of the English-speaking world and Europe too. This self-taught, superb artist was responsible, single-handedly at first, by his incredible voice and sound instinctive style, for the re-establishment of solo counter tenor singing in the secular concert world.

I recommend *A Singularity of Voice* for the story of the 'discovery', by Michael Tippett, of Deller in Canterbury Cathedral Choir. It is an amusing story and should be enjoyed in this, Deller's first official biography.

When Deller eventually sang Purcell's 'Music for a While', for Tippett, there in the Song School in Canterbury Cathedral, 'the years', according to Tippett, 'seemed to roll away'. He was hearing what he thought never to hear, *and* in Canterbury where Lionel Power and probably Thomas Tallis were once lay clerks and Orlando Gibbons' grave is situated.

Of course, nearly forty years later, it is difficult for us to imagine a musical spectrum without counter tenors: although there are those prejudiced enough to wish it were not so. But as has been said, counter tenors, admittedly weak ones, had always been hidden away in choirs. So Michael Tippett was not hearing a unique *register*, but a unique artist, a unique voice: the genuine *virtuoso* solo alto, extinct since the close of the eighteenth century or not long thereafter.

The woeful lack of this missing voice, essential in performing not just Purcell but all early music, had been noted and lamented by many. E. H. Fellowes asks sadly in his famous *English Madrigal Composers* (back in 1919), what can we do about these awkward and essential alto parts? Interestingly, he does consider that the altos of his time could manage well. Of course, sixteenth-century madrigals do not usually demand a virtuoso solo alto. Fellowes has no hang-ups: to him counter tenor equals alto and vice versa:

For practical purposes with modern singers a serious difficulty is presented by the awkward compass of the inner voice-parts of much of this music, both sacred and secular, though the difficulty is much mitigated when male altos are available. For the alto-parts sometimes extend for a compass of nearly two octaves, ranging for an octave on either side of middle C.

And the tenor-parts often lie very high, yet too low for female alto singers. It seems probable that in Elizabethan days male singers made very free use of the *falsetto* register. In order to meet this very real difficulty some editors have introduced drastic emendations into the text; such a course of action is inexcusable unless adequate annotation is printed which may enable the student to perceive the exact form of the composer's text, and may also make it possible to perform the music in its original design when circumstances admit of it. In Wilbye's *Sweet honey-sucking bees*, where two counter-tenor voices of equal compass are employed, the difficulty has been met in most reprints by a wholesale rearrangement of these two voice-parts without annotation, but it might be overcome by transposing the music down a tone; while if counter-tenors are available, the parts, as they stand in the original text, are exactly suitable for that class of voice. In many instances this type of difficulty can be solved by the readjustment of a single phrase and sometimes of no more than one note. Another plan is to include a few alto voices among the tenors, and *vice versa*. But all such minor matters are best left to the judgement of conductors, who must be guided by their own individual requirements, acting always on a wise discretion and with due reverence for the composer's text.

A. K. Holland, writing in 1932 in his book *Henry Purcell, the English Musical Tradition*, puts it more strongly. He does not even consider the possibility of using the altos of his time:

. . . a rather grave problem, applying equally to his anthems and his dramatic pieces, is the use of the alto voice in so much of Purcell's most difficult music. Purcell has had, in the course of time, almost every conceivable kind of bad luck, serving to hinder the performance of his music and the growth of a practical tradition. But this misfortune has lain more heavily upon him than any other. Had he been himself a tenor instead of an alto, we might not have had quite so much of his work pitched in this particular register, though there is no doubt that the male alto, besides being inevitable in cathedral music and particularly in the verse-anthems of the time, was a very popular solo voice in Purcell's day. Nowadays it is scarcely cultivated outside the sphere of male voice choirs, if we except the type of falsetto which usually does duty for it in church. 'Feigned voices', as Matthew Locke tells us, were not unknown in Purcell's day. Yet the male alto (or counter-tenor) is a real voice and a traditionally English one. Apart from the fact that in colour and texture it differs from the contralto, it has, or should have, a compass that is at once higher than the tenor and lower than the female alto voice, so that for contraltos much of Purcell's music lies in an awkward tessitura besides requiring an agility which few contraltos possess. But the problem ought to be faced and not evaded. Alto voices are not incapable of development. The difficulty is one which is met with frequently in the case of the madrigals and wholesale re-arrangement or transposition will not solve it. The older composers wrote for a wide range of voices. The study of Purcell would certainly tend to do away with the vogue of the nondescript type of voice which modern English composers in their vocal music seem so often to encourage. The characteristic English voice of to-day is a mezzo-soprano or a baritone, when it is not a tenor that is a baritone forced up. Purcell wrote for real sopranos and real basses and in his inner parts used the fullest range of voice. A diagrammatic analysis of some of his typical songs would probably reveal the fact that his music demands not merely a wide compass but a fairly prevalent use of the more extreme and characteristic levels of the voice.

* * *

There were other laments, equally as strong. In 1937, John Hough's paper to the Royal Musical Association, called *The Historical Significance of the Counter Tenor*, was an important event and a paper still very useful today despite some of its conclusions. I discuss elsewhere the falsetto versus high tenor argument in detail. Much of Mr Hough's lecture was concerned with this matter, as in 1937 it was puzzling to everyone why the altos then to be heard were either so weak, or strongly but *inappropriately* toned for music apparently written for them in earlier centuries.

During questions at the end of the lecture, Professor J. A. Westrup, the Purcell authority, remarked: 'One would not naturally assume from hearing modern [1937] counter tenors that much of the music of Purcell's period was so virile in quality. Thoroughly manly songs were sung then by counter tenors. What has happened to the voice in the meantime?' (His was surely a lament echoed by many who were concerned with effective performance of pre-Romantic music.) In answer, Mr Hough went on to state his view that the counter tenor is a naturally high tenor, and virile in tone; the alto, though beautiful at times, is unnatural and merely a mellow falsetto. Interestingly, Professor Westrup was not convinced by the lecture or the answers to questions on this point, for he, together with Frank Harrison, edited Collins *Music Encyclopaedia*, 1959, in which there is a highly revealing entry under 'alto'. (See Appendix B.)

It is fascinating to consider that within six years of Mr Hough's paper, Tippett had heard Deller at Canterbury and the revival had begun. E. H. Fellowes, writing in 1941, in his famous study *English Cathedral Music*, is still mourning by implication the lost virtuoso alto, never realising he had only two years more to wait:

> Tudway's reference to the exceptional excellence of the men's voices at Whitehall is significant. Among the basses was the famous John Gostling (an ex-Canterbury Minor Canon), for whose extraordinary compass Purcell and others wrote passages that are sometimes grotesque. But the altos must have been exceptionally good. Michael Wise was one who was evidently outstanding; William Child was another, and there were many more. The composers at the Chapel Royal had these singers in their minds when they wrote not only solos, but the numberless verses for men's voices with altos at the top. Tudway was right; it is still a mistake to attempt to performances, and it is idle to pretend that much of the [work of the] Restoration composers and later, which looks good on paper, has any real artistic value when the trios, and, still worse, the alto and bass duets, are rendered with such a want of balance of tone as they often are. The effect is often made more tolerable by a kind of false

tradition that all verse passages of this sort must be taken at a slow tempo, and after a short pause following the previous movement.

In 1943, *The Times* critic, presumably not H. C. Colles (see page 182) reviewing a concert at Morley College at which a certain Alfred Deller made his London debut, wrote: '. . . Mr Alfred Deller of Canterbury, in the anthem, and in an air, made familiar by Dr Whittaker as "Music Shall Now Proclaim" (Music for Awhile), but sung in its original pitch, showed by the purity of his voice and of the style how it was that the seventeenth and eighteenth centuries came to attach so much value to the high male voice.'

It now reads as a piece of history. It was the real start for Deller. But he had far to go to overcome the most extraordinary prejudices. Many upsetting comments came his way, sometimes *before* a performance, as when waiting to go on at the Royal Festival Hall in the 1950s. He was standing by Sir Malcolm Sargent and an orchestra leader Alfred Deller has been too kind to name. The leader said to Sargent, so that Deller could hear: 'I see we've got the bearded lady with us.' Apparently, Sargent, the epitome of the English Gentleman, affected not to hear and is said to have brushed some imaginary dust off his sleeve.

It is easy with hindsight to remark that it was after all only a matter of time before a singer great enough came forward to re-establish this vital voice in the revival and authentic performance of early and Pre-Romantic music. How difficult initially Deller's task was, even with Tippett and the B.B.C. Third Programme to help. Most of the musical establishment, trained, still entrenched in and guided by the prestigious music colleges, did not want to know. Again I recommend Deller's biography for an account of this. Also imagine selling the idea of the renascent solo 'male alto' to provincial choral societies and music clubs in the 1940s and 50s. Even in the 1980s, much work remains to convince those conservative bastions.

With Deller's recent untimely death, an era has passed, one filled with the excitement of great pioneer work. This book is dedicated to Deller and that era. Here is J. B. Steane in the *Grand Tradition*, 1974. Oddly, it reads as if Deller had retired by then, but he never did and was still singing well up to his death in 1979:

> . . . over the last twenty years or so they have learnt to accept the voice of the counter tenor as a regular part of the musical fare . . . Alfred Deller's great gifts were luckily at hand at just the right time to give a lead, inspire new interest and virtually to found a school . . . he gave some incomparable performances of songs by Dowland and Purcell. Of its kind his voice was unusually full-bodied and

vibrant. He could float it very beautifully, but many altos and falsettists can do this. Where (as far as I know) he is still unique is in his strong resonance; also, of course, in the style, which though often imitated was entirely his own. Ornate in its fondness for crescendos, sudden pianos, emphases, . . . knowledge of voice colouring, . . . most at home in Purcell . . . erotic languor . . . gentle mystical swing . . . the minor-keyed languishing chromatic comforts . . . When the poets spoke of making delicious moan and so forth, they must have had singing something like Deller's in mind. He could catch Elizabethan melancholy . . . in Dowland's 'In darkness let me dwell' we hear something essentially stronger than melancholy . . . a quite exceptional artist, who . . . brought volumes of old music to the light of imaginative performance . . . his resonant voice matching the sonority of the viols . . . folk songs . . . wealth of music from tavern songs to Monteverdi with his Consort, a fine body of singers . . . strongly directed. Benjamin Britten paid his tribute with Oberon's music in *Midsummer Night's Dream* which Deller recorded, using his full voice for this often aggressive part, and luxuriating in the Purcellian solo 'I know a bank'.

Thurston Dart, in *The Interpretation of Music*, commented:

Another obsolete voice, the solo male alto or counter tenor, has become familiar again during the last decade through the artistry of Alfred Deller. The tradition of counter tenor singing in English cathedral choirs has never been broken since the earliest times, but solo counter tenors of Deller's calibre must always have been rare. The voice itself seems to have been an especially English one – Purcell and Henry Lawes were both counter tenors – and its distinctive tone colour is an essential part of English choral music.

During the late 1940s and early 50s, Deller's brilliance inspired others to follow, notably John Whitworth, Grayston Burgess, Owen Wynne; and Russell Oberlin in the USA. By the time of the joint Purcell–Handel Commemoration in 1958, the solo counter tenor was re-established firmly in England, if not yet throughout the British Isles; re-established yes, popular in a wide sense no.

This London-based festival provided a comprehensive brochure which included various articles on each composer and his works. It also listed the London events in detail, and conclusions may be drawn which are interesting and informative. Out of forty-two concerts (including instrumental recitals, opera and oratorio performances, but not including lectures) eleven involved solo counter tenors. This sounds modest, but out of those forty-two, several events were re-peated throughout the festival at intervals:

The Tempest–Purcell,   (at The Old Vic, 17 performances, no counter tenor part in the original.)

Samson–Handel,   (Covent Garden, 3 performances, counter tenor parts taken by women.)

This is interesting, in that opera was the last bastion to be recaptured, if so it can be termed, for the situation is still not entirely satisfactory even in the 1980s. It is worth noting that opera was the first medium to fall to the castrati, back in the eighteenth century.

Dido and Aeneas–Purcell, (Great Hall, Hampton Court, 3 performances. No counter tenor part in the original.)

Semele–Handel,   (Sadlers Wells, 3 performances, with counter tenor–Grayston Burgess.)

If we take each of the above works as *one* performance, making four in total, the concert total, instrumental and vocal, has shrunk to twenty, out of which nine now involve solo counter tenor work.

The brochure had a large list of centres throughout Britain where other Purcell and Handel works were performed as part of the com-memoration. It would be interesting to know how many included counter tenors where the voice was originally specified or expected. The works included: *Acis and Galatea*; *Alexander's Feast*; *L'Allegro et Il Penseroso*; *Belshazzar*; *Dido and Aeneas*; *The Fairy Queen*; *Israel in Egypt*; *Jephtha*; *Joshua*; *Judas Maccabaeus*; *King Arthur*; *Messiah*; *Orlando*; *St John Passion*; *Saul*; *Semele*; *Solomon* and *Xerxes*.

The Times music critic, writing at this same time, was interested but not noticeably over-enthusiastic or hopeful for the counter tenor to prove more than a passing fad:

> The curiously sudden revival of the counter tenor voice is another vagary of taste, aided by scholarship which demands authentic performances of Purcell, who liked and used the voice. It is to be distinguished from the male alto, which is a baritone's falsetto and its tessitura lies a fifth higher than the tenor's – Britten writes Oberon's part up to D. A generation ago the voice was unknown outside books and certainly unheard: now counter tenors multiply, and there are even attempts to revive the sound of the male soprano (though without surgery).

The re-introduction of counter tenors into mainstream secular ensemble work happened naturally after the example of the five voice

68

Golden Age Singers, with Deller the sole voice of alto range. Then came the peerless example and excellence of the Deller Consort, founded in 1950; a similar group to the former, but directed by Deller himself. (John Whitworth replaced Deller in the Golden Age Singers in 1953.) Other ensembles followed, notably the Ambrosian Consort, which also included John Whitworth. But all this was in the world of early music – madrigals, motets, concert performances of early church music and so on.

Male-voice quartets or small ensembles, an honourable if by then rather stuffy sounding survival of the great tradition, sang as I have hinted, with a style and repertoire almost completely romantic. Yet they too soon became transformed with the impact of the new exciting alto sound and capability. John Whitworth's excellent 'Well Tempered Singers' made exciting and emphatically not lugubrious listening. Groups today include the popular 'King's Singers', 'The Scholars' (they have now added a very good mezzo soprano, but started without one), and there are many others, not forgetting the only trio, 'Canterbury Clerkes'.

Strangely, the voice has not yet really repenetrated the secular chorus, except in cases like the Three Choirs Festival Chorus, where the cathedral choirs themselves were the originators and founder members. Barry Still explains how the 'large' chorus formed by the three cathedral choirs was slowly but steadily augmented:

> Early in Festival history, a few ladies were 'imported' from the North, then members of other cathedral or collegiate bodies were invited, with the aim of giving extra strength to the choral forces. For the fashion was developing for more robust and opulent interpretations of the Baroque repertoire than could be attempted by the three cathedral choirs alone. (Even in 1835, the orchestra numbered seventy-one, the choral body 119.) Taste has turned a somersault in some ways, as this year's *Messiah* at Gloucester testifies – Cathedral choir with chamber orchestra!

Other than the Three Choirs Chorus, the typical choral society, despite its comprehensive repertoire taking in perhaps Monteverdi to Tippett, does not use altos at all. One argument is that the staple musical diet of a choral society still remains the last 180 years. Many of the alto parts are therefore not only more comfortable for contraltos, but written for them. Another reason is that the choral society tradition is conservative. Counter tenors were themselves supported and sustained in the nineteenth century by the same slowness to accept change. (Yet these same counter tenors must have been feeling the strain over range.)

A third point is sociological. In these days of women's liberation, who would dare push the ladies from the alto line for even one performance of Purcell or Handel? Also, it would be sadly difficult today to find *enough* counter tenors to populate the alto part exclusively in a choral society.

In my opinion the biggest reason, however, is aesthetic. The timbres of altos and contraltos do not mix well. Even on identical notes in the scale, the alto sounds higher and more piercing than the rather plummier contralto. Neither enjoys the sensation of singing next to the other.

Consequently it seems that there are few counter tenors of modest vocal endowment, in other words average choral society singers, who even apply for regular membership of a choral society. However rarely it may occur, they prefer to be asked to strengthen the contraltos for odd occasional early works and reserve their enthusiasm for the local all-male church choir or some smaller specialised chamber group in which the alto is usually sung exclusively by men.

England with its cathedral choirs stood to some extent apart, musically, at least since the sixteenth century, from Scotland, Wales and Ireland. Religious tradition being rather different in Scotland, the 'chorus' counter tenors survived, very tenuously if at all. Until its decline in the sixteenth century, Scotland had a proud musical history, but the Reformation hit hard, particularly hard in the cold north under the influence of John Knox. Then in 1601, when King James VI became King of England and came south, what was left of Scottish court music petered out.

Wales has another differing tradition over the past few centuries. It had never enjoyed the grand Medieval and Renaissance musical tradition of both Scotland and England. By the mid-sixteenth century only St David's Cathedral could boast an adequate cathedral foundation with music. Most Welsh musicians were in England. Since then, in the few cathedral choirs, there survives a slightly better situation than in Scotland. Llandaff has rather displaced St David's as the premier Welsh cathedral choir. The other modest foundations still support choirs on the traditional pattern. In Wales there have probably always been a few cathedral altos, despite the supremacy and popularity in male voice choirs of the high tenor variety.

An interesting sidelight on Welsh choral singing is shown in the October 1903 *Musical Times*. Dr Roland Rogers, organist of Bangor Cathedral, was credited with the 'discovery' of the contralto voice in North Wales at least:

He conducted the celebrated Bethesda Choir which won £1000 in prizes at various Eisteddfodau, and discovered the contralto in N.

Wales. Until then, the alto part in choruses was sung by boys whose voices were bordering on the 'breaking' point, and all the women sang soprano! He was quick to perceive that the beautiful deep-toned voices of Welsh women could be used with splendid effect in choral music, with results that are too well-known to need further comment.

Percy Scholes adds in 'The Decline of the Male Alto and the Rise of Contralto' (*Mirror of Music*, 1947): 'Rogers was born in 1847 and died in 1927. It would seem from the above that the adult male alto, for centuries so common in English choirs, was unknown in Wales until recent times, and that the introduction of the contralto came much later than in England.'

Scholes' remarks surely refer only to secular not cathedral choirs. It seems likely that mixed choral singing and male voice singing – for which the Welsh are now so famous – were very different forms of expression indeed. Some people hold the view that the mixed chorus in itself was entirely a nineteenth-century innovation in Wales, which seems surprising. Perhaps the Rogers article hides within its lines a hint of the remains of a boys and men male voice choir tradition. Scholes' comment that the 'male alto' was unknown in Wales until recent times (1947) is probably mistaken. Apart from the cathedral altos (who surely must have existed), sitting amongst the top tenors of the tenor–bass male voice choirs were possibly, even still are, a number of low counter tenors who never heard the term counter tenor in their lives.

Ireland was a different case: in the South mostly parochial Roman Catholic; in the North, mostly fierce congregational Protestant. The historical Church of Ireland was stuck traditionally and precariously between, and was different again. These 'Anglican' cathedrals, not-ably the two in Dublin, preserved from ancient times the English style and repertoire of choral singing, and so preserved the tradition of alto voices as a direct consequence. It was, after all, Christ Church Cathedral Choir, Dublin, which gave the first complete performance of Handel's *Messiah* in 1742. But these isolated centres apart, Ireland's high male voice tradition rested in the 'Irish Tenor', a curious but possible branch of the counter tenor family.

Scotland, Wales and Ireland then were not surprisingly slower than England in the acceptance of the 1940s renaissance of counter tenor singing. The fact that it seemed English might well have counted against it. It would be interesting to survey this whole question.

Considering solo and ensemble work in England in the 1980s, we can look about with confidence despite the reservations. There are many superb counter tenor singers heard regularly in concert, opera, records, broadcasts and oratorios. Most still emanate from England (surely the home of the counter tenor voice), but several are American, and several are from the Continent of Europe and elsewhere. Not all sound the same. Which is entirely proper considering the varied character of repertoire. There is some controversy about matters of voice production, referred to later in detail.

It seems appropriate to finish this general historical examination of the natural high male voice with a sideways glance. Clearly, European and North American Caucasian males are not the only ones to enjoy the use of what we would call the falsetto. Its use is probably as old as the human race. It has figured large in Negro music: African, American and Caribbean; indeed all places where there has been an influx of Negro culture for whatever reason.

Primitive peoples, like the Australian Aborigines, are known to use falsetto. Even the crude Swiss yodel can be seen as a folk instrument.

The falsetto was certainly developed to a highly sophisticated degree in the Near and Far East. As we have already seen, there is considerable evidence to suggest that the art of the falsettist formed very much the main tonal colouring of early medieval music. It is very likely that the travels of the Crusaders and the influence of the East were partly responsible. Such influence is discernible in medieval art.

Falsetto singing was certainly practised and admired in the Near East at least by the eighth century AD. By very early medieval times European singers seem to have adopted much the same nasal falsetto and vocal style. This can be seen in contemporary pictures showing the accurate physiognomy of singers.

The Moorish invasion of Spain in the eighth century resulted in the art of falsetto voice production passing into Spanish culture. Certainly the rise of the troubadour is connected with this. The art of Spanish falsetto seems likely to have originated very early on, and as we have seen was firmly established and acclaimed by the Renaissance. Because troubadours also moved freely round France and Italy, the art of falsetto was taken through Europe with obvious results. It was in France that the vocal style of the troubadour seems to have entered the world of the Church, probably as early as the eleventh century.

It might be suggested incidentally that the modern 'pop' use of falsettists is merely another manifestation of an outside creative influence on European music, and thus a healthy cross-cultural fertilisation in just the same way as the Moorish falsetto techniques were in the tenth and eleventh centuries. But the similarity between then and today is superficial.

Before the coming of the Moors to Spain in the earliest of medieval times, there was no rich commonwealth of music. No sumptuous European thousand year tradition was in existence in which had been created probably the greatest of musical works of art ever likely to be conceived by man. Also, the adoption of falsetto by the 'pop' industry is for the most part contrived and almost completely commercial.

So although on the positive side some good to the counter tenor movement could possibly come as a result of the public's common-place familiarity with the high male voice, the negative aspect is that the very poverty of 'pop' music itself seems likely to prevent any real lasting benefit accruing to music as an art form.

Be that as it may, the fascinating African or Eastern musical cultures by which it seems European music was once indelibly influenced must remain unexplored in a book of this nature. A separate study is needed on this fascinating aspect of ethnomusicology, but I mention this now as it must be understood that male falsetto singing is not unique to European sophisticated cultures, or merely a quirky English manifes-tation. As J. B. Steane puts it: 'There have been plenty of counter tenors in these years . . . they should all from time to time join in a fanfare for counter tenors in praise of Alfred the Great, the first of a steadily prospering line.'

What we underline is that this very high *natural* male voice, some semblance at least of which every man alive possesses, is utterly normal and its use is not at all 'quirky'.

Chapter 3

CASTRATI

HAVING TALKED at some length of natural high voices, let us now consider voices which can hardly be described as natural, those of the castrati. Yet, natural voice or not, they were some of the greatest vocal artists in human history.

The castrati, male sopranos, mezzos and (castrati) contraltos, who enjoyed a great vogue in Italian opera in the seventeenth and eighteenth centuries, still give rise to knowing smiles today. It is often assumed that the counter tenor is the same in origin.

Castrati existed for thousands of years. The practice of castrating young boys to preserve one or more of their boyish attributes (voice, looks etc.) or to provide sexually-safe guardians of the harems of the East was, if not widespread, at least not uncommon. However, although the study of the practice in antiquity is not without interest, it is not relevant to the more modern habit.

The attribute of the castrati which is relevant is the retention of the boys' singing voice. Castrati were also variously known as 'musici' or 'everati', which read like euphemisms. Eunuchs were used in antiquity as singers, and records exist in early medieval times of eunuchs singing. One factor which accelerated the rise of the castrati was the introduction of complicated 'a capella' singing in the middle of the fifteenth century. This demanded extremely competent and proficient treble singers, and using boys for this exposed several drawbacks, not least of which was the fact that by the time they had learnt their job their voices were about to break. In Spain, where the art of falsetto was highly developed, falsettists began to be used to supply the power and maturity needed for the new contrapuntal requirements. The Spanish had developed a method for greatly increasing the upward range of the voice in men – much higher than the counter tenor – without involving the singular disadvantage of castration. However, castrati did exist in Spain, and it has been argued that perhaps the Spanish falsettists

74

were castrati masquerading under another name. Be that as it may, the tone of the castrati was considered pleasanter than that of the falsettists. Furthermore, it was found that the vocal cords of the falsettists did not last well – the strain of such singing wore them out. With the approval of Pope Clement VIII, the numbers and popularity of the castrati increased by leaps and bounds.

How were castrati produced? This question (all too easily answered by modern Philistines as, 'They had their balls cut off!') must be answered remembering the standards of the day, which to us seem brutish and callous. Civil punishment for crimes was often barbaric: maiming and branding were common, and the death penalty for many crimes not now regarded as serious. Surgery was performed without anaesthetic and with scant regard for hygiene. Strangely enough, the Church refused to countenance maiming as a punishment, and yet still was one of the first institutions to use castrati (and the last to give up the practice), although it would not publicly agree with the means by which they were produced. Considering the above, there were three possible methods of attaining the required result. They were: (a) disease; (b) accident; (c) deliberate surgery.

Some diseases, such as mumps at the correct age, cause the hormones necessary for normal sexual development to be suppressed. Apart from the obvious drawbacks of such an occurrence, the secondary sexual development is also arrested – growth of body hair, and thickening of the vocal cords. Nowadays, the problem is easily remedied by the injection of the necessary hormones. Indeed, quite recently, before such hormone treatment was widely known, a director of an ensemble specialising in early music considered searching for such 'natural castrati' to take part in early music. He was, not surprisingly, unsuccessful.

Accidental castration no doubt does happen, but must be rare. Nonetheless, accident or surgery following accident was the accepted (and acceptable) reason for the Church to condone castrati as singers in church. The Church was naturally averse to publicity encouraging what was, after all, the deliberate maiming of children.

Deliberate surgical castration was the most widely used method of producing castrati. Disease and accidents simply could not have coped with the increasing demand. For the standards of the day, the operation must have been *comparatively* minor. Following the administration of some drug such as opium, the child was placed in a hot bath. This rendered him virtually insensible, at which point the ducts leading to the testicles were severed, so that the testicles eventually shrivelled and disappeared. The *removal* of the organs does not seem to have taken place in the case of the castrati.

In order to preserve the boy's voice, the operation would have had to be carried out *before* the vocal cords began to thicken. It would be no use castrating a tenor or bass and expecting him to sing treble immediately, as many people still seem to think. Nor would it have been much use castrating children at random. The boy would have had to show some aptitude first.

Despite many claims to noble birth, most of the castrati came from fairly lowly families, who hoped, no doubt, that eminence in their future profession would enable their sons to provide for them. Such was seldom the case . . . Only two well-known castrati came from well-to-do families – Farinelli and Caffarelli – and these two may well have been operated on as the result of accident or disease. Apart from any consideration on the part of the parents, it was the law that before the operation could be carried out, the child himself had to desire it. In one known case, apparently, the child *did* request it, in order to preserve his voice, of which he was very proud.

Following or just before his operation, the young castrato would have been apprenticed to a singing master or sent to one of the 'conservatorios' or singing schools which graced many Italian cities. Although originally set up as charitable institutions for the education and upbringing of children, by the middle of the seventeenth century they were music schools, pure and simple. To boost the insufficient foundations, the pupils were often hired out for public or private musical events (as in the major English choirs in Tudor England).

The life of the castrati in the conservatorios was a little less spartan than that of the other students. They were accustomed to better food, warmer living accommodation, and better practice facilities. On the other side of the coin, they do not seem to have had a very happy time. Their physical condition would have set them apart from the other students, and would have encouraged spiteful ragging, while their preferential treatment would have cause them to be resented. Although the normal students may have been thrown out for idleness or misbehaviour, they seldom ran away as the castrati were prone to do. The inference is obvious.

Provided his voice came up to expectation, the young castrato would make his debut at some opera-house in his late teens. From then on, if his acting ability and voice appealed to the cognoscenti, and provided he did not become too gawky or obese (as castrati often did) he would run the full gamut of 'stardom' – very much in the modern idiom. If he failed to make the grade as an actor, he could always find himself employment as a church singer.

Italian opera was (and still is) regarded as the highest form of operatic art. In the seventeenth and eighteenth centuries, other countries may have had their own native traditions of musical drama, but it was still Italy that led the field, not least because the chances of employment were much higher. In countries other than Italy which enjoyed opera, it tended to be the diversion of the court and the nobility, and was largely confined to the capital city. Openings for singers would, therefore, be rather limited. Hence the castrati did not enjoy a world-wide reputation even though, as is true today of soloists, they might well tour other countries, and give opera-lovers in other nations an appreciation of their style and mode of singing. National pride was also involved – Charles II sent the English counter tenor, John Abell, to Italy to be trained, and also 'to show the Italians the other nations had good voices, too!' Abel would have been what is now called a 'high counter tenor', with the ability to push his voice to the top of, and beyond, the treble stave. It has been suggested that Abell may have been a castrato, but there seems little evidence to support the theory. England only subscribed late to the use of castrati, relying on the home-grown counter tenor for high parts in opera and stage music, women or boys for feminine roles, and boys for the treble in church music.

Despite popular misconceptions, the results of castration did not seem to affect the future life, either emotional or physical, of the castrati. It did not lessen or alter their sexual urges – the stories of their amorous intrigues with their well-born female fans are legion, and differ little from the behaviour of 'stars' through the centuries. Nor did castration shorten or lengthen their lives or singing careers. They seem to have led perfectly normal lives, barring the fact that they were sterile.

The decline in the use of the castrati in opera began towards the end of the eighteenth century. The Italian musical climate of the 1790s had degenerated to frivolity, and the Napoleonic invasion with its political upheavals caused fashions to change. With the weakening of the conservatories, a new type of composer, notably Rossini, had little trouble in setting new trends, in which the castrati played small part. By the first few decades of the nineteenth century, the castrati were mostly finished, although a few, Velluti and Pergetti for example, lingered on a little longer.

Yet understandably, the castrati continued in employment in some Italian churches (notably the Sistine Chapel) for much longer. Domenico Mustafa (1829–1912) directed the Papal Music until 1895, when another castrato, Perosi, succeeded him. The last of the Papal castrati was Alessandro Moreschi (1858–1924), whose voice may still be heard on gramophone records made in 1903–4. These recordings, poor in quality though they may be, of a voice not of the best, provide us with the only audible link with those strange artists of another age.

We have verbal descriptions, however, and this does not only provide us with musical and physical evidence. Consider the sexual ambiguity noticed by Casanova in a café:

> An abbé with an attractive face walked in. At the appearance of his hips, I took him for a girl in disguise, and I said so to the abbé Gama; but the latter told me that it was Beppino della Mamana, a famous castrato. The abbé called him over, and told him, laughing, that I had taken him for a girl. The impudent creature, looking fixedly at me, told me that if I liked he would prove that I was right, or that I was wrong.

As a sexual expert, Casanova was clearly fascinated by these feminine men. He commented on one when visiting Rome in 1762:

> We went to the Aliberti theatre, where the castrato who took the prima donna's role attracted all the town. He was the complaisant favourite, the mignon, of Cardinal Borghese, and supped every evening tête-à-tête with His Eminence.
>
> In a well-made corset, he had the waist of a nymph, and, what was almost incredible, his breast was in no way inferior, either in form or in beauty, to any woman's; and it was above all by this means that the monster made such ravages. Though one knew the negative nature of this unfortunate, curiosity made one glance at his chest, and an inexpressible charm acted upon one, so that you were madly in love before you realised it. To resist the temptation, or not to feel it, one would have had to be cold and earthbound as a German. When he walked about the stage during the ritornello of the aria he was to sing, his step was majestic and at the same time voluptuous; and when he favoured the boxes with his glances, the tender and modest rolling of his black eyes brought a ravishment to the heart. It was obvious that he hoped to inspire the love of those who liked him as a man, and probably would not have done so as a woman.

To finish this brief account of the incredible castrati, here are some individual descriptions of witnesses to probably the greatest of them, Farinelli (1705–1782), whose real name was Carlo Broschi. The castrati must have been among the very finest singers of all time, and Farinelli was the best of even this exalted band. Mancini, the eighteenth-century singing teacher, wrote of him that:

> His voice was thought a marvel, because it was so perfect, so powerful, so sonorous and so rich in its extent, both in the high and low parts of the register, that its equal has never been heard in our times. He was, moreover, endowed with a creative genius which inspired him with embellishments so new and so astonishing that

no one was able to imitate them. The art of taking and keeping the breath so softly and easily that no one could perceive it began and died with him. The qualities in which he excelled were the evenness of his voice, the art of swelling its sound, the portamento, the union of registers, a surprising agility, a graceful and pathetic style, and a shake as admirable as it was rare. There was no branch of the art which he did not carry to the highest pitch of perfection . . .

Our own ever-present music critic, Dr Burney, heard him when the singer was only seventeen years of age, in 1722:

During the run of an opera, there was struggle every night between him and a famous player on the trumpet, in a song accompanied by that instrument; this, at first, seemed amicable and merely sportive, till the audience began to interest themselves in the contest, and to take different sides; after severally swelling a note, in which each manifested the power of his lungs, and tried to rival the other in brilliancy and force, they had both a swell and shake together, by thirds, which was continued so long, while the audience eagerly awaited the event, that both seemed to be exhausted; and, in fact, the trumpeter, wholly spent, gave it up, thinking, however, his antagonist as much tired as himself, and that it would be a drawn battle; when Farinelli, with a smile on his countenance, shewing he had only been sporting with him all the time, broke out all at once in the same breath, with fresh vigour, and not only swelled and shook the note, but ran the most rapid and difficult divisions, and was at last silenced only by the acclamation of the audience. From this period may be dated that superiority which he ever maintained over all his contemporaries.

Burney heard him again in England in 1734:

Every one knows who heard, or has heard of him, what an effect his surprising talents had upon the audience: it was ecstasy! rapture! enchantment!

In the famous air 'Son qual Nave', which was composed by his brother, the first note he sung was taken with such delicacy, swelled by minute degrees to such an amazing volume, and afterwards diminished in the same manner, that it was applauded for full five minutes. He afterwards set off with such brilliancy and rapidity of execution, that it was difficult for the violins of those days to keep pace with him. In short, he was to all other singers as superior as the famous horse Childers was to all other running-horses; but it was not only in speed, he had now every excellence of every great singer united. In his voice, strength, sweetness, and compass; in his style, the tender, the grateful, and the rapid. He possessed such powers as never met before, or since, in any one human being; powers that were irresistible, and which must subdue every hearer; the learned and the ignorant, the friend and the foe.

It is hoped that this brief section on the castrati will have cleared up definitively any lingering misunderstanding of the difference between the counter tenor and the eunuchoid voice.

Chapter 4

THE VOCAL MECHANISM

THE HUMAN VOICE, regardless of its tessitura, behaves like any other musical instrument. It needs a vibrating mechanism to produce the sound waves, and a resonator to amplify them.

Musical instruments use a variety of wave-producers – strings, single reeds, double reeds, sharp edges, the lips (in brass instruments). Their resonators usually use a captive body of air set in motion by a surface (stringed instruments), or a column of air (woodwind instruments). Solid resonators are also used in some instruments, e.g. the xylophone.

The human voice uses exactly the same principles. To produce sound waves it has a pair of *vocal cords* – these are caused to vibrate by air passing between them from the lungs, and to provide a resonating chamber it has the *pharynx* and the *mouth* plus secondary resonators above.

The production of sound by the vocal cords and mouth is as much akin to the method used by stringed instruments as to the woodwind. This may seem surprising to some people, who would consider the passage of air along a tube to be the hallmark of the woodwind, and this therefore resembles the human voice in production. However, a moment's thought will easily dispel this notion. Stringed instruments have a fixed body of air of constant size to produce resonance, while woodwind instruments vary their volume of air by covering or uncovering holes along the body of the instrument, thereby lengthening or shortening the column of air. The pharynx and mouth have, with minor variation, a fixed volume. Naturally, this volume varies from individual to individual, but the volume is not much variable within the individual. Individual members of the violin family, for instance, have different sized sound-boxes, but a viola cannot shrink to violin size, or swell to that of a 'cello. (Even with one type of instrument, sizes will vary slightly.) But the human instrument can vary slightly the size and shape of the resonators simply because muscle is elastic. Some adjustment of mouth and pharynx can do this, but not to any large extent.

Sound waves are caused by something vibrating. Reed instruments rely on the rapid opening and closing of a small aperture provided by the reed pressing on the mouthpiece (as in the clarinet) or on another piece of reed (as in the oboe). The flute and recorder rely on air eddying either side of an edge, and brass instruments on the vibration of the lips. Except by changing the length of the vibrating air column, woodwind and brass instruments are unable to change pitch except by overblowing, which will only produce notes of the harmonic series. Stringed instruments, though, have four methods of varying pitch, and these are directly analogous to the voice. The variables are: (i) thickness of string, (ii) tension of string, (iii) harmonic of string, (iv) length of string.

(i) The thickness of the string determines what notes *may* be played. The thicker the string the lower the note and vice versa. Although, in theory, a thick string and a thin string can produce the same notes, in practice a high note from a thick string would require very high tension, and a low note from a thin string would be rather weak and die away rapidly. The several strings of a musical instrument are therefore chosen to produce a satisfactory sound over each of their ranges.

(ii) The tension on a string will vary the pitch of the note within certain limits – it has to be sufficient to make the string taut, yet not enough to cause breakage. The greater the tension, the higher the note. Tuning of all stringed instruments is carried out by adjusting the tension of the strings by means of pegs.

(iii) The harmonic used can increase the frequency of a note by an integral factor. Normally the fundamental, the first or lowest note of the harmonic series, is used:

However, by plucking or bowing in different positions, or by using a finger to produce other nodes, other harmonics may be obtained:

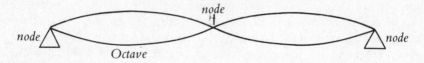

Purcell's home in Bowling Alley,
Westminster, is the first house on the
right.

Henry Purcell from a 1683 edition
of his sonatas for strings and
harpsichord.

The Sistine Chapel in Rome where many of the best castrati and falsetti performed.

The south west view of the Chapel Royal, Westminster Palace, as restored in 1800. It was destroyed in the famous fire in the 19th century.

Sandford's engraving of some of the 32 Gentlemen of the Chapel Royal at the coronation of James II in 1685.

The choirs of the Chapel Royal and Rochester Cathedral combine for the Maundy service at Rochester in 1961. The Chapel Royal choristers can be distinguished by their 17th-century dress. The Gentlemen wear the usual cassocks and surplices.

Counter tenors in a parish church, St Mary the Virgin, Northolt, Middlesex, in about 1949.
There were two altos in this choir (both on Cantoris, nearest the camera).

Contrasting arenas for the counter-tenor voice. Above: a stage set for Clayton's Arsinoe by Sir James Thornhill for 'a Room of Stait, with Statues and Bustoes', in which the counter tenor, Francis Hughes, took a leading role. Below: Canterbury Cathedral choir singing the daily office in 1981. The author is nearest the camera on Decani men's row.

Westminster Abbey choir in 1888 or 1889. Of the Decani altos Scharteau is in the centre of the second row and Sexton is second from the right on the front row. The Cantoris altos are missing.

Counter tenors of tomorrow? This is the song room in which Michael Tippett first heard Alfred Deller. The only genuine 'English hoot' likely to be heard today is being produced in the foreground!

Paul Esswood as Ottone in Zürich Opera's production of Monteverdi's L'Incoronazione di Poppea.

James Bowman, one of the finest counter tenors of today.

John Whitworth, who, with Deller, was largely responsible for the modern revival of the counter tenor.

Carlo Broschi (1705–1782), known as Farinelli, the greatest of the castrati.

Alfred Deller (1912–1979), who began the modern renaissance of the counter-tenor voice, seen here in a typical performing stance.

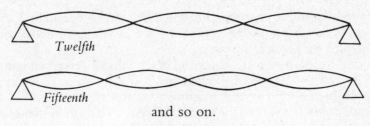

and so on.

Figure 1 *Harmonics.*

This principle is used in the fretted clavichord where one string may be used to produce two or three different notes depending on where the tangents strike the string.

However, although these three methods may be used to change the pitch of a note for a given length of string, none could be used for the actual playing of music because of the practical disadvantages. The exception is the clavichord, which is however almost inaudible except to its player. For practical music-making, (iv), length of string is the criterion.

Progressively shortening a string will result in a progressive raising of the pitch of the note produced. This is infinitely variable – we are not restricted to the harmonics – and a choice of string thicknesses will give the musician a sufficient range of notes on which to play. So it is also with the voice.

There is no great need in a book of this nature for a very detailed anatomical study of the larynx, provided the essentials of sound production by the vocal cords are understood. It would be all too easy to blind the reader with science when all he needs is a fundamental knowledge of the basic workings of the vocal cords. The various types of voice – soprano, treble, tenor, etc., rely solely on the length of the vocal cords, and the degree of strength possessed by their muscles. A boy's vocal cords are short and thin, and hence capable of rapid vibration and high notes (the same is true of a girl's). At puberty, his cords thicken up and become longer, and the larynx becomes visually more prominent. Because the cords take some time to enlarge, and the muscles therein also need time to develop, the voice 'breaks' and frequently becomes unmanageable.

The final length of the vocal cords will determine the tessitura of the adult chest voice. A tenor with rare short vocal cords may well have a range comparable with many counter tenors. A woman with long cords may well be able to reach notes on the bass stave which would make her the envy of many men.

Women's voices, from soprano to contralto (and lower, in the case of many American ladies' choirs) do not differ in any way from men's, at least in the means of *producing* sound waves. The *tone quality*, however, is another matter. This will differ, and we shall look at this later on in the chapter, especially where it cuts across the debate on the use of women's voices in early music.

In either speech or song, the vocal cords vibrate at the fundamental (see diagram). Change of pitch is made by the muscles within the cords tightening them and thinning out the edges – pulling cord material out of the way of the passing air. As with a violin string, there is a lower and upper limit to the possible notes produced. At the upper level, which is what we are concerned with in this book, the muscles reach the limit of their strength, and can produce no more tension.

The *vocal cords* are two short strips of muscular fibrous tissue covered with squamous epithelium (tough, elastic connecting tissue), which project, shelf-like, into the air-stream at the top of the trachea. They are not strings, but act like a double reed, with a narrow slit between them. Although they act like a double reed, the cords have means of adjustment whereby the *frequency* of the vibrations may be varied. In this way, the vocal cords act more like strings than reeds.

The cords in the adult male are around 0.5 inch long (12 mm); less than this in women and children. They are situated in the larynx, which is a cartilaginous box (visible as the 'Adam's apple' at the front of the throat). The larynx is made up of two large cartilages – the thyroid and the cricoid, and two small cartilages – the arytenoids (see diagram). The cartilages are held together by ligaments and muscles which nonetheless permit some movement. The vocal cords are attached to the thyroid cartilage at the front (anterior) and the cricoid at the rear (posterior) of the larynx. The arytenoid cartilages are embedded in the vocal cords at their posterior end, but the full length of the cord can still be used for vibration.

A simplified diagram will be used to describe what happens in sound production. (Anyone wishing to study this in greater anatomical detail might well look at *The Science of Voice* by D. Stanley, Carl Fischer Inc., New York, and *The Singer's and Actor's Throat* by Norman A. Punt, Heinemann, London.)

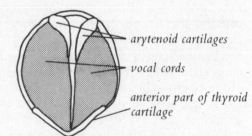

arytenoid cartilages

vocal cords

anterior part of thyroid cartilage

Figure 2
(i) Looking down into the larynx

The control of the vocal cords in breathing and singing is by the following movements:

(A) The cords themselves have an internal muscle, the vocalis, which can make the cords tighter and thinner:

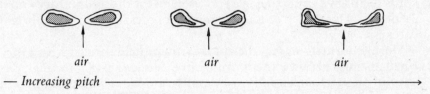

air   air   air

— Increasing pitch —————————————————————————→

Figure 2 *(ii) Diagrammatic cross-section of vocal cords. Pharyngeal production uses just these thinned edges.*

(B) The arytenoid cartileges can move in several ways, using the various groups of muscles attached to them:

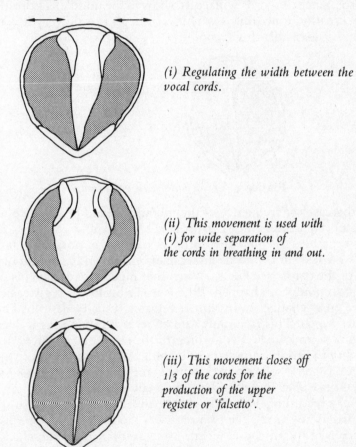

(i) Regulating the width between the vocal cords.

(ii) This movement is used with (i) for wide separation of the cords in breathing in and out.

(iii) This movement closes off 1/3 of the cords for the production of the upper register or 'falsetto'.

Figure 3 *Movement of arytenoid cartilages in larynx. These may be termed internal movements within the larynx itself.*

(C) Muscles attached to the outside of the larynx can cause it to move higher or lower in the throat, and can also put more tension in the cords themselves by acting in opposition on the thyroid and arytenoid cartilages. This will give a higher range of notes, but causes strain and soreness.

During normal singing, the vocal cords are held parallel with a very small opening between them. Air from the lungs passing through this slit will cause it to open and close rapidly, and the air will pass through in a series of discreet puffs. This generates the sound waves.

Control of the frequency is by the movements previously described. The lower notes are produced by slackening the vocalis muscles in the vocal cords and separating the arytenoid cartilages (Fig 3(i)). This may allow a leakage of air directly through the slit between the cords, since the cords will tend to bow in the middle. The result is a rather 'breathy' tone (this is why it is difficult to sing very low notes loudly – at least for most people).

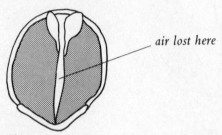

air lost here

Figure 4 *Air loss with slack vocal cords.*

To increase the frequency of the vibrations (and hence the pitch of the note), two things must happen. The arytenoid cartilages move closer together (keeping the cords as parallel as possible), and the vocalis muscles in the cords increase in tension and also thin out the edges of the cords (see Fig 2). When the singer has reached his upper limit, two things can happen. If he is using his lower register he will make a 'gear-change' to his upper register, usually described as the 'falsetto' voice. This is an unfortunate term implying, as it does, an unnatural sound when it is nothing of the sort. Every voice part has the ability to produce this type of sound, but of course, in a naturally light voice – lyric soprano, treble and some tenors – the changeover is hardly noticeable. Fashion plays no small part in this.

In early recordings of treble voices (those of Ernest Lough spring immediately to mind), the two registers can easily be distinguished. Nowadays, though the tendency is to smooth over the change as much as possible, large operatic female voices often still display clear register changes. These have as their basis some variety of chest-falsetto/head shift of mechanism. Even now the public seems happy to accept this as the norm, though Clara Butt would have to modify her technique today. The cognoscenti seem knowingly to maintain this odd 'double standard' – women have 'head' voices, men have falsetto. Crude though this idea may seem, and obviously mistaken, it is implied by more than a few textbooks.

The anatomical reason for the 'falsetto' voice is quite simple, as Fig 3(iii) shows. At the 'gear-change', the arytenoid cartilages press together and prevent the posterior one-third of the vocal cords from vibrating – just like shortening a violin string with the finger. There is no mystery about this – above all, no discreet surgical operation is necessary, as many seem to think.

At the very limit of a singer's range, when the internal and external muscles have been used to their maximum effect; when the 'falsetto' has been employed to its top limit, there remains a mortifying phenomenon known as 'cracking'. The singer attempts a note and all that comes out is air. This is caused by the air pressure from the lungs being too strong for the vocal cords to hold their shape – they distort and buckle, allowing air to escape directly to the mouth (compare this with the loss of air when singing low notes, except that in that case it is the slackness of the cords themselves which causes the loss).

It must be noted that 'cracking' does not just happen in the upper register. It can as easily occur at the top of the lower register if the singer is steadfastly refusing to 'change gear'. It will also occur more readily in an untrained voice, where the vocal cords have not been trained to hold themselves tight and parallel.

The volume produced by a singer is directly proportional to the power of his lungs. An adult soprano has a larger lung capacity and chest musculature than a boy, and if the top line of boys is mixed with *trained* women singers, the women will swamp the boys' singing – a reason why mixed choirs of boys and women are not usually successful. The castrati of Italy gained their reputation for powerful singing from a combination of men's lung power allied to boys' vocal cords.

Tone quality is a difficult thing to assess objectively. It is easy enough, in discussing instruments, to distinguish between the sounds produced by an oboe, a piano, and a clarinet each playing the same note, but to *describe* the difference is another matter. Terms such as 'reedy', 'sensuous', etc., are subjective – the only way to analyse the sounds is in terms of the intensity of the fundamental note produced and of its overtones. For this sort of analysis, one would need to delve into the depths of cathode ray oscilloscopes, acoustic spectrometers and the like.

In order to produce any sound at all, the vibrations must be amplified. Earlier in the chapter we saw that, just as a violin has a sound-box under the strings, so the human voice has the pharynx and the mouth. The size and shape of these will determine the quality of the sounds produced – certain of the overtones may be augmented, others suppressed.

One, perhaps the main, conventional school of thought claims that the sinuses of the nasal cavity do not have any effect at all on the emerging sound, despite the fact that many teachers of singing profess to use them. During singing, they say, the palate shuts off the nasal cavity from the mouth – no air passes down the nose, hence the sinuses cannot be brought into use as primary resonators connected with the other primary resonators of the mouth and pharynx. However, they admit that they do act as secondary resonators – sound waves can travel through the tissue of the palate and cause resonance within the sinuses, but it is claimed that the effect is only felt by the singer himself, not his audience. The sinuses can therefore be used to monitor the sound produced for the singer's own benefit, but any effect they have on the emerging tone is illusory.

The other school of thought claims otherwise. Because the singer employs the sinuses to help focus the voice, there is considerable effect on the emerging tone. The counter tenor uses this focus more than most, but tenors and other voices have also been trained in this way. A singer suffering from a cold-blocked nose soon notices the reduced resonance in his voice.

The sphenoid sinuses have more prominent development in men than in women. This is why at puberty the male voice change is more marked, more disturbed. As Arthur Hewlett says in *Thinking Afresh About the Voice*: 'A man using only his frontal sinuses produces a treble-like tone, the so-called falsetto, which in general is used in performance only by male altos.' Indeed, Ernest George White's school of sinus tone, of which Hewlett was a disciple, trained many to use the advantages of sinus focus. The tenor, Frank Titterton, one of John Whitworth's teachers, was himself an advocate of this production.

John Whitworth always explained that in counter-tenor vocal production a balance must be achieved between edgy sinus element – an almost buzzing sensation in the nose and across the cheekbones and behind the front teeth, resonating first on the pharynx, the curved soft roof of the mouth, then up into the skull. A true head tone, it is one of several voice adjustments.

Sinus production is probably the key to the amazing extension of upward range of the Spanish falsettists.

Incorrect use of the muscles of the tongue, or uneven breath pressure, can cause the production of a wobble in the voice. This is usually

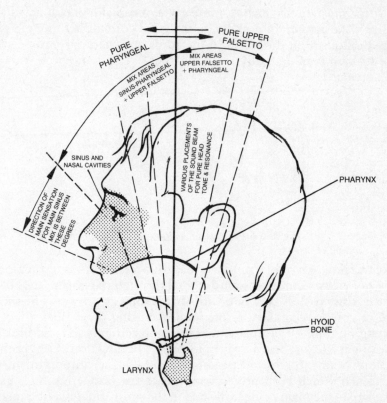

Figure 5 *High and low counter-tenor modes of voice placement and resonation. Pharyngeal and upper falsetto are used in a proportional admixture. Other male voices share something of this at the top of their ranges, at least in their historical production, but with much more basic voice in the mix.*

called 'vibrato', incorrectly. The exact nature of vibrato, wobble and tremolo is much disagreed upon by vocal authorities. What is certain is that continuous use of any form of undulation in the singing of early music is inappropriate. It is not an automatic phenomenon; unless present because of bad habits, it is *trained* in. Anyone can put some sort of undulation into their vocal tone if they want to, and likewise anyone can remove it with careful practice.★

★ David Wulstan, working with the Clerkes of Oxenford, has shown this. His soprano top line had eliminated it completely and the resultant sound is very like boys' voices. Talking in this case of the sixteenth century and about polyphony, Wulstan writes in his article on vocal colour: '. . . a blurred "fruity" tone is incompatible with polyphonic singing. So is vibrato: in its various forms, it seems only slowly to be loosening its stranglehold upon singing style. To forsake it requires effort both because it appears to amplify the voice, and because intonation poses no problems when the margin of error is so obligingly wide.'

A manifestation which can cause roughness and breathiness in the voice is the growth of nodules on the vocal cords. These are pin-head sized callouses on the edges of the cords and, naturally, prevent the cords from coming really close together. Their removal is usually a minor matter.

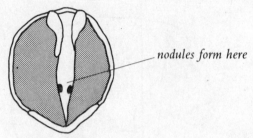

nodules form here

Figure 6 *Position of nodules on the vocal cords.*

To conclude, I would emphasise that advocates of sinus resonation do not normally claim that sounds travel through the upper facial bones and cavities to flow down the nose in a strong air stream. The sinuses are of course secondary resonators, but using them does affect the emerging tone – a sympathetic resonation certainly felt and heard by the singer and just heard by his audience. The direction of a hypothetic 'sound beam' in all head production signifies an important mental approach which both projects and keeps the resonation high in the pharynx – the main resonator – and in the sympathetic cavities above. Few would seriously suggest that sound actually emerges from the top of the skull or cheekbones.

Chapter 5

REGISTERS, RANGE AND REPERTOIRE

THERE ARE AS YET no books specifically on counter tenor vocal method. General principles apply of course, but until this voice is more commonly developed and voice text books include, automatically, discussion and exercises appropriate in pitch and character to counter-tenor singing, then there will be a problem. Perhaps the present work will be the spark needed for such a book to be written; it is certainly needed. In the meantime I hope the suggestions here are helpful and I recommend the student to search out the few extremely useful existing works by certain enlightened vocal authorities. (See the asterisked titles in the Bibliography.) It is outside the scope of this book to include vocal exercises, or hints on the answers to the varied individual problems counter-tenor students will encounter. These could and will be answered one day.

One important point to make is that even some eminent teachers of voice deny that the head voice and the falsetto are one and the same and require the same use of the vocal cords. Until erroneous thinking of this sort is straightened out, again we will have problems. As an example, take Kate Emil-Behnke's mostly admirable book *The Technique of Singing*. She gives a masterly description of the action and workings of the vocal cords, in chest register (upper and lower), medium (she never uses the term pharyngeal – or middle falsetto for obvious reasons, later seen) and head. She describes the thinning of the cords for medium and the employment of between half and two thirds of the cords for head register, then comes up with the following: 'If a man sings a high note so softly as to eliminate all tension of the vocal ligaments, he will probably sing in falsetto, a mechanism which is useless, offering no foundation from which to develop.' Other such odd views will be quoted before the end of the present work. It is of interest to report that Miss Kate's father, the great Emil Behnke, did not agree with his daughter. In his book, *The Mechanism of the Human*

Voice, he says: 'How widespread is this mistaken notion that the use of the falsetto is entirely contrary to art.'

We must examine further that incredible musical instrument, the human larynx, this miraculous but tiny organ about which there is so much argument.

Bel canto, that 'lost' art of the beautiful voice, the old Italian method or school, began to lose ground from the mid-nineteenth century. When the great voice teacher, Manuel Garcia, invented the laryngoscope, much speculation, excitement and curiosity was aroused regarding the probable and provable mechanics of the vocal function. Very soon there developed a quite definite purpose to control the larynx and the voice directly from a scientific point of view. The results have been chaos ever since and a continuous longing nostalgia for the lost 'golden age of singing'.

Early teaching and its traditions clearly worked, and did so on a practical level by principles handed down mostly by example and authoritative word of mouth. But with the advance of scientific larnygeal technology the proponents of bel canto methods were left without defence. Though clearly and demonstrably right by result, they could not prove their methods scientifically. As Cornelius L. Reid explains in his excellent treatise, *The Free Voice*:

> In the meantime, a new generation of teachers came along to confront a world in a process of change; a world which created in every area of life uncertainty and confusion. Some found it expedient to adopt a pseudo-scientific jargon, but the majority tried to remain faithful to a tradition which was in the process of slipping away from them without their being aware of it. Vocal pedagogy, and the functional principles upon which it rested, thus struggled against the contrary currents of two worlds, neither of which was clearly defined nor concrete.

It is therefore of the utmost importance for us to look back to these old 'pre-scientific' methods, for there we will find the historical technique which produced the counter tenor in whichever of its varieties or aliases are chosen to describe it. But unlike the old Italian teachers, we can also use modern scientific method where this is helpful.

The phenomenon of vocal registers is not a new discovery. Vocal theorists have been concerned with them for many centuries. Generally authorities have agreed that the human voice seems to be divided into two distinct sections, one 'true', the other 'false'. Before the Renaissance they were termed vox integra and vox filta respectively. Later they were known as voce di petto (voice of the chest) and voce di testa (voice of the head).

Teachers began to realise that the two mechanisms shared a direct functional relationship and for the greater good of the singing voice they should be united. To allow for differences of qualities and timbres, new names appeared. Derivative groupings were termed the mezzo falso, or half falsetto, and the voce di finte, or 'feigned' voice. The joining of the two main mechanisms became one of the first concerns of the establishment of a correct basic vocal technique. The 'break' still remains the 'bête noir' of most aspiring singers.

The term 'mezzo falso', half falsetto, is a strange idea, for what then is the other half? The logical answer is the opposite mechanism – the voce di petto, chest voice. The French describe the two together as the voix mixte, or mixed voice. As time went by mezzo falso began to be called, merely, 'head' voice. So where at one time the head voice was synonymous with the falsetto, the phrase head voice began to indicate a relationship of falsetto and chest registers, but with the falsetto as always the dominating element. But oddly, the head voice became thought of eventually as a legitimate functional process whereas the falsetto became discredited. The concept of 'falseness' became so firmly fixed in association with the falsetto that the latter was even considered quite wrongly for many years to be a product of the false cords.

So, after the mid-nineteenth century, Garcia, the laryngoscope and the discrediting of the old school, it was conveniently and even firmly forgotten that the head voice is basically the falsetto, usually developed and mixed with other elements. Cornelius L. Reid provides excellent tables in *The Free Voice*:

Table 2 *Terminology pertaining to registers.*

14th Century	15th to 19th Centuries		
* 1. Vox Filta	* 1. Voce di Testa or Falsetto	Combined to become	‡ Falsetto † Mezzo Falso 'Head' Voice Voce di Finte Voix Mixte
* 2. Vox Integra	* 2. Voce di Petto or Chest Voice		‡ Chest Voice

* Each of these two mechanisms divided by the 'break'.
† Falsetto derived tones cultivated for the purpose of obscuring the 'break' between the two register mechanisms. In reality, they represent a combined, or coordinated, registration in which both mechanisms form participating elements. The preponderance of balance, however, was always made to lean toward the upper of the two registers. With the passing of time, these conditions of blended registration came to be looked upon as being initiated by resonance – a tragic misconception.
‡ By the close of the 19th century the 'chest' voice and 'falsetto' gradually came to be regarded as isolated and unrelated entities whose functional importance was destructive rather than constructive.

93

Table 3 *20th-century terminology.*

Group 1.	Group 2.
*1. Falsetto	1. Falsetto
2. 'Head' Voice	2. Concepts of 'placement'
Upper Voice	a. 'high'
Voix Mixte	b. 'low'
	c. 'forward'
	d. 'back'
	e. 'up and over'
	f. 'in the masque'
	g. 'focus'
3. Middle Voice	3. Breath Control
	a. 'support of tone'
	b. 'sing on the breath'
4. Lower Voice	4. Tonal 'covering'
5. 'Chest' Voice.	

Group 1.

* These two mechanisms no longer recognised as presenting an opportunity for combined action to account for the 'head' voice or the voix mixte. Terms 'upper', 'middle', and 'lower' refer to a tonal change, not a register. Falsetto neglected and left unused. 'Chest' voice rarely employed, if ever.

Group 2.

Registration in all forms denied, with the falsetto considered an oddity, and the 'chest' register an abomination. Because this error led, inevitably, to 'pushing', tone qualities began to sound too 'open' and 'shouty' in the upper range. Thus there developed an obvious need to 'refine' the technique, a need which was met by 'covering'. A 'covered' technique always distorts the vowel and promotes tonal impurity.

(By kind permission of the Joseph Patelson Music House, New York.)

As has been described earlier, the head voice or falsetto register is produced by both 'shortening' and 'thinning' the vocal cords. The alto mechanism, as it has been called, is brought into play *at some stage* in the ascending scale of both so-called falsettist and so-called tenor altino. The former would expect to enter the head register earlier than the latter for the obvious reason that the average tenor has a higher upper chest range than the average baritone. Both varieties of male voice possess the need for a chest to head register change, however difficult to pick out; though of course, a counter tenor may choose to stay within the head register exclusively and extend and develop it downwards.

A most informative short article, written in 1967 by G. M. Ardran and David Wulstan, is included as a valuable appendix to the first edition (only) of Alfred Deller's biography *A Singularity of Voice*. Readers would be well advised to track down the complete article. (See Bibliography.) As Ardran and Wulstan point out, even today

slow motion cinematography has not given us the sort of incon-
trovertible evidence we would welcome on the workings of the head
or falsetto register. They therefore initiated a series of investigations
into the behaviour of the larynx to determine common factors in
falsetto production of all altos. This was to include a bass singing
ordinary undeveloped falsetto, through various different timbres, to a
singer of strong counter-tenor tone using his head voice. The idea was
to investigate whether the laryngeal mechanisms used were the same
in all cases, and if not, how they differed.

Apparently five male volunteers were chosen, some very good
singers with what is usually considered counter-tenor tone; one a bass
with a hooty alto sound, the rest with tone between these extremes.
Each man's neck was radiographed in the lateral projection, during
quiet breathing. All the necks were fully relaxed, revealing a wide
laryngeal airway, with the vocal cords up-turned into the laryngeal
ventricles. The result was that only a small amount of air remained in
the anterior of the ventricles. Ardran and Wulstan continue:

> When the note a (220 cps) was sung in the 'chest' register to the
> vowel 'ah', all the subjects showed the appearances of a vocalized
> larynx, that is to say, there were prominent air-filled ventricles
> delineating the vocal folds over practically the whole of their length,
> and there was evidence of the stretching of the vocal folds by the
> cricothyroid muscles both from the position of the laryngeal cartil-
> ages and also from the shape of the airway. When exactly the same
> note was sung in the falsetto or 'head' register, all the subjects
> showed the same type of change: the air content of the laryngeal
> ventricles was reduced, indicating that a shorter length (shorter by
> about a quarter to a third) of vocal fold was free to vibrate. In each
> instance there was evidence that the cricothyroid muscles were not
> contracting so vigorously, and the stretching of the vocal folds was
> therefore less. All the subjects showed a narrowing of the laryngeal
> vestibule from front to back, which was associated with the back-
> ward bowing of the intralaryngeal portion of the epiglottis and its
> ligament. Other studies (Ardran and Wulstan, to be published) have
> shown that this is associated with the reduction of tension on the
> false vocal folds, allowing them to bulge medially. This effect can
> be seen on radiographs showing (i) the subject producing the note in
> chest voice and (ii) the same note sung in falsetto. The two sets of
> pictures contrast A, a subject with the so-called countertenor voice
> production, and B, a bass producing a hooty type of falsetto. The
> pictures of the production of A and B are identical.
>
> It is suggested then, that when singing the same note falsetto as in
> the chest register, a shorter length only, in the middle of the vocal

folds, is free to vibrate. Associated with this, there is evidence of a reduction in tension on the vocal folds. The backward bowing of the epiglottis is associated with a decrease in the distance between the body of the hyoid bone and the thyroid cartilage, and in some instances with the relative backward movement of the hyoid as well. We believe that it is the movement of the hyoid bone relative to the thyroid cartilage which is capable of moving the epiglottis and its associated tissues so that it can alter the tension on the false vocal cords, which allows them to bulge inwards and effectively damp the vocal folds: for the vocal folds cannot vibrate adequately unless associated with an air-filled laryngeal ventricle.

It has already been stated that the vocal cords are often compared with violin strings: tightening raises the pitch of the note. But the range of pitch is limited by this method. So the violinist stops the string somewhere along its length with his finger. The tension remains exactly the same, but the pitch rises because the string is shorter. Ardran and Wulstan explain that not only is it possible to use this analogy for the vocal cords, but that in addition, there is in the human vocal mechanism a *lessening* of tension so that the pitch of the resultant note remains identical. This explains how singers can move from chest register to falsetto easily and without tension if they are able to control the falsetto mechanism with no effort.

All this underlines the fact that the head and falsetto registers are the same, and, however good or bad, however incompetent, there is no fundamental difference between the laryngeal mechanism of one alto as compared to another. So Ardran and Wulstan believe. Yet it does not seem quite right when one considers that there are two forms of falsetto, upper and so-called middle or pharyngeal voice (see page 108).

We referred earlier to the extension of the falsetto or head register downwards. Many English counter tenors, especially since Deller, have used this technique effectively, but those who to put it idiomatically 'change gear', like Whitworth and Bowman, have learned to match up head and upper chest registers so that the change in resonance is not apparent. Some singers, like Oberlin, do this unconsciously, but because it is an unconscious transition it does not mean that the change does not exist. Ardran and Wulstan express it well:

Here the analogy of the 'gear change', a phrase used by almost every alto, is a good one: a car with a crash gear box almost invariably gives an audible change. Less skill is required with a synchromesh gear box unless it is faulty. Another type of singer corresponds to the automatic gear box: here changes are made without effort, but a trained listener can detect the point of change in most cases. The last type of singer has an undetectable change, like the torque-converter on rather expensive cars. But, in common with all the other types, the torque converter box works to the same end: there must be a gear change (except, of course in the case of altos using falsetto exclusively), however gradual it may be, and no matter how involuntary.

Reid uses the piano as an analogy:

Examination of . . . the piano immediately discloses . . . two different kinds of stringing have been used. For tones extending from the lower middle to the top the strings are made of thin steel, for the lowest two octaves, steel strings are wrapped with heavy copper wire. Thus, bass notes on the piano are not only longer, but thicker and of different metal. Regardless of this difference, the piano has a smoothly graduated tonal scale with no point of mechanical transition detectable to the ear. A major transition is made, but the gradation is engineered so as to pass unobserved.

So despite the different mechanisms in chest and head, correct resonance and adjustment provide a smooth vocal transition.

We have of course reached two important points. First, that it is the *resonators* which are all important to all tone produced as a result of all laryngeal activity in any register. Like any other register, falsetto is a weak voice alone, like an old-fashioned gramophone needle held on the record merely by the fingers. Connect it to proper resonance and we hear the properly produced sounds which lie within the record. The second point is the usual one of dispute over what constitutes the counter tenor voice and what the alto, for those who maintain that they are separate. For this reason we will consider this question now.

Tenor altinos claim that their higher, lighter chest voices and smooth transition into head (if indeed they admit to any separation at all) makes them different from the other high voice type. They claim that the 'real' counter tenor is clearly and exclusively a species of tenor voice and that singers who use either head voice exclusively, or the 'synchromesh gear box', are by this reasoning denoted 'male altos'.

As we have seen, history does not bear out this reasoning. They are *all* counter tenors because they sing the counter tenor altus part. In fact, many English counter tenors argue just as emphatically that the tenor altino is not a counter tenor at all – just a very high tenor. They claim that the counter tenor altus, the voice type finally reached by the early sixteenth century, is *purely* a head voice. This, too, in our opinion, is probably mistaken, but it is a powerful argument, and *if* it did happen, it happened in the latter half of the seventeenth century for reasons which will become clear. (See page 99.)

What is certain is that in the late nineteenth century it was usual for altos to use both head and chest registers. Dr A. H. D. Prendergast, writing in 1900 in *The Man's Alto in English Music*, demonstrates this clearly:

> It is certain that even in the lowest register the chest notes are modified or veiled, in other words that some operation occurs in the throat by which the vocal cords giving chest notes are not allowed to vibrate to their full extent. The highest register is caused by some more decided limitation, or as it were pinching, of the vocal cords, so as to give an entirely new quality. The middle register, covering the 'break', is caused by a compromise between the two modes of emission, and is as everyone knows difficult to manage.

Prendergast goes on to reinforce what he says about singing across the register change, having already given us clues that he at least is familiar with the traditional use of the two modes of falsetto plus the chest register. 'Modified or veiled' is obviously a reference to the pharyngeal voice used on the chest. What is particularly interesting is that he describes the register change about a third higher than most altos today: 'The ordinary compass of a man's alto voice in this country is from fiddle G to C in the middle of the treble clef. The best notes are from B flat to B flat. The break is between Middle C and the E above.'

This seems to suggest that in 1900 the English alto was in spirit at least very much in line with tradition, with what obtained in Italian baritone and tenor chest-head technique. This question is discussed more fully later, on page 110. It is interesting to know that Prendergast himself was an alto, and was listed in that section of the Purcell Commemoration Choir in Westminster Abbey, 1895.

Alfred Deller's own view, just over sixty years later, is admirably explained in *A Singularity of Voice*:

> There are generally recognised to be two types of counter tenor voice. The first, and more usual, is where the fundamental voice is baritone or bass, and the head voice, or so-called falsetto, is developed to the maximum range. My own voice is of this type. You produce this head voice naturally, and you work on it as you would on any other voice. But, if you wish, you can still sing off the chest, so to speak. Purcell was a counter tenor of great ability; he also sang bass in the Chapel Royal choir.
>
> The other type of counter tenor is essentially a high tenor who can either dispense with falsetto entirely, or use it for the top fourth or fifth of the compass, without perceptible break. Some people say this is the true counter tenor; others, that it isn't counter tenor at all, but merely a very high, light tenor. Certainly, some singers one hears who are billed as counter tenors seem to be just tenors with exceptionally high range.

No less an early music authority than Robert Donnington seems unclear about the counter tenor question. In his excellent work *The Interpretation of Early Music* he writes (and I fully concur), as he talks of the castrati modern performance problem: 'Thus our substitution of a female soprano, mezzo soprano or contralto, though it is what Handel himself did when short of a castrato, is inevitably a misrepresentation. A good counter tenor (i.e. a male alto) makes a plausible substitute, if he has power and agility enough.'

But, illogically, lower down the same page, Donnington defines the male alto and high and low counter tenors differently and ambiguously. It really reads rather strangely:

(a). A male alto is a bass or baritone singing high parts in a falsetto voice, apparently produced by using only the edges of the vocal cords.
(b). The counter tenor is a natural voice often of extremely high tessitura, light and more or less unchested yet masculine in quality. The range is from G to D or even E".
(c). A normal tenor may sometimes go extremely high, as in the magnificent voice and musicianship of Hughues Cuenod.

Ardran and Wulstan have an interesting theory: they maintain that the two-register voice, while being needed in sixteenth-century music (and by implication, earlier), seems not so clearly useful or its use expected by the time of Purcell:

. . . distinction between the compasses of full and verse passages is indeed the reverse of that found in the early part of the sixteenth century. Whereas the chorus parts (in Restoration music) are of normal compass, the solo parts are extended either to a high or to a low tessitura. This suggests that the falsetto was now being cultivated for the low register, and the chest voice was abandoned; this resulted in the division of counter tenor voices into two specialist classes: the high and low counter tenors.

Unfortunately, some authorities have misinterpreted Purcellian alto ranges as either falsetto alto *or* high tenor, modern lyric type. Clearly, the idea is right, in that high and low counter tenors and basses used falsetto; the low counter tenor would hardly be an exception. Yet certain authorities continue to claim that all true counter tenors used no falsetto at all.

I would argue that low counter tenors always included singers like John Whitworth who blended high to low register and whose upward range may not have been as extensive as a Deller for example. Henry Purcell may well have been of this type, judging by solos he is known to have sung and by the fact that he could at least fill in some sort of bass part if required. Or perhaps he was a high counter tenor of the Deller type with pharyngeal development downwards, as Ardran and Wulstan have suggested.

It is always most difficult to sort out the middle ground: the Howells, Abells and Dellers of this world are clearly specialist head-voice men, falsettists (high counter tenors); but who apart from Oberlin are the tenor altinos (low counter tenors, type number one): Price or Saville?

Oberlin claims that he has lyric tenor tones up to F″, but I feel that his middle falsetto voice is likely to have been employed for several tones by then, probably at F above middle C, and that he has the expensive torque-converter. His last few tones *sound* like a mixture of pharyngeal and pure head voices.

The Whitworth and Ferrante type of counter tenor, full range, two-register voices, were written for and expected throughout the seventeenth and eighteenth centuries too. After all, cathedral choirs at least sang earlier music than that of their own time, though not of course to the extent of our present day enormous wide-ranging repertoire. Just examine the 1680 list from Durham. Twenty years after the Restoration there is *nothing* instantly recognisable as being in Restoration style, although there are a few unknown names.

David Wulstan is of the view that in sixteenth- and *early* seventeenth-century music, comparison of exposed passages for verse (solo, duet, trio or quartet or occasionally more) with full sections or full anthems very often reveals a clear contrast in ranges expected of the alto in two different situations. Though E flat below Middle C is reasonably commonplace in full sections, A flat under Middle C is normally the lowest note in exposed verse passages except for special effects.★ (Presumably he wishes us to assume allowance made for sixteenth- and seventeenth-century pitches.) He is led to the conclusion that composers of the period deliberately limited certain solo sections to the falsetto register, expecting the 'gear change' to be used in unexposed passages. This would be wise, says Wulstan, for many altos are not skilled at undetectable register changes. The sort of special effect to which he refers is present in the verse anthem 'Out of the Deep', by Thomas Morley:

(up a minor third)

Out of the deep have I call — ed to Thee O Lord Lord, hear

★ Study of the double treble/double counter-tenor verse in the Nunc Dimittis of Byrd's *Second Service* reveals a definite exception to Wulstan's hypothesis. There are others such as the S.S.A. verse in Byrd's *Salve Sancte Parens*.

The solo counter tenor would expect to use blended chest tones for the first few notes in order to underline the meaning of the words.

A successful technique is likely to be used to the full. It seems likely that the traditional register change, upper chest to head, remained part of the counter tenor's usual technique, and it was used in both verse and full sections by those who were skilled in it, just as it is today.

June	Morninge	Eueninge: Service: 1680
(Tusday:1)	[O. Gibbons] short service	[O.] Gibbons: [short] Eueninge service
	(Behold) [now praise the Lord] [R.] Allinsons	[Ravenscroft]: O lett me heare thy louinge kindness
(Wed:2)	[Byrd's] (s)hort service	Birds: short service
		Almighty god ye fountaine [T. Tomkins]
(Thursday:3)	[R. Farrant's] (sho)rt service	[R.] Farrants: Eueninge service
	[The Lord bless] us: R. White]	O lord yu hast searched me out [Batten]
(Fryday:4)	(Childs in D so) l re	Childs in D sol re
		Out of the deep [Full anthem]: Morley
Satt(erd:5)	[Pattrick's short] service	Patterick: Eueninge service
	(Deliver me fro)m mine Enemies [would be Byrd; should be R. Parsons]	God standeth in the congregation [Read]
Sunday:(6)	[Bryne's short] (s)ervice	Brynes: Eueninge service Holy lord god Almighty: Battins
Munday:7	[J. Farrant's in D] (s)ol re Arise [O Lord]: Tallis	[J.] Farrants in D sol re Blessed be thy name o God [Tallis]
Tusday:8	[?Nicholls short]service O	Nichols: Eueninge service Let god Arise: tow Basses: wards
Wed:9	Wil(kes shor)t service	Fosters second service o how gloryous art thou o God [R. White]
Thursday:10	Childs B(enedici)tie [in Gamut]	Childs: Eueninge service [in Gamut]
	O pray for (the pe)ace: Nichols	If the lord himselfe: [Edw.] Smiths
Fryday:11	Fosters: (secon)d service	Fosters: second Eueninge service O God the proud [Byrd]
Satterd:12	Wilkinsons (sho)rt service O lord give (ear) [Byrd]	Reads: short service When the lord turned: Fosters
Sunday:13	Tallis: short (ser)vice I will magnifi(e t)he[e] o lord: Hooper	Tallis: Eueninge service I will alwayes Give thanks: [W.] Kings
Munday:14	Shaws: short (se)rvice O pray for the (p)eace: Childs	Shaws Eueninge service I call and cry [Tallis]

June	Morninge	Eueninge: Service: 1680
Tusday:15	Hilltons: shor(t) service Blessed by the (l)ord god: Childs	Hiltons short Eueninge service I will give thanks Nichols
Wed:16	Childs in F faut	Childs in F faut Save me o God [? Byrd; or Hilton, Portman – both *v*]
Thursday:17	Childs: in E:# O clap yor hands: Childs	Childs: in E:# Behold how good and Joyfull: Portman
Fryday:18	Loosemore short service	Loosemore short Eueninge service I lift my heart to thee [Tye]
Satterd:19	[T.] Tomkins short service Give laud vnto [the Lord] [J. Mundy]	[T.] Tomkins short service Call to remembrance [Hilton]
Sunday:20	Gibbons short servi(ce) o Give thanks Willi(am) [Tucker]	Battins 3 for vers praise the lord o my soule Battins
Munday:21	Strogers sh(ort service) o thou God (Almighty) [would be Mundy; should be Hooper]	Strogers short Eueninge service If the lord himselfe Foster
Tus(day):22	Childe	I will magnifie ye lord Pearson [R.] Hinde: o sing vnto the lord
Wed:(23)	[R. Farrant's short service]	[R.] Farrants short Almightie [and everlasting God] [O.] Gibbons
Thursd(ay:24)	[Parsons of Exeter] (O) sing [unto the Lord] Child	Persons of Exeter Vnto the[e] o lord Wilkinson
Fryda(y:25)	[Childs in D] sol re	Childs in D sol re O pray for the peace Nichols
(Satterd:26)	[Bryne's] (sh)ort (Behold) it is Christ [Hooper]	Bryne short o lord I bow the knees of my heart [W. Mundy]
(Sunday:27)	(Tal)lis short lift up your heads [O. Gibbons]	Tallis short We praise the[e] ô father [O. Gibbons]
(Munday:28)	Wilks short o how gloryous [R. White]	Nichols magnific(at) Blow vp the trumpet [Peerson]
(Tusday:29)	[W.] Mundays short If the lord himselfe: Foster	Reads [short] O God my heart prepared is [R.] H[ucheson]
(Wed:30)	Hiltons short Behold [how good and joyful] [J.] Hutchinson	Hiltons short o lord Let it be thy pleasu(re) [J. Hutchinson]

Table 4 *A month's music at Durham Cathedral in 1680 demonstrating the almost complete absence of works in Restoration style. Cathedral choirs have seldom, if ever, confined their repertoire to the contemporary.*

Wulstan seems to confirm that Purcell was a *low* counter tenor. It is thought that he could sing some sort of bass. As he says: 'This [singing bass] is by no means a unique occurrence, and, in any case, all counter tenors are able to sing bass of some sort, even if the quality differs.'

I would however maintain that most tenor altini could not sing even a light baritone variety of bass, so the counter tenors we agree on are the most usual type, those whose baritone extends into a developed head voice.

In our opinion, then, the traditional technique of the English cathedral and Chapel Royal counter tenors always embraced the use of two registers; but it was the secular use of the voice which encouraged the great extension upwards into specialist high counter tenors like Abell, Howell and Hughes. Howell sang the high first part of 'Sound the Trumpet' from Purcell's *Come ye Sons of Art*, a part which hits several top E's. Deputising for castrati would have developed higher ranges, too, a need which never arose in ecclesiastical surroundings because there were always boys present to take the higher parts, that is to say from about 1660. Anyway, solo alto church music in England never really called for castrati.

As on the Continent, the development of opera and oratorio in the eighteenth century must have hastened the development of these high counter tenors, singers who specialised in head voice work with little or no need to use their chest registers, because the music seldom reached down to that level. The low counter-tenor voices of both varieties would probably have had less employment than the high, except for cathedral music where both low counter-tenor types were as valuable as ever, and in Continental music for men's voices.

As the eighteenth century wore on and volume became of greater importance, the full tenor would probably have been more useful in secular circles than the tenor altino type of low counter tenor, because of its greater sound in 'dry' theatres and crowded halls. The sympathetic resonances of echoing cathedrals were alas not transferable. So it is likely that the most useful forms of the counter-tenor voice in secular music throughout the eighteenth century were the high counter tenor followed possibly by the low (baritone) counter tenor because the latter's falsetto could maintain almost as high a tessitura as the higher voice, yet it had a strong lower range.

The undeveloped falsetto, alone, is a weak unfocused voice, incapable of anything more than a mellow gentle tone with neither ring nor resonance enough to hold its own against other developed voices.

What is known of medieval and Renaissance music suggests that such a sound would quickly be smothered. It could not possibly cope with the music written for counter tenor, either in range or volume. When we say falsetto alone is a weak unfocused voice we mean that without proper *focus* and *resonance* it is so, as too are all other undeveloped voices. Resonators focus the tone, amplify, change and produce it as a mature voice on an equal footing and balance with others.

We have seen how most counter tenors had and have 'baritone' chest voices. Tenors must surely always have enjoyed using their higher chest and basic voice range, almost as they do now. The difference could be that they used to know the truth about the head voice. Certainly the tenor was always in the minority: the average man has a baritone voice, both in speaking and singing (if he ever sings). There seems no reason to doubt that the human vocal organ has always been distributed in range and pitch throughout the population in much the same random manner as today. We know of course that certain countries acquire reputations for producing more than their particular share of one variety, like the Russian bass for example; but besides climatic and possible genetic reasons (discussed on page 171), surely usage and demand also build these reputations. Thus it is with the English counter-tenor tradition.

Many fine voices belong, tragically, to the utterly unmusical, or perhaps to people who by accident of birth or environment are brought up to believe they are unmusical. It is surely true to say that the finest voice in the world, brought up in an environment in which fine singing has no place, will, likely as not, never be used. The weakest baritone voice may well, in the possession of a musician, be capable of development into a superb counter tenor.

Let us be quite clear. In men, the chest voice is the only truly 'natural' voice, approximating as it does to the talking voice. The chest voice is not, as is often supposed, one register, but two: lower and upper. The upper chest, used lightly, is the beginning of the pharyngeal or middle register. Together this vocal state is usually tenable up to about E' natural in men and F' natural in women.* Add to this the head voice, and we have a crude description of the human vocal organ in both men and women. Some teachers insist that whereas women possess three registers, head, medium and chest, men only have two. (This is quite wrong. Just as in women, the three registers are available to men.) If only the chest is completely natural, it follows that the head voice is to some extent *always* a developed voice. Yet we know that the falsetto is present in almost every adult larynx to some degree. This suggests by implication that the falsetto is

---

* Some chest voices, of course, end a tone or two earlier, depending on the individual larynx.

more natural alone than in the mixed, mezzo falso state. It is interesting to see what the vocal authorities, past and present, think of this.
First let us take *The Tenor Voice* by Anthony Frisell:

In its undeveloped state the head register is often referred to as the falsetto. Many think of it as a carry over from the child's boy soprano voice and unrelated to the matured male voice. Nothing could be farther from the truth. The misconception is due to lack of technical knowledge for developing and uniting its quality and action with the lower register. The upper register is often referred to as the head voice and the mixed voice. The lyric voices are more familiar with the falsetto than the dramatic ones. However, both must utilize the register in the same manner. Qualities both associate with it are soprano-like, flutey, lyric, soft and sweet. These terms only describe the register's undeveloped condition and fail to indicate the power that is acquired with advanced development.

Lilli Lehmann in *How to Sing* writes that: 'Most male singers – tenors especially – consider it beneath them, generally, indeed unnatural or ridiculous to use the falsetto, which is a part of all male voices . . . They do not understand how to make use of its assistance . . . Of its proper application they have not the remotest conception.'
E. Davidson Palmer, in his *Manual of Voice Training*, writes:

The term 'falsetto' is a most misleading one, and its indiscriminate use has been mischievous in the extreme. The man who invented it has much to answer for. He has caused right to be mistaken for wrong, and wrong to be mistaken for right . . . what is false appear to be true, and what is true appear to be false. Had it been his desire to do all the injury in his power to the male voices of his own and succeeding generations, he could not, by the exercise of the utmost ingenuity have devised means better calculated to accomplish his purpose . . . *The way to get rid of falsetto is to use it*. Let it alone and it will assuredly remain. It may grow weaker, but so long as voice of any kind remains, it will never disappear. Use it judiciously and perseveringly and in course of time it will lose its falsetto character and become firm and sonorous. It will then no longer sound strange and artificial, but will have the true manly quality and will seem to be what it really is, the natural voice. Wherever a separate falsetto register exists, it, and it alone, is the rightly produced voice. Its extremely high notes, however, are not the notes to practise upon.

E. Herbert Caesari, in *The Voice of the Mind* writes:

The term *falsetto* (diminutive of the Italian *falso*, false) means 'false little voice'; by itself it is worthless for purposes of vocal expression.

The old Italian School used to call it *falsettino di testa*, 'false little head voice', because, as a sensation, it seems to be generated high up in the head cavities. By no means is it a false voice, as the tone is generated by the thread-like upper edges of the vocal cords which, in order to produce the so-called falsetto, separate much more than is the case for the production of either the pharyngeal or normal tone. And because of the greater space or slit between the cords while producing the falsetto, a much greater quantity of breath is expended, in that not all of it is employed in producing tone (as is, or should be, the case with normal tone) but escapes through the slit, thereby 'diluting' the product. It is a 'head' voice, but of a pale, insignificant, breathy sort: the tone is anaemic and static. Most voices, male and female, are able to produce falsetto. But some basses, and baritones of the heavier calibres, apparently do not seem able to produce it at all. In its usually undeveloped state, the falsetto is weak, and has little tension-resistance (due to the separation of the cords). We hold the falsetto tone in contempt only when it is produced by itself.

(By kind permission of Robert Hale.)

In *The Art of Singing*, Sims Reeves, the great English tenor of the Victorian era, wrote:

As the term implies, falsetto is a false voice. It is produced by a coup di glottis – that is, by a sudden, forceful shock of the voice. A falsetto note, to give a startling effect, must be high, and must be attacked from a chest note lower in the scale. Any attempt to add vibrato to falsetto will at once result in the production of a nondescript tone of very bad quality. It is impossible to make a crescendo on a falsetto note – it may swell out a very little, but a full, genuine crescendo cannot be done. This fact will help the learner to distinguish between the head register and falsetto. I consider falsetto to be merely an illegitimate way of getting an effect which, at best, is only vulgar; good voices never have occasion to adopt such an inartistic trick. Bass voices usually have the best falsetto tones.

Michael and Molly Hardwick writing in *A Singularity of Voice* consider that:

Much of the modern neglect of falsetto may be due to the cult of the ringing tenor, who, in accordance with one of the many dubious conventions of Italian opera, must attack his high notes at full bellow, or be derided for a ninny. Falsetto was valued by earlier generations of Italian singers; even the castrati used it to extend their range, and Farinelli's incredible ability to span three octaves certainly owed something to it.

G. Edward Stubbs in *The Adult Male Alto* makes the point that: 'Now if the falsetto was an unnatural and injurious production it seems incredible that the greatest teachers of singing the world has ever known failed to make that discovery.'

Grove's Dictionary of Music and Musicians, Fifth Edition, defines falsetto as:

> A particular form of sound production at the larynx sometimes adopted by male singers and in the majority of cases employed only when it is desired to reach a note above the ordinary range of the individual voice. By some singers falsetto is habitually adopted, as in singing alto, and in such cases tones of wide range, extending to a comparatively low pitch and of powerful volume, may be produced. But in most instances the tones of this mechanism are high-pitched, of feeble volume, of short duration and of poor quality.

Percy Scholes in *The Oxford Companion to Music* (1938) writes: 'Falsetto. The head voice in adults, an unnatural effect producible by practice (as distinct from the voice of a castrato produced by means of a surgical operation). The male alto sings falsetto. Falsettist is a falsetto singer. Counter tenor – see alto voice.'

E. Herbert Caesari again in *The Voice of the Mind* holds that: 'As the Old School used to say, the *falsetto* is the pile of the *pharyngeal carpet*. The pharyngeal puts life, lustre and intensity into both the falsetto and the basic; this is particularly true of the tenor's high notes. Falsetto is the velvet cloak for the steely pharyngeal, and the latter provides a solid base for the falsetto.'

Remembering the enormous range and power of the castrati, here is Pietro Francesco Tosi's comment on falsetto:

> A diligent Master, knowing that a Male Soprano, without the Falsetto, is constrained to sing within the narrow compass of a few notes, ought not only to endeavour to help him to it, but also to leave no Means untried, so to unite the feigned and the natural voice that they may not be distinguished; for if they do not perfectly unite, the Voice will be of diverse Registers.

We must surely smile at the idea of the 'natural' voice as opposed to a feigned one in a castrato!

We have explained what falsetto is, then how it is variously described by contrasting and often painfully mistaken vocal authorities, even though for centuries it was an honoured and celebrated technique. By the close of the nineteenth and first part of the twentieth century not only was it scorned as a specialist voice, but its uses in general vocal technique were increasingly denied and repressed by all except a few older teachers.

The tone of an undeveloped falsetto is usually soft, flutey, pleasant, rather weak and if by unusual chance it already has a reasonable upward range, it is most unlikely that notes below middle C will be audible except from close by. This is the theory, and often the case. But it is also clear that *correct* training of other vocal areas, other than non-pharyngeal tenor production, helps the unused falsetto lying above. So many baritones may well find a developed counter-tenor head voice awaiting use (like Elford, see page 113). Such a discovery underlines, in the opinion of the most enlightened singing teachers, the correctness of the vocal development already made. Many teachers put it another way. If the head or falsetto voice is understood and produced properly, then the other vocal registers will also be produced properly. So what of this production? Why is it so important to other vocal types? How can this soft head voice be amplified to widen other ranges in strength and ringing power?

The truth is that the falsetto or head voice embraces not one register, but two – 'middle falsetto' and 'upper falsetto'. The latter is by most men easily encountered and produced; and even undeveloped makes the singer feel detached, aeriated, a mile away from the chest or basic voice far below. When taken down by a counter tenor to middle C (where the upper falsetto used *alone* will be especially weak, i.e. in the area where the upper chest voice lies waiting), the *upper* falsetto feels separated from the chest by a gulf. The singer has a feeling of buoyant flexibility; he is free to pirouette vocally like a skater on ice. All vocal weight has gone. He exists in the free world of the head.

By contrast 'middle falsetto', sometimes called mezzo falso, remains quite definitely related to the chest, even though in itself it has a falsetto quality. This middle falsetto is termed also the 'pharyngeal' voice and is the source of the power, edge ring and essentially masculine timbre of the mature, developed counter-tenor singer. The properly produced tenor voice also uses something of this production, as should the high baritone, though many are unaware not only of their employment of it but of its very existence within them.

The pharyngeal voice uses the same edges of the vocal cords as does the upper falsetto, but the vocal cords are now completely aligned. Pharyngeal used alone does not require the use of the whole length of the thinned cords; unlike the upper falsetto it uses only about two-thirds. But it requires more diaphragmatic breath support than the upper voice. As Anthony Frisell says in both his books *The Tenor Voice* and *The Baritone Voice*: 'Its flexibility is limited by its attachment to the chest register, and the physical demands [in] producing it are greater than the detached falsetto and the singer senses both register characteristics in his throat simultaneously.'

It must be said at this point that the pharyngeal voice cannot be obtained or developed by the beginner, but must be found after the full development of the upper falsetto. The essential sound made by the whole falsetto range changes with continuous exercising. The original soft lyric timbre turns into a rather piercing, sometimes unpleasant, sound. The reason is that the first exchange of power from the chest register has taken place. We then await the roundness and polish to join it. Though but a transitory stage this piercing quality is never completely banished, but mixed and coloured by other added qualities. It was nicely termed the 'witch voice' by the early Italian singing teachers.

When the 'witch voice' is finally tempered and the full beauty of the finished pharyngeal voice has taken its place, as Anthony Frisell says: 'The singer acquires security in the area of the register's break, and passing from one register to the other (in both ascending and descending directions) while maintaining full resonating quality is no longer a problem. The middle falsetto is operative throughout the range.' This is borne out by E. Davidson Palmer (see page 105).

The term 'pharyngeal voice' derives from the Italian voce faringea, and was used much in the old Italian school of singing to describe the tone of a peculiar and distinctive mechanism. Its strength and its use are that it can be engaged alone, or in combination with the basic or chest voice, or upper falsetto, or indeed both together. Thus it is a link, a forging together of the chest and upper head voice: a true medium register, and except to the (falsetto) male soprano, it is essential.

Its use is ancient, and certainly covers the last three hundred years, and includes the 'golden era' of singing. But nowadays the knowledge of it, as related to 'conventional' voices, seems possessed by few. Yet most modern counter tenors use it continuously and often instinctively. Some form of it remained throughout the counter tenors' long years in the shadows, though it was never taught, for few altos were ever trained as such for about one hundred years. E. Herbert Caesari said in 1951 (ironically as Deller had just reached full flow), 'The male alto, heard in churches and choirs in England, employs mainly the pharyngeal, which for lack of real schooling never attains, however, perfection of development.' At any rate, those altos who throughout the dark years remained specialist falsettists, had at least some familiarity with the pharyngeal production even if it stayed mostly undeveloped.

Up to the end of the nineteenth century, Italian tenor singers were certainly trained to use it. Specialist users of voce faringea were traditionally known as 'contraltos'! This male 'contralto' (*not* the same animal as the old castrati contralto) was surely the linear descendant of the low counter tenor altus. When vocal fashion changed, surely the new Romantic tenor voice retained this ancient technique, while those high voices who specialised in it remained not tenors but 'contraltos' – the final Italian diminution or corruption, if you like, of contra-tenor-altus. The eighteenth-century ambiguity had remained. Contralti could be male or female, rather in the same way that, if fashion continues here in England, the *alto* voice will soon be permanently (but still wrongly) a bi-sexual term.

It seems that the Italian 'contralti' were not tenor altinos, whose voices would probably be too light, but developed baritone or normal tenor chest voices with the full-toned pharyngeal head development. It has been suggested that their title of contralto derived from their resemblance to the female contralto voice. It is more likely that it came about because of the similarity in the upper range to the castrato contralto – a voice still existing in nineteenth-century Italy.

E. Herbert Caesari writes about the term falsetto, which was: 'something applied to . . . tenor vocalists because the latter's head voice was an admixture of pharyngeal and falsetto. When exercised to the maximum (over a period of about four years, depending on the individual voice of course) these two mechanisms, properly amalgamated, are capable of producing a head voice of extraordinary power.' By 'falsetto', Caesari means upper falsetto. The reader will have noticed how he too underlines the importance of vocal *maturity* in the development of the full range head voice. His own teacher, incidentally, was the celebrated Giovan Riccardo Daviesi (1839–1921), the greatest 'contralto' singer of the Sistine Chapel in the nineteenth century.

Remembering the presence of soprano castrati in the same Papal Choir in the nineteenth century, one realises that something of the traditional Sistine *sound*, if not the style, had survived there against the odds in much the same manner as in English cathedrals. The Sistine castrati were by now heard almost exclusively in their ecclesiastical surroundings like the English alti, yet the Italian male 'contralti', despite their strange title, but perhaps because they had a tenor chest voice, were not only acceptable in the secular world but celebrated in it.

Caesari reminds us that the pharyngeal voice or mechanism is situated between the basic and the falsetto mechanisms. He suggests that the student will find it easier to envisage the mechanisms as:

three horizontal layers, superimposed, three *depths* of the vocal cords' mechanism producing three different tonal qualities, each of which is characteristic and quite distinct from the others. Taken by itself, the pharyngeal voice, without any admixture of basic or of falsetto, has a certain quality of steely intensity which is the reverse of beautiful particularly when produced forte. Mixed however, with either the basic or the falsetto (and still better with both simultaneously), it assumes very considerable importance.

It should be remembered that the technique described is not restricted to the male voice. Just as the female voice has registers and an upper falsetto, so it has also the middle falsetto. It is, however, says Caesari, 'built into' the larynx in a different manner, into the back half of the vocal cords, while in the male it is at the front. Women cannot combine the pharyngeal with the head notes.

In the upper falsetto of both sexes, the vocal cords oscillate with about the same thickness as in the medium (pharyngeal) register, but more apart, about half or two-thirds their total length, the oscillating section being in the middle. This varies depending on whether or how much the pharyngeal register is carried up and mixed with the upper falsetto. The expertly developed upper falsetto – for example that of Alfred Deller – is usually produced with a raised larynx.

Some laryngologists and teachers still maintain that all falsetto uses only the middle or central section of the cords, and this alone produces falsetto tones. They ignore the two varieties of falsetto and three different uses of the same anatomical equipment.

The basic or chest voice uses the cords full length, full thickness. This is the only really 'natural' use or register, if assessed by the nature, pitch and character of the individual's speaking voice. As we said, the medium, pharyngeal, or middle falsetto voice, unless used in a mixture of head and chest registers, uses two thirds of the length but greatly thinned cordal edges (less cord depth). The pure head or upper falsetto voice uses less than two-thirds of the cords. With the closing up of the arytenoid cartilages the now slight 'oval' tendency of the cords has separated their centre, leaving less than two-thirds of the full length to oscillate. As Caesari says:

> To engage the second layer, mechanism responsible for the so-called pharyngeal voice, *the cords approximate considerably more than they do when producing (upper) falsetto*. As the pharyngeal mechanism comes into action the feeling is one of flexible firmness and resistance (that are lacking in undeveloped falsetto). Being the second 'layer' it is, as a tonal sensation slightly lower than the falsetto, and by this we mean that it has slightly more vertical depth, definitely more substance, and is more lifelike.

The pharyngeal or head voice comes into play at *about* the same point despite the characteristic voice type of the singer. A tenor or baritone would expect to engage *no higher* than:

111

Male

Female

A soprano, mezzo, or contralto enter *in at the same area* because, though written an octave higher, the tenor's high F is *acoustically* on the first space, the identical note to women's voices. For detailed explanation of this see Caesari's *The Voice of the Mind*.

To take Purcell's high bass parts (see page 128), it now becomes clear how those high basses and baritones extended their range into their head voices. There can be no mystery. It was the ancient and proved method. The great Purcellian bass John Gostling had the most enormous range. We can now see how. The deep chest notes were never weakened by the stretching of chest notes high above the stave – which would happen today. Gostling used his head.

The counter tenor is in a different position. He is a specialist head voice singer, and unless a tenor-altino, *he will usually engage middle falsetto at a lower point in the scale*. This is necessary as he has usually to maintain a much higher tessitura than the tenor or baritone. (Though interestingly, if we are to believe Prendergast in 1900, the nineteenth-century altos, at least by the close, engaged head voice between C' and E'. At a guess, this may have been from lack of weighty enough development of the lower pharyngeal tones.)

The average two-register counter tenor, depending on his chest quality, would expect today to engage the pharyngeal at about B natural below middle C, and use it for forte singing mixed with upper falsetto to about the B flat above. Beyond that the pure head voice is in command, and though there may not be in the tone of a skilled singer much obvious difference, an equally skilled singer may choose to emphasise the change of timbre for musical effect, like Deller.

Of course, at other times the upper falsetto will be retained much lower than at B' flat. This would probably be for works requiring a soft mezzo voce, cantabile tone, probably when the other parts too are low in their range and the music is post-Classical.

The one-register high counter tenor (i.e., not the Oberlin-type extended low counter tenor, but the singer who extends his pharyngeal register down in what Ardran and Wulstan suggest is the late seventeenth-century manner) will find at (A) that his effective range will be approximately:

(A.)

(B.)

At (B) it will be noticed that Richard Elford's extremely puzzling, seemingly unique low counter-tenor range (A, first space, Bass Clef, up to B', Treble Clef) is interestingly bounded at the top by the ending of the middle falsetto voice. If he chose not to use upper falsetto, this would grow weaker with the extensive use of the pharyngeal with his chest register. This does not happen if the chest register is employed almost full time as with the specialist baritone or bass. The quality of the upper falsetto might or might not be good, but it does not disappear or weaken.

As we have already seen, the well-trained baritone's pharyngeal voice is often excellent, but he still regards himself as a baritone because that is his speciality. What if he were to call himself a counter tenor and specialise in low alto parts? We could have a Richard Elford. Ardran and Wulstan seem not to have thought of this possibility:

> Freaks undoubtedly did exist from time to time, but they cannot be regarded as the norm. The fact that Elford had a range as low as A at the bottom of the Bass Stave is a musicological red herring for either Elford was a tenor, as Mr Hodgson suggests, in which case he should not have called himself a counter tenor, or, more likely, this note was falsetto. It is not an impossible note to reach in this way, but to sing it in performance would make Elford very unusual.

It is quite possible then that Elford had an *acquired* low counter tenor and did in fact specialise in low alto parts. (His famous lowest notes would hardly ever be used in the normal run, though if he sang baritone parts as well on occasion he would have opportunity to bring his low A into play.) Extensive pharyngeal development, plus chest register, could well have lost him first the quality and eventually the use in public of his upper falsetto.

If Elford were a tenor, as Ardran and Wulstan think possible and Hodgson believes, why then call himself counter tenor? Perhaps he was an ordinary high tenor but enjoyed singing counter tenor parts, a phenomenon not unknown today. He would have become known as a counter tenor: much as those who are really 'forced-up' baritones are referred to as tenors because they sing the tenor part.

Discussing Thomas Tomkins's counter-tenor parts, which are much earlier than Elford, Dr Bernard Rose seems to imply a belief that seventeenth-century altos probably used no falsetto (see 'Vocal Pitch in Sixteenth and Seventeenth Century Music' in *English Church Music*, 1965). As an undisputed expert on Thomas Tomkins, he writes:

> In Tomkins's *Musica Deo Sacra*, for example, the range of the counter-tenor is from bottom E flat to C, a thirteenth above (this is at modern, transposed pitch). There is no documentary description

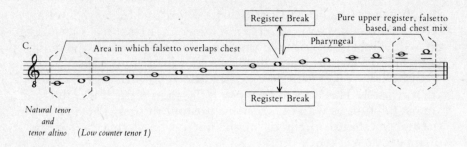

C.

Register Break

Pure upper register, falsetto based, and chest mix

Area in which falsetto overlaps chest

Pharyngeal

Register Break

Natural tenor
and
tenor altino   (Low counter tenor 1)

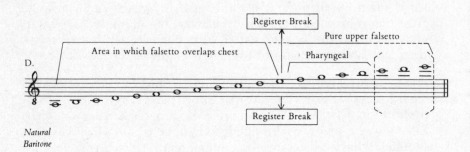

D.

Register Break

Pure upper falsetto

Area in which falsetto overlaps chest

Pharyngeal

Register Break

Natural
Baritone

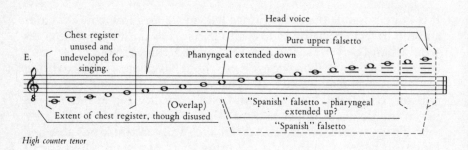

E.

Head voice

Chest register unused and undeveloped for singing.

Pure upper falsetto

Phanyngeal extended down

(Overlap)

Extent of chest register, though disused

"Spanish" falsetto – pharyngeal extended up?

"Spanish" falsetto

High counter tenor

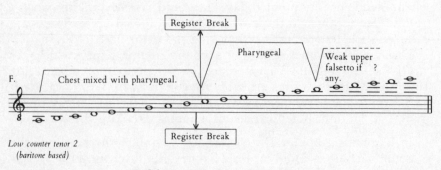

F.

Register Break

Pharyngeal

Weak upper falsetto if any. ?

Chest mixed with pharyngeal.

Register Break

Low counter tenor 2
(baritone based)

Table 5 *Male vocal registration.*

of the type of voice production which was used by this counter-tenor. It was a much favoured voice – this is evident from the fact that most five-part works are for S.A.A.T.B., and that many of the finest verses are for counter-tenor. The normal alto of today, who tends to sing falsetto, can manage the higher notes of this wide range but is very ineffectual in the lower part. There can be little doubt that he was either a very high tenor such as the present American singer, Mr Oberlin, or a bass with a high and probably strident top octave. With the mellifluous falsetto-alto of today it is vital that he should learn to sing the lower notes in his low speaking voice, and effect an unnoticeable 'gear-change' round about the B flat below middle C, otherwise much of the finest music of the period just does not 'come off'. Obviously, if one has a really high tenor in one's choir, it is far better that he should sing the big alto verses than a falsetto-alto who does not possess a good low register.

(By kind permission of The Royal School of Church Music.)

Dr Rose is correct in that it is vital to use the singer who can be heard in the lower notes. Our very point is that the properly produced alto is just as much the counter tenor as the Oberlin tenor-altino.

The Oberlin type is most certainly *based* on an abnormally high tenor. He himself claims not to use falsetto notes which lie untouched at the top of his range. It seems that their quality is, like most tenors' upper falsetto, weak. Few tenors possess an upper falsetto of any merit, either because they never did, or because their normal everyday production has weakened or banished it completely.

As an illustration of the Elford theory, I assure the reader that used in a particular way, the pharyngeal weakens the upper falsetto while itself attaining enormous strength. I know because I experimented with this production over a few weeks and noticed a weakening of my previously floated easy upper notes from B' upwards. If I had continued (having a baritonal chest register myself), my range would have become like that of Elford. In his later years as a full-time professional, John Whitworth seemed to have Elford's range exactly.

So I suggest that low counter tenors like Elford, in restricting their upward range and concentrating on the strengthening of their lower notes, might actually have vetoed any possible later use of upper falsetto if and when they wished to use it. *The Times* music critic, writing at the end of the 1950s, puts it well:

The vocal cords, though a small organ, are infinitely adaptable provided their owner will limit their infinity to one thing at a time. No one can sing both high and low . . . if a man finds that his vocal cords are adjustable to high notes he can cultivate that end of his range and become a counter tenor, just as Per Contrarium a trumpeter or hornist cannot be expected to play Bach's high solo parts if his normal work is ordinary orchestral playing where the tessitura is anything from a fifth to an octave lower.

So, in bringing in *intention* as an important factor, we are not just introducing mind over matter but matter over mind. For once intention has been successful, then the range, not to forget tone and style, is surely prescribed? *The Times* critic continues:

> All these musical faculties depend on elasticity of tissue . . . The vocal cords, like the trumpeter's lips, cannot be both tense and loose. The singer's pitch range is of course primarily given by nature: a low bass is not convertible into a high tenor or a light soprano into a deep contralto, but short of that the muscular adjustment of the larynx can with practice produce almost anything desired, if there is a model to imitate . . . Men who would be undistinguished baritones astonish the world by singing whole Handel opera roles in the soprano range.

We have discovered then that prior to the development of the high, powerful, chested, operatic tenor, all male voices employed a large amount of pharyngeal, often plus upper falsetto in their *normal* production. It was the basis of what is now thought of as the old Italian school of singing, itself the direct descendant of the catholic Classical and pre-Classical method. The counter tenor or alto voice is part of this ancient family tree.

We have a valuable first-hand description of pre-Romantic tenor technique. It is of considerable interest to us for obvious reasons.

Writing to Bellini in 1831, when the part of Pollione was being composed for him, the famous tenor Domenico Donzelli said:

> I do not consider it amiss if I give you some idea of the compass and general nature of my voice, for you will then know better how to write for it and I shall be sure of successfully interpreting in the dual interest of your music and my art. My compass is almost two octaves: from D to high C; I employ chest voice to G only, but up to this pitch I can sustain a vigorous declamation. From this G to high C, I employ a falsetto which, when used with art and strength, is extremely ornamental. I have adequate agility.

Clearly, by falsetto from G to high C he was referring to the pharyngeal voice nicely mixed with what we today know as upper falsetto. Caesari comments:

> By 'chest voice' Donzelli meant the normal voice. In accordance

with the training at that time, Donzelli used his normal voice up to F sharp or G, and then the pharyngeal-falsetto combination for the head notes. Several arias in Bellini's and Donizetti's operas include high D″ natural, obviously intended to be sung with the pharyngeal-falsetto schooling.*

It is therefore quite clear that today's muscular operatic tenors are a comparatively recent breed. But the influence of this powerful type on our contemporary tenors of other types is definite. Can you imagine a tenor of today *admitting* to the regular use of falsetto of any sort? As Anthony Frisell says in *The Tenor Voice*:

Present day singers are expected to sing upper tones with a great amount of resonance drawn from the lower register, which limits their upper extension. If our present day tenors were to sing upper tones in a falsetto manner their production would be criticized as being false and unrelated to the natural voice. The castrati of the early 'Bel Canto' era were the only males to posses extreme ranges, due to their altered nature . . . recordings of [great tenors] . . . reveal that none display any more than two octaves' range, with D flat above high C as the utmost top.'

It is quite true. Even particular tenors renowned for abnormally high singing did not possess this facility for more than a brief part of their total singing careers. But even Frisell seems here to have overlooked the fact that the castrati's phenomenal range was largely due to the use of falsetto techniques. The irony is that although the lyric tenors use or should use the pharyngeal mix, many either do not know or do not *wish* to know that they are using it.

The tenor roles in the operas of Rossini, Bellini and Donizetti show that they were clearly written for voices trained in the old method, for the 'tenore di grazia', or light, graceful tenor. The tessitura, the melismas with phrases touching high D or even F, were never written to be delivered in the so-called 'chest' or basic mechanism alone, or to sound as if they were.†

Those authorities who pooh-pooh the use of falsetto happily talk of 'head voice', apparently without understanding how it identifies with the two main forms of falsetto production. Presumably they do not consciously set themselves against what is by common agreement the most glorious era in the history of singing; yet they appear to preach against one of its basic tenets.

* The famous tenor Rubini (contemporary with Donzelli) is known to have had enormous range but a 'weak' middle to his voice and a powerful 'freak' (so called) extension at the top. The implications are clear enough.

† A light tenor with a noticeable three-register range, like Rubini, sounds familiar.

Caesari tells us how the break with vocal tradition began. It was:

Initiated by the tenor Marcel Duprez, whose success, however, was all too ephemeral. He is credited with being the first tenor to produce all the head notes, including the C and C sharp, with the normal voice (unmixed basic mechanism) . . . Duprez's vocal collapse and eclipse are instructive under the circumstances. Might is not always right; and in this respect the following extract from *Cantanti Celebri del Secolo XIX* [Celebrated Singers of the Nineteenth Century], by the impresario Gino Monaldi, is illuminating.

We now quote the passage referred to. It might be as well to reflect that not only do many heavy operatic tenors lose their voices relatively early: they lose their lives early too. They are not notably a long-lived race. Gino Monaldi:

Duprez through sheer willpower and determination became one of the most famous tenors in the world. In his case, Nature had not been lavish, his voice being both weak and dull; yet by dint of hard unremitting work he succeeded in making it exceptionally robust. After hearing Duprez in *William Tell*, Rossini complimented him with tears in his eyes . . . I weep because those who heard *William Tell* tonight sung by Duprez will not enjoy hearing it sung by other tenors; but unfortunately, poor Duprez cannot last long.

It was a prediction not long in coming true. But unfortunately, Duprez's technique was imitated. The celebrated Russian singing teacher, Panofka, declared:

Duprez sang . . . with a tenacity and energy worthy of a better cause; and who can deny that afterwards most tenors set themselves the task of imitating Duprez's mistakes, seeking nothing but the brutal force of the high C ? . . . Who can deny that such tenors had to engage in an athletic contest with their voices, a struggle from which the voice came out second best? Who can deny that the sopranos, in order to compete with the 'tenori di forza', were obliged to force their voices beyond the normal?

We must remember, though, that only Italian church tenors (the so-called contralti) employed just pharyngeal-falsetto without any basic or normal voice on the head notes. The operatic tenors of the Rossini–Bellini–Donizetti era produced their head voice mostly in pharyngeal-falsetto plus a *modicum* of basic voice. The reasons are surely either that the church or oratory acoustic does not need the same amount of sheer sound as the dry theatre, or that the style required something different.

The student would be well advised to acquire Caesari's book, *The Voice of the Mind*, in order to study especially the last chapter in minute detail. Caesari might have been thinking of the counter tenor (of which actual term he seems never to have heard) when describing that rare occurrence of a tenor or baritone appearing on the scene with a perfectly integrated voice after no particular study. He writes of a singer who can progress from basic, through pharyngeal to (upper) falsetto and back with no break in the mechanism:

In these particular cases nature has, through recondite circumstances completed her work – as sometimes she thinks fit to do, to show us one and all what a completely natural voice is, and how it operates, and what tonal effects it produces. On the other hand, she is generally very remiss in this sense and apparently is content to leave things in an unfinished state, albeit with full mechanical potentialities, under the assumption that man will exert himself to complete the work. Indeed it is far better so, for such industry, such striving, is creative of both art and the artist.

At this point it is perhaps appropriate to comment on an interesting, well-documented article in *Music and Letters* (1969) called 'Alfred Deller, John Freeman and Mr Pate', by Olive Baldwin and Thelma Wilson. The article discusses the counter-tenor question through the medium of these three important singers, and two Shakespearian operas in which, separated by three centuries, they sang: Britten's *A Midsummer Night's Dream* and Purcell's *Fairy Queen*. The role of Oberon was written for Deller. It is not by any means certain that the counter-tenor solos in *Fairy Queen* were written for Freeman and Pate, though it is possible. They were the resident counter tenors in the company which first performed it.

The general thesis of Baldwin and Wilson is that because the Britten counter-tenor solos are approximately one third higher than the Purcell parts, then *ipso facto* they were written with different voices in mind: in fact it is a reiteration of the old falsetto alto versus high tenor argument.

The reader is urged to study the article in its entirety. But he would do well to remember that Britten chose the excellent upper falsetto of Deller for its special ethereal quality. There are carefully calculated effects using excursions into strong pharyngeal territory but the disembodied tone of upper falsetto is exactly right for the role of Oberon, King of the Fairies.

Purcell on the other hand uses mainly the pharyngeal register – the exact range of the low counter tenor of either type – perhaps because the addition of (upper) chest pharyngeal will have much the same effect as the contrast of upper falsetto plus pharyngeal in the Britten work. Incidentally, he was concerned to build a particular vocal and dramatic character, while in the Purcell, no singer was asked to portray one role throughout.

Baldwin and Wilson also suggested that the Purcell counter-tenor solos are near impossible for the modern type of counter tenor. How wrong this view is can be demonstrated by hearing the record of *The Fairy Queen* (Britten edition with Peter Pears) featuring Bowman, Brett, Partridge and Pears himself, to name the counter tenors and tenors. There is little difference in the effect of many of the solos rendered by these superb artists. In others, the different voices exactly express what I am sure Purcell intended: a similarity but not an identical sound.

The article suggests that English pitch has risen since Purcell's day. It has not. Elsewhere it worries that there are very few tenor solos in *The Fairy Queen*, wondering how tenor soloists could be engaged for only two solos and a trio (one tenor only). The suggestion is that the counter tenors were also the tenor soloists. This may well have been the case, but not quite as Baldwin and Wilson imply. Counter tenor was undoubtedly the favourite voice of the period. Perhaps no real tenors were engaged on this occasion? (Alternatively, the tenor soloists may have been specially drawn from the semi-chorus for those few numbers.) It is worth recalling that in his 1683 ode, 'Welcome to all the Pleasures', Purcell gives the one major solo to counter tenor: tenor and bass get a miniature flourish each. Other than in the trio work, *The Fairy Queen* fits a general pattern.

The article concludes with a reference to the Anthony Lewis recording of *The Fairy Queen* in which Pears is heard singing against a trumpet the counter-tenor solo 'Thus the Gloomy World', and which he sings very well. Baldwin and Wilson take this to demonstrate that all the opera's counter-tenor solos should thus be allocated henceforth to tenors. They fail to mention that Whitworth, who sings the rest of the alto solos, sounds much the same in timbre: both were using pharyngeal production, Pears with more additional basic voice than Whitworth. It is indeed ironic that Whitworth was indisposed the day they were due to record that particular important solo. Also, it must be remembered that the tonal strength and volume of a modern orchestral trumpet such as was used on that occasion is one thing; the light trumpet of Purcell's day is quite another.

If, as Baldwin and Wilson advocate, a tenor sings the counter-tenor solos, the comic possibilities of Mopsa are diminished (or indeed when the duet is transposed for mezzo soprano and tenor as Britten did). If ever a part demonstrated by its style and range that it required a counter tenor, and preferably not of the tenor altino type, then this is surely it. A modern tenor is unlikely to achieve quite the bizarre effect which Purcell undoubtedly envisaged.

The answer to Baldwin and Wilson is surely that the alto solos in *The Fairy Queen* were written for either a low counter tenor of either type, or high counter tenor with the greatly extended strong head pharyngeal range downwards, and no use of chest at all, and that Freeman and Pate were performers of one of these types.

Chapter 6

STYLISTIC CONSIDERATIONS

THIS CHAPTER looks at music written and available for counter tenors to sing. Let us leave choirs and ensemble music for the moment, and deal first with solo works intended for a counter tenor of one type or another. The student will not find here a complete list of all such music with its composers but an indication of what is available. Even today, much solo counter-tenor music is unpublished. Like half-forgotten works for other voices, songs for alto often lie waiting in manuscript in the British Museum and other collections. But a good proportion of works suggested here *is* published and obtainable, and more appears all the time from various rich archives. Check the edition before you buy, the most recent the better is a worthwhile but not infallible guide. (See page 176.)

Identification of songs as specifically for counter tenors is sometimes difficult. Even though identified by the alto clef, the music often seems absurdly low. The whole question of early pitch and variations in performing has been discussed in learned detail by Arthur Mendel, David Wulstan and Robert Donnington, to name but three. Careful study of their conclusions is recommended.

An indication of the size of the problems is given by two authorities. First, Frank Ll. Harrison, in considering medieval choral pitch and vocal range, discusses the Eton Choirbook, then the Old Hall manuscript:

The Eton music shows the extension in the range and pitch in choral music which came with writing for five and more parts, with the highest parts for boy trebles and the lowest parts in the modern bass range. The written pitch of the Old Hall music and of that of Dunstable's time had tenor C as the lowest normal note, the B flat a tone below being rarely written. Though the actual pitch was partly a matter of convenience, it is clear that the range of polyphony until the second half of the fifteenth century corresponded to that of the tenor and counter tenor voices of today . . . the regular compass of pieces in five or more parts in the Eton manuscript is twenty-two or twenty-three notes. The compass of each piece is given in these terms in the manuscript, together with the number of voices, both in the index and at the head of the piece, probably to show which works needed trebles and which could be sung by men only or, with transposition, by boys only. A few five- and six-part antiphons keep within the range of fourteen or fifteen notes, but none of the four-part antiphons exceeds fifteen notes. Of the ten four-part Magnificats, only one of which remains complete, six had a range of twenty-one or twenty-two notes, one of seventeen, and three of fourteen. The sonority obtained from the wider range in the full sections and the greater possibilities of textural contrast in the solo sections were among the major 'discoveries' of the later medieval composers, whose liking for the sound of rich and full chords is also evident in the common practice of dividing one or more parts at important cadences.

Secondly, Dr Bernard Rose is interesting on the problems of sixteenth- and seventeenth-century choral pitch. He is discussing the rarity and question of extreme keys. Most vocal music of that time was written and printed in a very narrow range of keys, and they are seldom those with ambitious key signatures. It is tempting to think simplistically that this was surely to relate to keyboard instruments – likely to be used for rehearsal if not accompaniment – which were tuned to 'mean-tone' as opposed to our modern equal temperament in which nothing is actually in tune except the octave. Mean-tone provided the player with about twelve central keys in which all the most essential chords were purer than on the modern keyboard. But the question of simple keys and keyboard pitch is highly complicated. Organ pitch was a fourth higher than choir pitch in the sixteenth century. What of the equivalent of the vestry piano – the practice harpsichord which one might assume present? Consult David Wulstan's excellent paper on sixteenth-century vocal colour, but as Dr Rose says:

Does the fact that 'a capella' choral music was not 'written down' in extreme keys necessarily prove that it was not 'sung' in extreme keys? When one realises that different pitches for different 'media' ran parallel throughout this period – church pitch, chamber pitch and so on – and that different parts of Europe used different pitches from each other – witness organ tuning – it would lead one to conclude that the expression 'absolute pitch' is a recent one and would have been an unlikely and an embarrassing attribute at that time. Surely it is possible that if a composer desired to have a piece sung in, say, A flat minor he would write it out in A minor and the director would hum A flat! Those of us who have daily experience with choirs know well that a choir will sing a piece better at a low pitch on one day and at a higher pitch on another day. So many factors affect singers – the time of day, temperature, atmosphere and the proximity of meals! My conclusion is, and here I am at variance with most scholars on the subject, that there is nothing sacrosanct about pitch in 'a capella' choral music of this period. Verse anthems and verse services are an entirely different matter, since the tuning of organs permitted the use of only certain keys.

(Ninety-five per cent of keyboard instruments in England remained tuned to mean-tone until the mid-nineteenth century.)

Until fairly recent times it was confidently thought that in the period roughly from 1600 to about 1820, the internationally used pitch for instrumental music remained at slightly more than a semitone below $A' = 440$ (the modern pitch). It was realised that there were inevitable local departures from this normal standard. (1711 saw the coming of the tuning fork, though it is doubtful whether this standardised an international pitch immediately. Yet it must have happened fairly rapidly so far as England was concerned.)

What was not generally realised until suggested by fairly recent research was that the usual secular pitch of Blow, Purcell and English composers of their time differed from that of Handel by a full tone, possibly more. English late seventeenth-century church pitch was still high – up to one tone higher than the 'printed note' considered at our modern $A = 440$. Church pitch had remained fairly steady, about a minor third above $A = 440$ earlier in the seventeenth century, but after the Commonwealth a new start was made. It is possible that the influx of French musicians and influence resulted, in secular music, in the adoption of lower pitch which was similar to today's.

Some authorities insist that the distinction between church and secular pitch had disappeared, and that both were about a semitone up from today. This would help the low Purcell alto parts. Others believe that in meeting at a common pitch, both church and secular music was performed at what amounted to our modern pitch.

What is certain is that when Handel and large numbers of other German musicians, instrumentalists and instrument makers came to England in the early eighteenth century, they brought with them German pitch. This was between a tone and semitone *lower* than the 'printed note'. This took English pitch down past $A = 440$ and therefore probably mainstream opera, certainly oratorio and other secular music, was performed in excess of a semitone *down* from today's pitch.

The recent practice of performing seventeenth-century English music a semitone down from what was intended is the result of using foreign instruments, thus their pitch, for earlier music. The aesthetic effect is undoubtedly superior to that obtainable on later Romantic period instruments; but this practice should cease when authentically built instruments for seventeenth-century music are used instead. Purcell and his contemporaries will thus be heard at nearer their true pitch.

Traditionally, certain instruments were tuned higher or lower than what was normal. Cornetts, for example, sounded slightly more than a tone higher than their written music would suggest, organs slightly in excess of a semitone.

Clearly, pitch has a most important effect on discussion of music for the inner voices. We can be certain that the lowest part in works for S.A.T.B. was sung by a bass of some variety, and the highest normally by a treble. But the inner parts are obviously more ambiguous, and affected by considerations of pitch. This is especially so when the parts are subdivided for example into S.A.A.T.Bar.B.

The difficulty with old pitches is further complicated by the question of the Chiavette device. Detailed extra study of this is recommended to the student, but we may define Chiavette as involving the use of certain 'high' clefs which indicate that the music should be performed a fourth or fifth down from what is written. Obviously, this could suggest that counter-tenor voices might well have been used for works apparently intended for other vocal ranges. The principle of transposition when 'high clefs' are used is precisely stated by Michael Praetorius in his *Syntagma Musicum*, vol. iii (1619).

Briefly then, Chiavette (meaning key or clef) means that the tenor clef

might be used for a bass part instead of

Alternatively, there was the use of the G clef on the second line:

for a soprano part instead of the usual

The idea was to avoid the need for leger lines, but as leger line notes may well lie outside the effective compass of the voice, they were used also to indicate transposition down a fourth or fifth. So a soprano part written in the G clef with this compass:

might possibly indicate that it was to be sung thus:

with a similar transposition indicated by the Chiavette of the other parts. Do not forget that the *pitch* involved is not likely to be our modern standard pitch. Monteverdi is an example of a composer some of whose works are now thought to be associated with the Chiavette device. The effects that pitch and clefs may have on all parts merit further study (see Bibliography).

Having read of the origins of the counter-tenor part, you will no doubt recall how the part has risen gradually from early medieval times when it did duty for a rudimentary 'bass' and 'alto'. It was a gradual process, and arrived at what we consider comfortable alto range – i.e. a range which for purposes of discussion tires the average voice least – in the sixteenth century. Alto parts remained much the same in tessitura for about a further 200 years, after which, as described earlier, with the Romantic influence the upper range rose and continued to rise further. Although this was chiefly in secular music, it affected and influenced later church composers like Stanford and Wood, and through them Bairstow, Vaughan Williams, Howells and others.

The resulting tessitura of the alto part in twentieth-century English cathedral and church music is usually as high as is possible for most counter tenors to manage; sometimes it is decidedly uncomfortable.

In October 1956, Stuart Humphry Ward, in a *Musical Times* article of all too short a length called 'The Male Alto in Church Music', made the point that the modern alto part can actually damage the young adult voice before it has reached enough maturity to cope with this sometimes cruel upward range. This in turn spells doom when he has to deal with classical counter tenor parts, yet composers continue to write ever higher alto parts. Mr Ward makes the plea for slower vocal training to avoid this damage, and adds another plea that modern composers might break the vicious circle by keeping their tessituras down in the alto line.

He takes two excerpts from important works for alto and demonstrates the change. We are *not* now discussing a different voice, i.e. an abnormally high tenor as compared with a falsettist, but the traditional English cathedral counter tenor (Purcell himself sang Example A in the opening performance). It matters not that this Example A is probably for a *low* counter tenor (second alto) and Example B is for high (first alto).

Example 16a *Purcell's* Ode to St. Cecilia, *1692.*

Example 16b *Vaughan Williams's* Te Deum In G *(first alto line).*

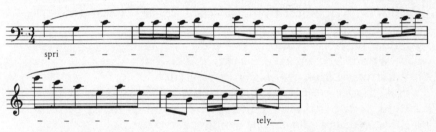

Example 16c *Purcell's* Ode to St. Cecilia, *1692 (first bass solo).*
(By kind permission of *The Musical Times.*)

As Mr Ward says, the tessitura of *Te Deum* (B) is cruel, and yet it is a work frequently – even mostly – performed by altos in our cathedrals. In fact, this particular *Te Deum* was written for and performed by Canterbury Cathedral Choir at Archbishop Lang's enthronement in 1928, and at several since.

Which counter tenor would wish to sing a typical Purcell solo immediately following the Vaughan Williams *Te Deum* in G? Very few. And what is not fully appreciated but often felt by singers; who would care to reverse this? It bears out my feelings about low counter tenors' lack of upper falsetto. It should be noted that Example A was for pharyngeal voice in full strength, Example B, upper falsetto with the added strength (since it is a forte passage) of added pharyngeal *support*.

One of the most interesting aspects of the article is Mr Ward's random choice of ten works written for cathedral choirs, five older works, five newer, in order to compare the alto tessitura. Conscious of the pitch differences which might be brought into consideration, he points out that an inspection of the tessitura of the other voice parts in the older works shows the fairness of comparison. Purcell makes his bass soloist sing Example C in the same piece as heretofore mentioned. This, like Example A, *could* have been performed at 'secular' pitch. Regarding the range of Example C, the reader will recall discussion on page 112 and the chart on page 114. Also, compare the ranges of A and C. They are almost identical. There is now no problem in understanding how Purcell could be both counter tenor and take a bass part too, with bass parts like these especially. As T. S. Eliot says of St Thomas Becket: 'There is no mystery about this man who takes a certain part in history.'

Here are Mr Ward's conclusions. He calculated the percentage duration of the alto part spent above high A.

Vaughan Williams, *Te Deum in G*, 37 per cent.
Howells, Magnificat from *Collegium Regale*, 25 per cent.
Stanford, 'Jubilate', 21 per cent.
Bairstow, *Blessed City*, 18 per cent.
C. Wood, *Jesu, the very thought*, 17 per cent.
Palestrina, *Christe Redemptor*, 7 per cent.
Purcell, *Ode to St. Cecilia*, 1692, first solo alto, 6 per cent.
Byrd, four-part *Mass*, omitting Credo and Gloria, 3 per cent.
Blow, *Salvator Mundi*, one semiquaver B flat.
Purcell, *Remember not, Lord*, 0 per cent.

Of the five modern works, none descends lower than A flat, whereas low Gs and Fs are not infrequent in the older works.

We have extended his idea and analysed a well-known collection of Tudor works in the same manner. Here again, it must be stated that we are to some extent in the hands of editors; but most modern editors, acutely conscious of musicological scholarship looking over their shoulders, are generally scrupulous in their decisions over pitch, and always indicate the original. A few works give the alto voice a part originally labelled with another name. These are mentioned at the foot of the list. Knowing of the origins of the counter tenor, it will be realised readily that we have here a reminder of the nomenclature ambiguities of the past. The *tenor* parts in these few cases are often worthy of special study!

Where there are two counter-tenor parts, two percentages have been given.

	Anthem	Composer	Voices	%above A'
1.	Alleluia, I Heard a Voice	Weelkes	Tr.Ct.T.B.B. (S.M.A.T.B.)	13.66
2.	Almighty and Everlasting God	Gibbons	Tr.Ct.T.B.	2.85
3.	Ascendit Deus	Philips	Tr.Tr.Ct.T.B.	10.6
4.	Ave Maria	Parsons	Tr.Ct.T.Bar.B. (Trip.Med. Alt.T.B.)	8.4★ 2.9
5.	Ave Verum Corpus	Byrd	Tr.Ct.T.B.	0
6.	Call to Remembrance	Farrant	Tr.Ct.T.B.	3.3
7.	Factum Est Silentium	Dering	Tr.Tr.Ct.T.B.	4.27
8.	Give Almes of Thy Goods	Tye	Tr.Ct.T.B.	6.89
9.	Gloria in Excelsis Deo	Weelkes	Tr.Tr.Ct.Ct.T.B.	7.3 1.19
10.	Haec Dies	Byrd	Tr.Tr.Ct. T.T.B.	2.5
11.	Hide Not Thou Thy Face	Farrant	Tr.Ct.T.B.	7.0
12.	Hosanna to the Son of David	Gibbons	Tr.Tr.Ct.Ct.T.T.B.	8.0 5.16
13.	Hosanna to the Son of David	Weelkes	M.M.Ct.T.B.B.	1.93
14.	If Ye Love Me	Tallis	Tr.Ct.T.B. (Ct.Ct.T.B.)	9.92
15.	I Heard a Voice	Tomkins	Tr.Ct.T.B.	1.3
16.	Justorum Animae	Byrd	M.M.Ct.T.B.	.75
17.	Laetentur Coeli	Byrd	Tr.Ct.T.B.B. Sup.Med.Ct.T.B.	19★ 0
18.	Let Thy Merciful Ears	Mudd	M.Ct.T.B.	0
19.	Lord, for Thy Tender Mercy's Sake	Hilton	M.Ct.T.B.	1.49 1.16†
20.	Miserere Mei	Byrd	Tr.Ct.T.B.B. Sup.Med.Ct.T.B.	3.04
21.	O Clap Your Hands	Gibbons	Tr.Tr.Ct.Ct. T.T.B.B.	4.5 6.3
22.	O Lord, Arise	Weelkes	Tr.Tr.Ct.Ct. T.T.B.	4.08
23.	O Lord in Thy Wrath	Gibbons	M.M.Ct.Ct.T.B.	2.7 6.55
24.	O Lord the Maker	Mundy	Tr.Ct.T.B.	.4 .39
25.	O Nata Lux	Tallis	Tr.Ct.T.T.B. (Sup.Disc.Ct.T.B.)	3.37
26.	O Praise the Lord	Batten	Tr.Ct.T.B.	1.07

	Anthem	Composer	Voices	%above A'
27.	O Quam Gloriosum	Byrd	Tr.Tr.Ct.T.B. (Sup.Med.Ct.T.B.)	8.98
28.	Salvator Mundi	Tallis	Tr.Ct.Ct.T.B.	0
				0
29.	Sing Joyfully	Byrd	M.M.Ct.Ct.T.B.	5.83
				3.45
30.	Teach Me, O Lord	Byrd	M.Ct.Ct.T.B.	4.44
				3.45
31.	This Day Christ was Born	Byrd	M.M.Ct.Ct.T.B.	16.9★
				2.18
32.	This Is the Record of John	Gibbons	Tr.Ct.Ct.T.B.	3.4
				4.0
33.	When David Heard	Tomkins	M.Ct.Ct.T.B.	9.3
				1.06
34.	When David Heard	Weelkes	Tr.Tr.Ct.Ct.T.B.	2.12
				1.0

★ In anthems 4 and 17 the first counter-tenor part in the modern edition is that described as 'medius' in the original, while in anthem 31 the first counter-tenor part is described as 'sextus'.

† In anthem 19 the second figure includes the notes of the final 'Amen', which may not be original.

Mean percentage of counter tenor part lying above A' in the above sample is 4.62, customary pitch adjustments made.

Tr = Treble, A = Ct (Counter tenor), M = Mean, Sup = Superius, Med = Medius, Dis = Discantus, Trip = Triplex.

Table 6 *Analysis of counter-tenor voice parts in anthems in* The Oxford Book of Tudor Anthems.

Now for contrast a similar chart of conclusions using a collection of modern anthems:

Anthem	Composer	Voices	Counter Tenor notes	Notes above A'	%
A Hymn to the Trinity	K. Leighton	SSATB	226	17	7.5
A Litany	W. Walton	SATB	124	9	7.26
A Prayer for Peace	D. Lord	SATB	58	3	5.17
A Pure River of Water of Life	A. Ridout	SATB	118	9	7.6
Christ the Lord is Risen Again	J. Rutter	SSATB	170	54	31.76
Faire is the Heaven	W. H. Harris	Double SATB	1.266	26	6.74
			2.370	12	3.24

Anthem	Composer	Voices	Counter Tenor notes	Notes above A'	%
Give Us the Wings of Faith	E. Bullock	SATB	35	17	48.57
Greater Love Hath No Man	J. Ireland	S(A)A (T)TB	308	41	13.31
Jesu Dulcis Memoria	P. Drayton	S(S)A (T)TB	78	7	8.97
Let All Mortal Flesh	E. Bairstow	S(S)A(A) TB(B)	312	22	7.05
Lift Up Your Heads	F. Jackson	SATB	179	51	28.49
Like as the Hart	H. Howells	SATB	103	8	7.77
Lord, Thou Hast Told Us	A. Bax	SATB	33	0	0
Make a Joyful Noise	W. Mathias	SATB	192	48	25
O Clap Your Hands	J. Rutter	SATB	256	57	22.27
O Clap Your Hands	R. Vaughan-Williams	S(S)A(A) T(T)B(B)	285	135	47.37
O How Amiable	R. Vaughan-Williams	SATB	141	97	68.8
On This Day, Earth Shall Ring	H. C. Stewart	SATB	223	46	20.63
O Taste and See	R. Vaughan-Williams	SATB	57	4	7.02
O Thou the Central Orb	C. Wood	SATB	214	5½	25.7
Puer Natus	A. Hoddinott	SAATBB	161	95	59
Set Me as a Seal	W. Walton	SATB	110	5	4.55
Thou, O God, Art Praised in Sion	I. Hare	SATB	122	43	32.25
Turn Back, O Man	G. Holst	SATB	241	50	20.75
We Wait for Thy Loving Kindness	W. McKie	SA(A)TB	115	13	11.3
O Be Joyful	B. Britten	SATB	169	46	27.22

Mean – 20.68% above A'

Table 7 *20th-century anthems from* Anthems for Choirs 4.
(By kind permission of Oxford University Press.)

Although these anthems were written for cathedrals and collegiate churches, and cathedral-type parish choirs, so were those from the Tudor book – no distinction need be drawn between the uses to which the two types of anthem would be put. No confusion arises, either, over the allocation of parts – we *know* which parts would be sung by which voices. (Bracketed parts imply splitting in individual parts, e.g. S(S) mean 1 soprano part which splits occasionally into 2.)

One cannot present a book on the counter tenor without at least some discussion of the alto clef. All alto parts are now printed in what is often a quite infuriating manner – the treble or G clef is used universally which naturally takes most earlier alto parts into a web of leger lines. Compare this with the neater layout and instant legibility of the alto or C clef and one is left wondering why it was ever abandoned. One reason is surely expediency: the fewer clefs, the easier music reading became to the less skilled. Also, women contraltos prefer a treble clef for obvious reasons. The rise of the contralto produced a strong influence on all voices. A glance at plate 12 demonstrates the rather irritating similarity of alto and tenor parts placed on adjacent lines in similar clefs.

We should consider why the C clef was used for so long. As I have explained, it was useful to show a voice line able to be sung by either a counter tenor or a tenor (see the discussion on pages 139–44). Avoiding leger lines was much more important to publishers and music printers, for the setting up of music type was considerably more difficult when coping with more leger lines. Movable lead type is a vastly different matter to today's litho printing. For the singer, perhaps the best reason for employment of the C clef was that it placed the alto part fairly and squarely *into* the stave. There is, too, a psychological effect on the singer. Continuous use of the C clef induces the development of a tone colour as a direct result of a 'high-looking' as opposed to a 'low-looking' part. Listen to recordings of John Whitworth who sounds high and tenor-like even in a 'low' alto part.

Dr A. H. D. Prendergast underlines our point in his paper 'The Man's Alto in English Music' (1900). Speaking of the Alto clef he says:

> Its disuse in England cannot be too strongly deplored. When the man's alto part is written with the G clef, . . . and in a score where the tenor is notated in the G clef an 8ve above, as is now the almost universal practice, the alto part has the appearance of being lower than the tenor part. There seems no reason why even where the G clef is used for the tenor, the C clef should not be retained for the man's alto. Every Cathedral alto is quite familiar with the C clef.

It has been pointed out by some writers on the subject that a particular clef does not necessarily indicate a specific human voice. For example in madrigal part-books it was common to find 'alien' parts printed in amongst those of the indigenous voice. (See E. H. Fellowes's excellent *English Madrigal Composers*.) Certainly, as we have seen, it is possible on occasion for one voice type to perform the part allotted to another, but we should remember that vocal compasses and clefs were not only known of, but noted academically by such important men as

Thomas Morley, in his famous *A Plaine and Easy Introduction to Practical Music*, 1597. Yet even in Morley we may discern the ambiguity between alto and high tenor:

> The musicians also use to make some compositions for men onely to sing in which case they never passe this compasse. Now you must diligentlie marke that in which of all these compasses you make your musicke, you must not suffer any part to goe without the compasse of his rules, except one note at the most above or below, without it be upon an extremity for the ditties sake or in notes taken for Diapason in the base.

| Altus | Tenor Primus | Tenor Secondus | Bassus |

Allowing for pitch changes the following should help our twentieth-century eyes and minds to visualise Morley's instructions. We have adjusted upwards by the customary minor third.

| Alto | First tenor | Second tenor | Bass |

Observe:

1. How in twentieth-century placing, the alto looks a *low* part.

2. The bass appears baritonal, suggesting that its favourite low notes are to be thought of as 'diapason in the bass' – a special underpinning effect used occasionally.

3. 'An extremity for the ditties sake' could suggest, perhaps, 'if the logical movement of the voice part demands it in the harmony'. This could extend the part by several tones, up or down, momentarily.

4. That the first tenor could easily be a low counter tenor part. While this could suggest that low alto parts were sung by first tenors, the reverse is also possible, that 'high tenors' were sung by 'altos'. The range is nicely that of the alto. If, as we have seen, tenors sang with falsetto technique, then by modern definition they were altos. The rare tenor altino could, like the other counter tenors and tenors, opt or be directed to one part or the other for the particular occasion.

5. That there is no suggestion by Morley of high falsetto singing in the Spanish/Italian manner. Perhaps our well-established treble technique made it unnecessary in his opinion, but he must have known of the Spanish falsetto tradition.

I now present an outlined repertoire which should prove useful. Most items suggested are already at a suitable pitch, but in some cases songs and arias eminently rewarding for counter tenors can be found by judicious transposition. I emphasise that the list is *not* comprehensive but a suggested initial one.

Solo Voice

A) FOLK SONGS: A rich source, accompanied or unaccompanied, European countries especially Italian 'Lauda'. And of course English folk songs.

B) MEDIEVAL: Plainchant, sequences, conductus, troubadour and trouvere songs, and music from Royal and other courts. Note particularly Landini, Machaut, St Godric (b. 1060 d. 1170!), Adam de la Halle.

C) 16TH CENTURY: Consort songs, songs by various lutenist composers such as Dowland and Rosseter; Byrd; two-part canzonets (here counted as solo) by Morley. Verse anthems and services by Byrd, Gibbons, Morley, Tomkins, Weelkes, Batten etc. Songs by Caccini and the Italian school, Spanish songs to the vihuella.

D) 17TH CENTURY: Consort songs by William and Henry Lawes, Monteverdi, the sacred and secular works of John Blow, Michael Wise, Pelham Humphrey. Odes, operatic and stage and welcome songs of Henry Purcell. John Weldon, the Scarlattis, Buxtehude, Viadana, Lully, Marcello, Charpentier, Schutz, Carissimi, Couperin, Lallouette, Bassani, Cavalli.

E) 18TH CENTURY: Solo parts in opera, oratorio, and occasional songs by Handel; Bach cantatas and Passions, down a tone or semitone to original Bach pitch (and look at some of the highest tenor solos at modern pitch – certain voices can handle them); Gluck, Rameau, Vivaldi, Pergolesi. Verse and solo anthems by Weldon, Greene, Boyce, Croft, Samuel Wesley. Songs from the stage.

F) 19TH CENTURY*: Particularly as the century progresses, little if any English secular solo music is suitable; but some large-scale anthems have some incorporate alto songs – S. S. Wesley and others. But certain lieder, by Schubert for example, can be handled by a voice with a sympathetic timbre and style.

G) 20TH CENTURY*: Rimski-Korsakov: *The Golden Cockerel* (opera), certain very carefully selected later romantic songs by the English school (Head, Gurney, Quilter, Vaughan Williams, Finzi, Warlock particularly; almost all to be transposed). See the warning on lieder. Britten: Canticles I, II and III, solos from *A Midsummer Night's Dream*, and *Rejoice in the Lamb*, *Death in Venice*; Tippett: *Songs for Ariel*, *The Ice Break*; Michael Howard; counter-tenor songs; William H. Harris: alto Shakespeare songs; Alan Ridout: solos from the opera *The Pardoner's Tale*, *Three Sonnets of C. Day Lewis*, *Love Poems of John Clare*, *Ballad of Reading Gaol*, Sir Thomas Wyatt songs, solo cantata (Bonheuffer) *Prayers from Prison*, *Becket Cantata* solos, Malcolm Williamson: solo from *Symphony for Voices*, Peter Racine Fricker: 'The Tomb of Saint Euliah'. Walter Bergmann: 'Pastorale' and *Three Lute Songs*; Carl Orf: solo from *Carmina Burana*. Anthony Hewitt-Jones: solo songs for counter tenor. Various material by Geoffrey Burgon and Edmund Rubbra. Peter Maxwell Davies: solo work from the opera *Taverner*.

There is at last a projected anthology of counter-tenor songs. Mark Deller has undertaken this welcome move towards true parity with other voices.

Small Ensemble

Most of the composers already listed have provided a rich source of works which include counter tenor. Many of these and the following too can be performed with a handful of solo voices in ensemble.

1) MEDIEVAL: Early harmony (Ars Antiqua, Ars Nova and all European schools too vast to list.) Consult specialist books on the period such as *Historical Anthology of Music* edited by Davidson and Appell, Oxford University Press.

2) 16TH CENTURY: All European schools, especially music from the Court of Henry VIII, and Spanish National collection. Madrigals, chansons, especially Josquin, Arcadelt, Lassus, canzonets, ballets, part songs, motets, masses, anthems, dialogues. Further consort music.

---

* In practice, when considering Romantic solo songs written for other voices, and suitably transposed, the only real guide to the counter tenor remains this: is the individual voice concerned *convincing* for the song even when transposed? A contralto song may have unsuitable words for an alto. Many songs for bass and baritone are possible untransposed but sung an octave higher. The greatest care must be exercised in choice: if in doubt leave well alone.

Example 17 *Schubert's* Nachthelle, *ostensibly for tenors solo and T. T. B. B.*
(By kind permission of Peters Editions.)

3) 17TH CENTURY: Madrigals, canzonets, ballets, part songs, motets, anthems, glees, 'scena' and dialogue by composers like Purcell and Schutz. Catches. Late consort music.

4) 18TH CENTURY: Glees by Samuel Webbe and the rest of a large English school, part songs, catches, quartets. Music for the haute-contre tradition in France.

5) 19TH CENTURY: English glees, part songs, quartets. Certain composers like Cherubini wrote for the late 'haute-contre' tradition, also Schubert in works like 'Nachthelle' (plate 17), which though set for 'tenor' solo and male voices is surely no more intended for an ordinary high tenor than 'But Who May Abide the Day of His Coming'! The range is absolutely that of a counter tenor; a low counter tenor would fit beautifully, but even a high type with strong lower notes could sing it happily. The tessitura is clearly intended for the 'falsetto' tenor, male (natural) 'contralto', tenor altino, counter tenor, call him what you will. There is one F below Middle C, no G or A flat, the rest flies high with more than several B′ flats. The mean average note is E′.

6) 20TH CENTURY: Certain part songs are suitable, but more importance comes from various works especially composed for the re-emergent counter tenor, such as Tippett, 'Lullaby' for counter-tenor solo and five other voices. Britten: 'Journey of the Magi' (A.T.B. and piano), Wilfred Mellers: 'Two Monodies for counter tenor and three male voices', Christopher Brown: Five Chinese songs and 'The Harper of Chao' for two counter tenors, gamba and harpischord. Bergmann: 'The Passionate Shepherd to his Love' for two counter tenors and accompaniment. John Hastie: Song Cycle for counter tenor, baritone, flute and spinet.

While considering repertoire, let us examine that very revealing area of study, the glee club. The English glee tradition is a valuable help in determining certain points of (a) performance (seventeenth- and eighteenth-century verse anthems should not sound too *churchy*) and (b) vocal assignment.

The word 'glee' is thought to emanate from the Anglo-Saxon 'glig', meaning 'joy' or possibly just 'music'. We must remember that glees were often composed by cathedral organists, lay clerks, university professors, even clerics. With this background we may quickly see a useful parallel between what appertained in serious music, secular and religious, and the lighter glee and ruder 'catch' which were composed for the entertainment of the singers themselves in gentlemen's drinking clubs. The subject matter of the words concerned drink, and love almost invariably, often, as David Johnson has put it, 'making the sort of remarks men make about women when women are not present'.

Towards the end of their existence in the nineteenth century, the glee clubs began to admit ladies and new soprano parts. One senses then that the drinking, roistering and catch-singing activities declined. The glee faded into polite part song, the catch to harmlessness, and eventually the glee club itself into musical or choral society. But in its hey-day, the glee gave many opportunities for the counter tenor, and it does still.

When examining original editions of glees, part songs and catches, one is struck early on that many do not specify particular voices by name. Most are in three or four parts, most common being A.T.B., T.T.B. or A.A.T.B. (from their apparent vocal ranges). Later glees moved into more parts, clearly with added soprano voices in mind.

Most early glees specifying alto or counter tenor (the terms used interchangably as in normal practice) are written in the C or alto clef. But most top lines in later pieces were written in treble clef transposing down an octave like a modern tenor part. The reason for this appears to be expediency. As David Johnson says in his article 'The 18th Century Glee' (*Musical Times*, 1979): 'It seems likely that tenors were expected to be able to move unobtrusively into falsetto at the top of their range, and altos to change gear at the bottom. Unspecified treble clefs often make it impossible to tell S.S.B. from T.T.B. or S.S.A.B. from T.T.T.B.; this ambiguity was probably a deliberate device to increase sales.'

Whether the whole thing was for commercial reasons or not, the musical expectations of the composers seem clear. Altos or tenors could be called upon to sing the same part with success. The vocal accomplishment referred to by David Johnson is surely just that which the traditional English singer has been able to do. Today with most tenors there is pride in *not* using falsetto, though this is mostly from ignorance of the essential oneness of the falsetto and the tenor head voice. Commercial considerations apart, the abnormally high 'tenor' or low 'alto' line in the glee was none other than our friend, the second counter-tenor part.

It is always interesting how the obvious takes time to sink in. Take, for example, J. Merrill Knapp, writing in the United States in 1952. His *Selected List of Music for Men's Voices* has the following:

> In general the musical quality of the glees is of a higher order than the Männerchor literature, and these have the advantage of being in

English. On the other hand, their availability is often complicated by the selection of the alto voice for the top part in a three or four part voice composition. It is a well-known fact that the English, particularly in cathedral choirs, think of the alto as a male voice part taken either by boys or trained tenor falsettists. (There is still some confusion about the counter tenor in the music of the seventeenth century onwards.) When women sing the alto part in England it is generally called contralto to make a distinction.

There is no counterpart to this in the United States. Male choruses here almost invariably have tenors on the top part, and while they are often capable of great range, they cannot maintain the same tessitura that an English alto can. This precludes the use by American choruses of not only many English glees but also a great deal of fine music by men such as Byrd and Purcell, who often write for an alto and not a tenor in the top voice. The problem of the top part in the sixteenth century is different.

It is not clear why J. Merrill Knapp does not advise the training of tenor or baritone falsettists to cope with the wealth of music which lay waiting. However, when we examine other contemporary vocal music for this range in aria, song or chorus from cantata, opera, stage music, anthem and oratorio, we realise that this expedient may well have occurred there too, at times.

Roger Fiske's excellent and comprehensive book *English Theatre Music in the Eighteenth Century* is highly recommended for full discussion of all music performed in the theatre of that period. It throws especial light on policy and procedure regarding stage songs especially in ballad operas. He is here making the point that almost all ballad-opera songs seem to be intended for high voices, for their top notes are seldom lower than F, and quite often there is G or even A!

> Yet singing actors with untrained voices can have been no more inclined to sing tenor in the 1730s than they are today. In modern productions of *The Beggar's Opera* nearly all the airs are transposed down, some of them by as much as a fourth or fifth . . . Male singers expected to have to sing their top notes falsetto . . . Because of this, baritones and even basses could manage notes which today look possible only for tenors. When the castrati became the rage, baritones continued to toy with falsetto because men had so sung for generations, either occasionally or regularly.

Fiske is correct; but his phrase 'toy with falsetto' is misleading. They were not playing at it, but using the traditional head-voice technique. Of course, just as theatres today are not always renowned for the display of excellent vocal techniques, so it must have been in the eighteenth century at times. Fiske also suggests other aspects to remember when considering vocal range and pitch on stage: 'It does seem that the key in which ballad opera airs were printed was sometimes of the publisher's choosing, for it is suspicious that the tunes should so often be in whatever key results in the fewest leger lines.' (See page 132.)

Let us see what Fiske can tell us in detail about tenor-bass head voice. It bears out nicely much of what we already know; but it is presented to underline my thesis that the last 150 years are not remarkable for the eclipse of the counter tenor, but more for a fundamental change of technique for all voices. Fiske, while discussing the universal use of falsetto production for higher notes, tells us of a minor singer called Robert Owenson (1744–1812) who was told by Arne in about 1771 that he had 'one of the finest baritones he ever heard, and particularly susceptible of that quality of intonation then so much admired and now so out of fashion, the falcetto'. Thus baritones sang their high notes falsetto as well as tenors. At the turn of the century Dibdin wrote of Leveridge and Beard having given way to the use of effeminacy and falsetto, and though the remark is the less valuable for the fact that Dibdin can never have heard Leveridge, it is of interest for its pejorative undertones. But until the 1790s people found falsetto singing something to admire rather than condemn. Despite Dibdin and fashion, it is worth bearing in mind that falsetto–head voice technique continued here and abroad during much of the nineteenth century.

Richard Leveridge (1671–1758) and John Beard (1716–1791) were perhaps the John Shirley-Quirk and Peter Pears of their times. Fiske confirms the use of the pharyngeal voice as normal practice as discussed in Chapter 3, and agrees on the note at which the pharyngeal was engaged. He suggests that tenors and baritones usually entered it at D' or E' and states that baritone songs – no doubt of the bluff heavy variety – were often purposely kept below this pitch in order to avoid any falsetto timbre. He confirms too that normal tenors 'changed' at the same point and could thus extend their range as counter tenors.

Yet we are probably talking of special effects, because by the mid-eighteenth century, singers, though versatile and not so conscious as we are today of niceties of nomenclature, were nevertheless specialist tenors, baritones and counter tenors in almost the modern manner. The head voice was in universal use: the singer used it whenever he encountered the appropriate points in the vocal scale. Each singer *chose* his favoured pitch and specialisation according to what felt and sounded most effective in his particular case. He thus *became* a tenor, for example, his voice being named after the ancient part in which he specialised, as had been normal for centuries.

Fiske reminds us:

> Shield wrote Cs and Ds for both Incledon and Johnstone, the leading Covent Garden tenors towards the end of the century. Examples can be found in *Fontainebleau* and *The Woodman*. In *The Choleric Fathers* (1785) Johnstone even had a high E. His falsetto was praised by both Kelly and O'Keefe. *The Thespian* for September 1793 found it 'pleasingly expressive', though the writer was worried by the jerk between his natural and counter tenor qualities. Most people seem to have accepted the jerk as inevitable.

The Musical Quarterly, 1818, has an article on Incledon and states:

> He had a voice of uncommon power, both in the natural and the falsetto. The former was from A to G, a compass of about fourteen notes; the latter he could use from D to E or F, or about ten notes . . . His falsetto was rich, sweet and brilliant, but totally unlike the other. He took it without preparation, according to circumstances, either about D, E, or F, or ascending an octave, which was his most frequent custom.

We can see from this and implications elsewhere that even for an important singer like Incledon, there was little attempt or suggestion of the desirability to blend the two registers. As Fiske says: 'We today accept falsetto notes from some of our tenors when these notes are both high and soft, but we expect the singer to conceal the change in quality so far as his skill allows, and in theory we regard it as a small weakness that he should resort to falsetto at all. This is not a viewpoint of any antiquity.' (I cannot agree with Roger Fiske's rather odd statement that the falsetto range of a baritone, 'was naturally lower and smaller than that of a tenor'.)

There are today very occasional performances and a few recordings of minor English operas or semi-operas of the eighteenth century such as *Rosina* by William Shield (1748–1829). Today's production always gives all roles which reach high into the falsetto to tenors exclusively thus creating no variety of timbre. The original intention was to perform them with different types and weights of voice, bass, baritone, tenor, and presumably counter tenor 'in reverse'. So today, as Fiske points out, 'the only solution is for our singers to cultivate falsetto once more'.

Readers desirous of detailed discussion of the stage music at this period are urged to study Roger Fiske's excellent and large work on the subject. His account first of the growing unpopularity then scorn and finally embarrassment of the public towards the castrati makes interesting reading.

In the light of what we have discovered regarding eighteenth-

Example 18 Music for a While *by Henry Purcell, an edition in the 18th-century format from the author's collection.*

century vocal range and stage custom, we may now see extra significance in the reproduction of the famous counter-tenor solo 'Music for a While', from Purcell's Masque *Oedipus*. It is reproduced here from an eighteenth-century edition. It will be readily seen that though most successful with and traditionally written for specialist counter tenor, a high tenor could take it. The late seventeenth-century original was in the alto clef, this one a few decades later is still in C minor but now in a G clef, inviting alto or tenor as alternative. The range of choice is easier since it is printed in neither alto nor tenor clef.

This common ambiguity of voice parts seems likely of all countries to appeal to the English psyche (see Appendix C), just as the specialist solo counter tenor, while by no means exclusive to England, was nevertheless seemingly longer lived, more popular, and ultimately more readily revived. To be present in certain lay clerks' vestries after service can be educative. Young basses unwind as sudden tenors or altos; young tenors burst out as baritones or altos and young altos surprise as tenors or basses.

The tendency for the English sometimes not to take their music seriously could best be epitomised in the persons of John Liptrott Hatton (1809–1886) and William Hawes (1785–1846). Hatton was an entertainer, raconteur, musician and serious composer. He is now chiefly known for some favourite glees. Hawes was Master of the Children of St Paul's Cathedral and a prominent member of the London musical world of his time. Amongst the other activities of great and amusing diversity, he 'was remarkable', so John S. Bumpus tells us, 'for natural flexibility of a somewhat uncultivated voice – a circumstance which elicited the joke of Tom Cooke that he could take alto, tenor or bass *indifferently*'! But Hawes was surely the lunatic fringe. To specialise but also to be adaptable and imaginative cannot be a bad thing.

This chapter first discussed the main areas of interest in the repertoire and mentioned considerations of clef and pitch. When examining the repertoire open to any singer today, one cannot ignore the sheer variety of the music involved within the span of, say, 900 years. It is unfortunately true that so many otherwise excellent singers, some counter tenors included, seem unwilling to adjust vocal tone and style sufficiently between, for example, a Britten canticle and an Elizabethan lute song, between Brahms lieder and a Gluck aria. As Julian Gardiner rightly says in *A Guide to Good Singing and Speech*:

> The failure of teachers and performers to discriminate between music which is romantic or subjective, and music which is non-romantic or objective, results in their pumping false sentiment into non-romantic music which of its very nature demands a cool, sympathetic and exclusively musical approach. The old Italian arias for instance and the works of Bach, Handel, Haydn and Mozart do not demand the same intimate approach as the songs of Schumann and Faure. Naturally all vocal music suggests a more subjective

approach than does instrumental music. Nevertheless a great deal of the vocal repertoire is evocative; it calls for an active imagination and a sympathetic knowledge of the style and period of the composer, but no personal sentiment. For a teacher to tell a student to feel this kind of music is no more or less than an invitation to tell musical lies. Any work of art which is predominantly objective must be performed with the keenest ear for tone quality and variations of colour, rhythm and tempo, and with a respectful though not necessarily reverent regard for traditional readings. A sympathetic and active imagination is needed also, but no more personal involvement than would be found in an actor who plays Macbeth.

There are those who question the possibility of knowing how earlier voices sounded. It was certainly the case that vocal tone in the Middle Ages, for example, was utterly different from today's, and possibly had an Eastern quality, perhaps due to the influence of the Crusades. The answer is surely that though written contemporary vocal description can only go so far (and it can be extremely valuable up to a point), we do have one powerful help in determining long-past vocal timbres: any surviving or accurately reconstructed early musical instruments.

Though very early *playable* unrestored specimens are rare, instruments, unlike the human larynx, do not utterly decay away in a grave. Replicas can be built. Provided the player knows or can make an educated guess how to produce their sounds correctly (and who could fail to, remembering the example of the brilliant late David Munrow, and also others) then instruments, especially wind instruments, are extremely valuable to singers, for their timbres and those of voices have always been related. Yet conversely, in the 1950s, when genuine concern first began to be widely felt regarding authenticity in musical performance, a *Times* music correspondent wrote in an article on Austria's bid to develop the study of early music:

> The factor which has changed least during the intervening period is probably the human voice. Assuming the possibility of ridding ourselves of the dubious benefit of Italianate voice production, a lot can be done to bridge the gap which would otherwise separate us from the thirteenth, fourteenth and fifteenth centuries. In this respect, the desirability for early music, of using a hall with a resonance time of six–nine seconds . . .

We now know all too well the difficulties of modifying the human voice to produce timbres expected by an earlier age. Though there has now been some success, it *is* nevertheless, despite our *Times* correspondent, far easier to begin with the instrumental sound and contemporary description.

We are in search of style. There are now many experts on the subject. Books and records abound with excellent advice and examples based on impeccable musicological research. Arguably, style is an amalgam of the physical limitations of a given period instrument, augmented by what is known through research into a period, plus physical human considerations like hand-size, breathing capability, reach and the like. With knowledge of style and the tones still available from any early instrument in playing order, or more likely, modern exact replicas, we may surely deduce a great deal about the voices which they once accompanied or in whose close proximity they were once played.

We know that the tone of any singer would obviously be conditioned by custom, accompaniment and the style and type of music to be performed. For example, a late sixteenth- or early seventeenth-century singer would be expected to deal with crisp, clear, contrapuntal parts of equal importance in ensemble or choral works, be capable also of soft languishing tone when singing to a lute. He might also need ringing power against a band of instruments. Such a variety of sound should be available now, not just in volume but character. It should be possible for a modern singer to adjust his or her style and tone according to the style and date of the composition. Yet how many singers do? How often one hears a Schubert song performed in vocal manner almost identical to a Handel aria!

All this is not just true of singing; yet the human vocal organ is capable of tonal and stylistic variation in a way no other instrument can be. Many singers, even noted soloists, seem unaware of this, preferring to sing music of all periods beautifully but almost identically, therefore wrongly for most of them. To take the Renaissance for example, Brian Trowell says in *The Pelican History of Music*: 'We moderns can only hear the music of the Renaissance sung by voices whose training has been influenced by conditions unknown at that time – the need for one solo voice to carry over the sound of a large orchestra, for example in theatre or concert hall.' But there is no need for the modern automatically to transform the ancient. Conscious adjustment can be made from knowledge of what is required.

Other than contemporary verbal description, and the sound of instruments, there is one more available source of information on the sound made by at least medieval and Renaissance singers: the painting and sculpture of the time. The change to choral polyphony clearly initiated a change in vocal tone production. Early fifteenth-century paintings often portray singers with creased brows and strained features. Brian Trowell explains:

We sometimes see today such contorted features on our concert platforms, and they are associated with a strident, tightly-produced, nasal tone-colour. This appears to have been the noisy, penetrating sound which the Middle Ages enjoyed. If soloists were to be heard in the huge cathedrals of the Gothic era, there would certainly have been a tendency to strain. Later on, however, the faces become relaxed. This suggests the modern approach of relaxed muscles and open throat. Vibrato, however, is condemned.

It would however be a mistake to describe all pre-mid fifteenth-century vocal tone as crude or barbaric. We must remember that the artist's only method of suggesting the sound singers made was to exaggerate. It is not necessarily true that because a singer looks strained and tight that his throat actually felt the strain. Clever vocalists can create purposed tension in their tone for artistic reasons without the slightest physical effort. No, it is far more likely that tight-focused tone and skill, not crudity, underlined the music.

In any case, we must be aware here of possible differences in the vocal production of different countries. As Wulstan points out, the stained glass faces in the fifteenth-century Beauchamp Chapel of St Mary's Warwick show no sign of the tense production found in representations of Continental singers of a similar date. Although we are considering *pre*-fifteenth century timbre, it is likely that certain national characteristics had developed regarding singing style before the soaring quality of the English fifteenth-century school evolved.

There seems little doubt today then that the acceleration of concern for appropriate techniques is healthy. A good start has been made. There has been progress even since the mid-1970s. An excellent fairly recent record of Machaut's *Messe de Notre Dame*, sung by the Purcell Choir, has a programme note by the director as follows: 'Much medieval music demands and contemporary professional singing techniques certainly include methods of rhythmic articulation and dynamic control *which few singers trained by modern methods possess*' (my italics). J. B. Steane, in *The Grand Tradition*, commenting on this same record adds:

If the singing of the choir is anything to go by, a 'pure', unvibrating tone is also required. Now, again it looks as if the extension to the singer's repertoire is likely to have some salutary effects upon singing methods. Just as the vocal lines of Stravinsky's songs or of Schönberg's 'Herzgewachsc' forbid a spreading, unsteady tone (the notes have to be placed purely and accurately as by an instrument), so a medieval ballade or virelai (or a vocal-line in a choral work or part song) imposes a discipline. Where there is any unsteadiness, there intrudes something which sounds immediately anachronistic; and since melisma, elaborate and often strenuously rhythmical, is also a prominent feature, then the singer is compelled to dispense with aspirates – their habitual use, always regrettable, would be grotesque in this music. The notable thing here, however, is that good singers like Hafliger and Partridge do not appear to change their method or to have cause to do so.

Singers of the past were not burdened by the same problem. It was not lack of conscience but the fact that they sang mostly contemporary music. Our present age knows more music than any before it and is the first in which, armed with knowledge, advanced research capabilities, recording, communication, we are able to determine how music of the past should be performed. So we have a responsibility. We cannot now ignore the fruits of this knowledge. Having said all this, it is true to say that stylistically no one voice can be all things to everybody. Each has its own predominating timbre and character. These can be varied, appropriately, and to reasonable degree, but not totally and not perpetually. After this, the decision is aesthetic: is this musical work suitable for my voice or vice-versa?

So stylistic specialisation creeps in inevitably, and why not? We have early music voices who should never and probably do not ever open a book of lieder, and lieder recitalists who should not touch Lully. This raises the question of 'created' voices, especially those for esoteric performances of early music. Few singers are so clearly specialist as the 'mezzo soprano' Jantina Noorman, who sings medieval music so effectively with Musica Reservata. The inverted commas round mezzo soprano are self-explanatory to anybody who has heard her. Noorman's voice, so perfect for medieval music, is practically unacceptable for anything later. As J. B. Steane puts it in *The Grand Tradition*:

> One should really speak of 'voices', for she has two (maybe many more). One is a dulcet, piping sound, quite gentle and entirely without vibration; and when singing in this way she achieves exceptional precision in rapid ornamentation. That voice can be heard in Emilio de' Cavalieri's 'Godi turba mortal'. Then, in the same record, called Florentine Festival, she sings in some trios where one would not recognise the voice, which is itself revealed more fully in some anonymous dance songs. Here is the voice of a peasant, and the technique of a virtuoso: an uninhibited primitivism of tone, with the sophistication of modern musicianship.

How does all this affect counter tenors? Absolutely identically with other voices. And it teaches us all a valuable lesson. For if there be different colours and tones within the same voice range then surely argument over the nature of counter tenor sound is affected? We can instantly know that a given voice suits Tallis but not Gluck, until adjustment, and perhaps not then. Yet both voices could equally well be excellent solo counter tenors of their different type.

The question is only partly one of production, and the last chapter went into this in detail. A rounded falsetto alto may sound pleasant and appropriate in Romantic works, even in certain quiet lute songs, but he is perpetually handicapped should he attempt most Classical works without somehow altering not only interpretation but his production. If he does not or cannot adjust, even though he sings most of the classical counter-tenor range, it will be with tone so unlike what is and was required, that critics will claim that it is the wrong voice. He is 'only a male alto'. They are only partially correct. It is the right voice used inappropriately and by the wrong individual. The 'male alto' is the Romantic version of the counter tenor, in this instance singing music unsuited to his particular variety of voice.

Frederick Hodgson, himself an experienced alto, and knowledge-able writer on the alto–counter tenor question, ex-lay clerk of Lichfield Cathedral and St George's Chapel, Windsor, has written certain articles of value, well argued and worth reading (see Bibliog-raphy). Regarding alto tone, in *The Musical Times* of April 1965, he writes lamenting the loss of what he terms *real* alto tone:

> This is recognisable in the full, mellifluous head voice, resembling that of the contralto, but with a quite definite masculine depth of quality, by which the bona-fide alto becomes something of a vocal paradox. There is nothing 'weak and effeminate' about the voice. It is neither 'fruity' nor 'hooty', and substantiation of its claim to be real alto is borne out by the fact that as it is chiefly on aesthetic and dramatic grounds any singer stands or falls, it cannot be argued that the cold, white, edgy type of voice so prevalent among many young contemporary singers, who sound all alike, is to be compared with this warm, rich and beautiful alto quality which has always met with unanimous acceptance. The difference is that one is a gimmick; the other is a rare gift.

'Unanimous acceptance' surely cannot be right, and the young con-temporary singers 'sounding all alike' is no more the case, we contend, than any other type of voice, soprano, tenor, what you will, fashion and usage being what they are. Mr Hodgson is mourning a particular ideal, one which is or was surely just as sought after by just as many altos in the past, perhaps between 1850 and 1940. In fact since 1965 the wheel has turned slightly and alto 'voce bianca' is itself slightly sus-pect. The pharyngeal mix, with its supported ring, happens to be more in vogue.

B. Forsyte Wright, in *The Musical Times* of November 1959,

explains his view, which Mr Hodgson fully shares, that the counter tenor and alto voices are utterly different:

> By way of contrast, the alto voice, which is still fairly common in Anglican Cathedral Choirs, is an artificial voice and in that sense 'falsetto'. Being relatively weak and unsupported by a full resonance, it has no great value for solo work, on account of its lack of power. It is very useful, however, for the purposes of harmony in the way that it blends with boys' and men's natural voices.

David Wulstan's view seems to be between the two extemes. While endorsing most of the following, I would disagree with his statement that the alto differed markedly in tone from the tenor.

> The alto was therefore a predominantly falsetto voice of 'edgy' but not raucous quality; shrill, but sweet. Its tone was not unlike the treble or castrato. Its quality was certainly dissimilar from that of the tenor; and the change into chest register would have been masked in such a way that the lower notes would appear to be low in the voice – otherwise there would be no point in setting a lower limit to the range.

Wulstan is of course discussing the sixteenth-century situation, but for reasons discussed earlier in detail in the present work, for once we feel that he is either partly mistaken or partly misleading. The voice could hardly have been shrill in the pharyngeal area, where there must have been some affinity with the tenor tone. Butler's use of the word *shrill* (page 36) was perhaps somewhat loose, or the word has shifted in meaning since.

What is most interesting is that these two relatively recent writers, Hodgson and Forsyte Wright, are talking presumably of the same voice. Yet nobody is surely going to accuse one example of describing the alto and the other of something else. The truth is that their two views reflect the very best and the worst examples of the same Romantic alto voice!

Julian Gardiner, in his interesting book, *A Guide to Good Singing and Speech* (1968), seems first to agree with Frederick Hodgson then more with B. Forsyte Wright, then vice versa. In his chapter on 'Mechanisms', and talking of the alto mechanism in men's voices, he says:

> An untrained baritone singing up the scale on these notes, comes to a point where he has a choice of doing two things. Either he can continue brazenly and uncomfortably up to G in his normal voice, or he can drift into falsetto. This is a noise which may be comic or pleasing, but either way will be ineffective, and quite inappropriate to the rest of his voice and to his own personality. The true alto

mechanism is no breathy little pipe, but a tone of full-blooded contralto quality such as is heard in English cathedral choirs. In Victorian days male altos were popular as soloists and as leaders of quartets, but times have changed and today they are seldom heard outside the cathedral choir stall. Nevertheless, in the training of men's voices the alto mechanism plays an important part which singers are unwise to neglect. In breath management and vocal cord approximation the technique is precisely the same as for the normal male voice. Tenors and basses are as a rule nothing like such good alto singers as baritones. Even so, however modest their range and tone quality, all singers should make use of what they have. No matter what strange sounds they produce, they will enormously increase the quality and the steadiness of their normal voice. Of course, if they start singing exclusively in the alto mechanism, their ordinary voices will soon disappear. Similarly women who habitually sing in chest lose their ordinary voices, while their chest notes acquire surprising depth and range. I am assuming however that my male readers have no intention of becoming cathedral altos, nor that my female readers aim to excel as night-club singers, so that in both cases they will use their extraordinary voices to promote their general well-being.

It is not possible to sing a truly legato descending scale of four notes in alto voice, unless a correct technical preparation and follow-through is maintained – and let it be clearly understood that alto invariably means alto and not a quavery little falsetto. No forward production specialist can manage it. A high centre of gravity, raised cheeks and chest, retracted jaw and contracted tongue muscles, all these are indispensable adjuncts for a true alto voice. It is indeed significant that the average cathedral alto has a much steadier and purer quality and a rounder tone than have his colleagues in the tenor and bass sections. The voice itself has little individuality and is decidedly limited in range and power; yet it seems to remain as good as new through fifty odd years of cathedral services. This suggests that the male alto possesses an elixir of vocal life, but the explanation is much simpler. He cannot sing at all unless his technique is correct, and good technique keeps voices young.

(By kind permission of Julian Gardiner.)

Mr Gardiner is puzzling in the light of statements on altos and counter tenors throughout his book: first admiration, then grudging approval, finally the absolute execration quoted on our pages 183–4. But in the quotation above there seems more than enough contradiction to make my point. His remark about counter tenors 'seldom being heard outside the cathedral choir stall' could not be true in 1968 unless by altos he did *not* intend to mean solo counter tenors. Is he thereby implying correct recognition that the solo counter tenor differs greatly in tone and timbre from the 'old fashioned' (Romantic) cathedral alto?

Here are G. M. Ardran and David Wulstan on alto tone in their useful appendix to the first edition of the Deller biography:

> If no historical justification can be found for distinguishing two different voices by the two terms – a conclusion that Mr Whitworth, in his article on the counter tenor voice [*English Church Music,* 1965], also reaches – what is the difference between the patently falsetto 'hoot' associated with the term 'male alto' and parish sextons, and the clear tone of singers usually called counter tenors, such as Alfred Deller? The fact that the two types of singer produce sounds of rather different quality cannot justify the use of two separate words unless a further range of terms, such as 'throttle-tenor' and 'bull-bass', are to be called into use to describe differences in voices other than the alto. Unless they are tenors rather than altos (in which case there is no historical or logical reason for describing them as either counter tenors or altos) all altos, however named, must produce their voices by the same basic mechanism. Such refinements in tone-colour as distinguished one singer from another must be a question of natural ability and/or training in the 'placing' of the voice, that is, the control of resonance. It is clearly the larynx that must be studied in order to determine the mechanism that is common to all altos . . . To sum up, the alto voice today is produced in basically the same way by all singers. Such differences as there are depend on good voice production as in any other voice. There can be no doubt that the classical alto produced his voice in the same way with various modifications in the finer points of technique from period to period.

I sympathise with but do not fully share this view, for reasons given in Chapter 2, unless by 'various modifications' they refer to varieties of alto, producing their different voices in one of perhaps three slightly different manners. After the Ardran/Wulstan appendix, Alfred Deller himself commented:

> This is quite the most sensible thing I have read; but, in my opinion, the view that the alto voice today is produced in basically the same way by all singers, and that such differences as there are depend on good voice production as in any other voice, is an oversimplification. It is much more complex than that, not to say mysterious. I believe that with all first-rate – certainly with great – voices, the possessor is physiologically and psychologically predisposed to the making of the actual sound, the timbre and quality of

the voice. Of course, hard work is also necessary to acquire technique, but no amount of work will produce a clarion sound from what Nature has (inscrutably) designated a bugle.

A bugle is *appropriate* to a bugle band, a clarion to a Baroque ensemble, but we can surely share Deller's meaning!

So, to sum up, because music, as any other art form, reflects the age in which it is composed *and* performed, it is surely not surprising that counter tenors vary and have varied in order to meet the demands of the age in which they serve. With the exception of the Romantic period, when it was heard almost only in church music, and with tone round or even lugubrious, the counter tenor has always been exciting, ringing, nasal, piercing, clear and strong. Some or most of these qualities would always have been in evidence. Yet his palette of colours also included the delicate, the subtle and the languishing.

Chapter 7

WHAT'S IN A NAME?

WE HAVE SEEN the problems of adjusting the voice for a particular musical period and acknowledged that voices will always differ though they sing much the same range. Now we must consider the question of the tenor-altino, and the effect it threatens to have on the modern situation.

We should now be clear how the counter-tenor mechanisms work. It was explained how the tenor-altino voice could be included amongst the counter tenor *family*, it being perhaps one of three vocal types which make up that family. One main reason for the development in the United States in the 1950s and 1960s of a different breed of solo counter tenor is Russell Oberlin, a distinguished singer of the tenor-altino type.

After Deller had begun the renaissance in England in the late 1940s and early 1950s, followed closely by Whitworth, Oberlin started to become known in America as a soloist, teacher and a member of the group known as New York Pro Musica Antiqua. He did many of the things Deller was already doing in this country, broadcasting, recording for gramophone records, giving recitals and concerts to audiences for most of whom the idea of the counter tenor was utterly new.

Deller toured the United States and Canada, Oberlin came to England, Whitworth went to America as a member of the Golden Age Singers. As people were gradually given the opportunity of hearing several contrasting singers, each with his own distinctive timbre, it began to be suggested that the term counter tenor was right for one but surely not the other: they sounded so different. Few thought that there could be varying types of vocal sound singing at much the same pitch, and for each of which the same title would be valid.

There is no question that the Oberlin type of voice is very rare indeed – which proves that it alone could not have been the voice which provided easily half the counter-tenor singers in every English medieval, Tudor and seventeenth-century collegiate and cathedral choir, and in European choirs up to the end of the sixteenth century. Altos were also included in every opera chorus and cantata choir of the seventeenth and eighteenth centuries. Physically the tenor altino also seems to be a very short-lived voice.

We should consider the reasons for Russell Oberlin's original success in America, other than his skill as a singer. The United States is a country where the ideal of rugged masculinity dies hard. It is still strong in the 1980s despite a battering in recent years. Yet Oberlin was singing in the 1950s. Anything male but which seemed to smack of effeminacy, musical or otherwise, was surely terribly suspect. Baseball giants and huge football players, tough he-men in the all-American tradition were the heroes in the United States. Small wonder that the American solo counter tenor, when he appeared, despite having in Oberlin's case a rather effeminate upper register, always maintained that the counter tenor was really a very high rare tenor. Oberlin could certainly demonstrate a tenor-like lower register, although it sounded unusual. The American situation remained markedly different from the European for many years mostly through Oberlin's own characteristic techniques and influence. The Americans are more shy than most of the word 'alto' applied to a man.

They originally wanted no part of its (to them) feminine associations, or of suggested links with what they call the English cathedral falsetto tradition. (By the latter is meant the Romantic round sound.) Also, however much they admired the techniques of Deller and Whitworth, and, later, Bowman and Esswood, most regarded them as merely developed falsettists and as such, questionable. As if to emphasise their distinct positions, they used and still use the term *countertenor* as one word, perhaps to wipe out any suggestion of two registers.

In Europe, and America with its originally predominantly German Protestant musical tradition, the word *falsetto* is still anathema. As in much of Europe, 'alto' had naturally become associated with (a) a low, mature female voice – strangely in many countries they prefer to dock the prefix 'contra' – and (b) a low boy's or girl's voice. So for much of the musical world, alto has a feminine or child-like association.

In England, the renaissance of the secular solo alto voice happened because it came back out of the ecclesiastical shadows. Alfred Deller was a unique cathedral alto who had made himself into a virtuoso singer of a type not heard for perhaps 140 years.

He was so utterly different in sound from any alto anybody remembered, that amazingly he was unsuccessful in his first two attempts at a cathedral choir lay clerkship (Lincoln and Salisbury). When Dr Gerald Knight appointed him to Canterbury in 1939, he no doubt realised what a prize he had just obtained! (Deller stayed until 1947 when he moved to St Paul's, the London musical scene, and world fame.)

Like Deller, all or nearly all English counter tenors for twenty years came from a cathedral, collegiate or church background. Many still do. Most had been boy choristers, and if in a parish church, like Deller, had remained to sing alto when their treble voices faded, this often happening at an incredibly advanced age. Often, too, it was not their voices, but their own mature bulk and their worried choir-masters which had dictated the move.

It is and was different for cathedral choristers who are (now) required to leave the choir at the age of thirteen-and-a-half or fourteen, in order to move to a senior school, irrespective of whether their voices are gone. Although the physical treble ends earlier than ever, cathedral choirs are nevertheless often deprived of excellent boys six months or even sometimes a year earlier than necessary.

These ex-choristers usually move straight into a public school choir as mature trebles, and most to alto, tenor or bass in due course, some to oblivion. But many reappear aged eighteen, as choral scholars in university college choirs like King's, Cambridge, or at cathedrals with a limited number of choral scholars attached to their local university like Norwich, Canterbury and others.

Those youngsters who settle as altos have seldom or never sung at any other pitch, and like their humbler parish church choir brethren are thus specialists from the start: possible solo counter-tenor material if nature has provided them with a suitably sophisticated vocal organ. As Julian Gardiner has said, good male voices are invariably voices which never broke, but which gradually deepened, so that at no time were they incapable of singing.

This ecclesiastical and/or university background was almost exclusively, then, for twenty years, the source of English counter tenors. There could be few if any who were never choristers, lay clerks, choral scholars, parish church choirmen or some combination of these. This happened because of the English male choir tradition, single-sex school and university college. There was nothing odd, unusual or effeminate in singing alto in English ecclesiastical or academic musical circles and never had been. It was the norm until the days of co-education.

As we have seen, the position in secular music had differed for many years. As colleges of music ran no courses,★ trained no alto singers and did not really recognise the voice officially, there were no purely college-trained altos until much later when prejudice had been worn down. Paul Esswood was, I think, one of the first.

★ Although the Royal College of Music had allowed for 'Male Alto' in its Associate-ship Examination for years, there could surely have been few candidates – the voice was an entirely self-taught one.

Returning to the United States, we can see immediately that a difference would be expected. There were, and are, choirs of men and boys, but they are very few indeed. Fewer still are yet recognised as outstanding. The tradition there is precarious, and of course very recent by European standards. (Their situation should mature and develop having survived intense sexist pressures and attacks.) There is now a healthy young Canadian counter-tenor musical scene. The British influence seems to have been a contributing factor.

The original transatlantic (American) counter tenors were, like Oberlin, far more likely to have emerged from either a mixed choir background, or a college training, and thus almost certainly from the tenor line, the alto part being exclusively occupied by females. When these young tenors found themselves in possession of the highest head voice – the alto range – it was probably a pleasant surprise. It is most important for us to remember when considering them, that they probably never sang as choral altos or even trebles to any proficient degree. They thus *began* adult musical life as young tenors. This is a huge statement; one which demands investigation and probably a book in its own right, but I maintain that my view of the American situation until recent years is likely to be correct at least in essentials.

One American counter tenor to emerge in the 1960s, William Cobb, is an interesting case. He trained first at Oberlin Conservatoire, U.S.A. (no relation to Russell Oberlin as far as I know), then Trinity College of Music, London. He sang recitals in London and broadcast; then, dropping out of sight, he appeared as a tenor in Europe. John Ferrante, who seems not to sing this side of the Atlantic, has also sung as a tenor. Influenced by Oberlin, his style nevertheless employs admitted falsetto.

It is interesting to note that the counter tenors in American and Canadian choirs of men and boys are usually in the English tradition and vocal pattern. But until recently they were encountering problems in the United States, at least should they call themselves anything but altos. It was for the old reason that a little learning is a dangerous thing, and there was beginning to be a little learning. 'What's in a name?' many might ask, yet, for reasons later disclosed, the question of name is very significant.

English counter tenors, calling themselves such, have continued to enjoy success on the American continent despite prejudice, since Deller's early days. Some might explain this popularity in terms of the eighteenth-century English voices and the Italian castrati: visiting celebrities are one thing, *native* 'effeminates' another.

Where the Oberlin school was always convincing is in the matter of vocal timbre. For apart from the question of registers, it is the 'Romantic' falsetto which has worried them. It worries more than the

Oberlin school. It is the whole reason why Deller was such a revelation in England. Though it should be acknowledged that the ordinary alto is a *variety* of counter tenor, the very round unsupported unfocused falsetto of the old-fashioned English cathedral alto – late nineteenth-century style – will not do for the counter-tenor solos written up to the end of the eighteenth century, and those after, say, 1945. Few would claim otherwise on this side of the Atlantic, either, except Frederick Hodgson, and he would seem to agree with those who maintain that the low alto solos were for what we term tenor altino, and he terms 'true' counter tenor.

Once we have got away from the English alto being beautiful but lacking in power, in other words the Romantic-toned chorus or cathedral alto, then the Oberlin argument on tone fades. It is easy to see why. Listen to recordings of Whitworth, Bowman and some of the younger men for sheer strength and full, supported sinus tone. Ironically, the fine young American counter tenor John Angelo Messana is so unlike the Oberlin school that his middle register peters out below middle C, perhaps because he specialises in quasi-castrato repertoire.

The Times review of the first London performance, in 1959, of Britten's opera *A Midsummer Night's Dream*, contains two telling phrases: 'The new Oberon, Mr Russell Oberlin, is *gentler of voice* and more mercurial of gesture and gait than Mr Deller . . . but extremely musical. "I know a bank", is here treated not as a *soloist's show-piece* but as part of the drama.' (My italics.) 'Gentler of voice' suggests weaker. Subtle, effective perhaps, but weaker. Listen to Deller's recording. He uses much contrast – first heavy pharyngeal tone, now thin upper falsetto effect. It is strong stuff. Judge by the complete recording of the work. You can imagine what the reviewer meant. Yet by some definitions, Deller is merely a male alto, and Oberlin a counter tenor, supposedly that strong, ringing, 'natural' voice so different from mere falsetto.

If you listen to Oberlin's other recordings, his upper range, the more alto areas, do not really *ring*. It is my contention that the more brilliant English sound is not merely the result of highly developed pharyngeal and cutting upper falsetto tone, but also comes from the ecclesiastical ambience, which is the training ground of so many English counter tenors.

My own experience has a bearing here. When I was first appointed to Canterbury in 1967, I found that the acoustic of the Quire and Nave (both different) had to be adjusted to. Coming most recently from Lichfield, where the acoustic is strangely dry, and before that, Ely, which is different again, it required several months of experiment to get it right. Canterbury's particular ambience favours high tones but rather swallows lower voices. Accordingly, the cathedral choir really needs larger bass voices than many other comparable buildings. It occurred to me that if not the origin, then something of the development of Deller's unique sound must have been influenced by this Canterbury acoustic. I never discussed it with him, but I know personally that the acoustic encourages one to use less body in the alto tone, more light edge and a thinner, brilliant sound when catarrh permits!

The trio 'Canterbury Clerkes' recently completed their second long-playing record in Boughton Aluph Church, near Canterbury, where many of the most beautiful Deller Consort recordings were made. Boughton Aluph is the annual centre of Deller's brainchild, the Stour Music Festival. As Canterbury Clerkes sang, here again one felt the acoustic's influence which made us use our voices in a different manner, and the results are interesting when comparing our first record, made in an utterly contrasting acoustic.

Singing in a 'dry' theatre, opera house or ordinary recording studio necessitates a change of approach, yet one's instinctive or customed timbre must remain. In Deller's case the *resonance* was somehow trapped magically in his voice. Oberlin's 'dry' technique was in direct contrast.

Concerning *The Times* review of the Britten opera, the phrase 'a soloist's showpiece' merely suggests that the two artists differed greatly in their interpretation, and which one the reviewer preferred. But here again, we can glimpse the solo virtuoso counter tenor in the grand tradition as compared to the more modern technique of the light lyric tenor.

Properly resonated and produced, the English solo counter tenor is as crisp, clear, masculine and strong in tone as the tenor altino. The pharyngeal voice can even be stronger than the lyric tenor in the middle range and above.

Chapter 8

THE POST-WAR RENAISSANCE

FROM THE 1980s WE can survey forty years following the renaissance of the counter tenor. We are able to see just how successful it has been in various musical spheres. 1943 seems ancient history in many ways. Much of the prejudice against the highest male voice has faded, yet there still remain powerful 'anti' pockets, some of them surprisingly in the worlds of early Classical and twentieth-century opera.

As we have already said, opera seemed most likely to welcome the re-emergence of the counter tenor or alto voice. For one thing, the performance of much very early opera had been handicapped without this voice, both musically and dramatically. For another, considering the 'castrati' operas, there were clearly roles written for castrati well within the range of a large-voiced counter tenor, roles with no need for transposition; Gluck's *Orfeo* is a possible example. Handel's *Julius Caesar* is definitely suitable – indeed many of Handel's so-called castrati roles might have been written for the counter tenor. Certainly, Handel kept his eye on both voices as a performance insurance. Of the higher castrati parts, there are surely possibilities in suitable slight downward transposition, involving little or no difficulties with the accompaniment, but which still retains the *essence* of the eunuchoid voice. (Far more than using a mezzo soprano, or employing a tenor an octave lower. The latter has wrecked many an instrument/vocal balance.)

As Robert Donnington says in *The Interpretation of Early Music*, after first advising the use of a counter tenor as a substitute:

> One alternative is the transposition to a low octave. In Handel operas this has the unfortunate consequence of dropping the voice deep as a tenor (or still worse as a baritone) into an orchestration composed by Handel to support a soprano or alto part. A female voice may well be the best compromise, and *can be* [my italics] musically although not quite dramatically satisfactory.

Anything more than the half-hearted use of counter tenors in post-war productions of opera took a long time to happen. The apparent conservatism of the opera world, even amongst some of those purporting to stage authentic performances, was considerable. Despite the availability of Deller, Whitworth, Burgess, Oberlin, Bridger and Wynne from the mid-1940s and 1950s onwards; Mitchell, Bowman, Brett, Jacobs from Belgium, Mark Deller, Esswood, Ferrante (U.S.A.), and Tatnell from the 1960s on, the world of opera did not take much interest. Since then for some of the names mentioned matters have improved in the sphere of opera, but there is room for more opportunity. Smith, Davis, York Skinner, James, Penrose, Messana (U.S.A.) and Cheng-Jim surfaced in the 1970s; there are more young names all the time. There is no excuse for opera producers and casting directors with such an array of contrasting voices on which to call for pre-Romantic works. In some cases, of course, counter tenors have been and are being used. Here is Rodney Milnes, writing in the magazine *Opera*, in January, 1981, of a performance of a Handel work in the Wexford Festival:

> Reactionary elements muttered about the unsuitability of the counter tenor voice to Handel's castrato roles, and I could not disagree more violently. John Angelo Messana's singing of the title role was something of a milestone in the continuing process of the emergence of the counter tenor in *opera seria*. His phrasing was extremely expressive, and he fielded more variety of tone colour and dynamic than many of his *confrères* could muster. His delivery of the long finale of the second act, a sequence of glowing genius, held the audience breathless. All right, it might not have worked at Covent Garden, but we were not at Covent Garden. Mr. Messana's powerful stage presence was both exploited and controlled . . .

With very few exceptions, like Britten's *Midsummer Night's Dream*, Alan Ridout's *A Pardoner's Tale*, and Peter Maxwell Davies' *Taverner*, modern opera composers have rather held back from writing roles for counter tenors. This is surely not because of failure in performances already staged: we can single out a number of thrilling quasi-castrato or counter tenor roles taken by some of these singers, for example Deller and Oberlin in the *Dream*, and Bowman in the *Dream* and *Taverner*. (Deller unfortunately was never a strong opera actor so perhaps for once we must discount him. Yet his weak acting would not have proved a problem in *recorded* opera of which he did too small an amount.)

Perhaps in the case of modern opera, composers have felt that the counter tenor by its very nature does not reflect the contemporary world? As Frederick Hodgson pointed out in a *Musical Times* article in 1965:

> Most modern composers seem to fight shy of writing for the solo alto, and the Britten Oberon problem raises questions as to what comprehension they have of the potentialities and peculiarities of this voice. After the question of writing specifically for the alto had been put to a famous song-writer, he gave the ambiguous reply that it was difficult to find 'suitable words' for an alto! Another composer made play on a verse of the Psalms: 'I do not exercise myself in great matters which are "too high" for me!'

Time and again, early, Baroque and Classical opera has been staged without a counter tenor when one is obviously needed, either for original counter tenor or castrati roles. So many great opportunities have been lost for hearing, if not exactly the voice written for, the next best thing.

Greater success can be reported in opera's close cousin, oratorio. From soon after the Second World War, John Tobin's annual authentic performances of *Messiah* at the Royal Festival Hall in London were an inspiration. They were authentic in much more than voices – style, orchestration, ornamentation and so on. The only contraltos were in the chorus, and although it is known that Handel intended women for the alto solos on occasion, the ironic twist is that the style of writing and range are so clearly masculine that few contraltos are successful. Another twist is that even when Handel employed a solo contralto, the chorus altos were all male. Tobin actually did not go far enough.

The Watkins Shaw edition of *Messiah* appeared in 1960. Like the Tobin edition, it suggests the castrato, Guadagni, solos should be sung by an alto – meaning a counter tenor – for the most part (he does allow for versions using a 'woman alto' too). Hearing arias usually associated with a bass or a woman contralto sung by a counter tenor, is like first experiencing an old painting without its dull varnish. Recordings have appeared with Deller, Bowman, Oberlin and Esswood giving brilliant accounts of these *Messiah* arias. So pre-nineteenth-century oratorio, cantata and similar forms have proved a fruitful field for the multiplying counter-tenor voices.

Vocal ensemble again has had great success; not surprisingly, for male voice quartets and glee singers still existed anyway, and other mixed small specialist groups could quite easily adjust to the inclusion of counter tenor(s). Their chief musical literature, madrigals, early part songs etc., so clearly demanded a male alto line. Several such mixed or all-male groups were in fact brought together and/or directed by counter tenors, notably the Deller Consort, The Well

Tempered Singers (Whitworth), the Purcell Consort of Voices (Burgess); the original Clerkes of Oxenford (Wulstan), and later the Canterbury Clerkes (Giles). Many seemed built round the counter tenor, like the earlier Ambrosian Consort (directed by Denis Stevens), New York Pro Musica (originally directed by Noah Greenburg), St George's Canzona (directed by John Sothcott) Pro Cantione Antique (director, Bruno Turner). The King's Singers, The Scholars, and other democratically run, one voice per part groups abound in the glee tradition. Some larger groups like the Renaissance Singers (director Michael Howard, then John Whitworth, to name but two) and the later Clerkes of Oxenford use counter tenors exclusively for the alto parts: in the case of the Renaissance Singers an even more interesting experiment was tried. Falsetti were used for the soprano line. Perceval Bridger was the principal voice involved. A number of records and broadcasts were made which were stunning in impact. As John Whitworth writes in his short paper 'The Solo Counter Tenor and its Repertoire in England', for the Royal School of Church Music Journal, *English Church Music*, 1965:

> Some years ago, an experiment was made to recreate the sound of the Sistine Chapel Choir by performing this music with a soprano line made up entirely with falsettists . . . [it was] . . . partially successful in this, and I think the system broke down mainly because they had to sing two hour recitals almost without a break. The sound was quite thrilling before the voices began to tire, which they unfortunately did after about half an hour, and one was left wondering how good it would be if the system had about ten years or so of tradition behind it.

Some years later, the smaller ensemble Pro Musica Antiqua have followed the Renaissance Singers' example, though not attempting their very highest reaches. Vocal and instrumental ensembles multiply like the superb Early Music Consort of London (directed by David Munrow), featuring the excellent James Bowman, although the Munrow group itself has ended with Munrow's tragically early death.

English cathedral choirs and their treatment of the repertoire have been almost transformed by the modern counter-tenor movement. Almost completely gone from the major cathedrals at least are most of the round, often self-taught Romantic altos. Instead, there are firm, ringing, properly trained voices able to cope well with music previously performed weakly, or not at all. No longer, except in unusual cases, are counter-tenor solos like Gibbons' 'This is the Record of John' transposed down and given to a tenor.

The boys' tone has changed too, as part somehow of the drive towards a different attitude to choral blend: S.A.T.B. are now four equal parts, more in the Classical tradition than the Romantic. English cathedral choirs now sound for the most part exciting where once they had sounded vaguely lovely, or merely mellow. There are occasions, however, when one hears such admittedly superb choirs as Christchurch, Oxford, or St John's College, Cambridge, tackling Wesley for example, when one wishes for some tonal adjustment along the lines we suggested earlier for solo voices. So perhaps something has been lost too. I sometimes cannot wait to put on a record of Boris Ord's King's Cambridge Choir, and others, made before the pendulum had swung quite so far!

Coming to the solo scene today, there seems no problem. Solo counter tenors may often be heard on record, radio, concert platform, and stage: seldom for some reason, on television. Perhaps that is truly the last bastion? A general public which enjoys the lighter offerings of, say, the King's Singers (*two* counter tenors with no sopranos above to mask them) still seems nervous of the *solo* counter tenor in a way not true of any other voice. Television aside, and still with a slight frown towards the opera scene, counter tenors seem here to stay barring any cultural about-turns.

Let us take several solo voices now considered to be of especial note and selected for particular qualities of style and voice. *I would emphasise that the following list is utterly subjective.*

Alfred Deller. 1912–1979. Parish church boy chorister then alto lay clerk at Canterbury, later St Paul's Cathedral, London, until 1962. Largely self-taught, he used only the head voice in his prime. His earliest records, begun aged thirty-seven, are remarkable. The music chosen features his incredible upper sinus tone, a dreaming, delicious sound with no vibrato, but a piercing edge lightly covered with the thinnest of rounding. As he grew older this upper range gradually came down but never left him. The lower, pharyngeal section of the voice was richly edgy and penetrating, occasionally used with vibrato, able to hold its own against a lyric tenor. It did not deteriorate with age. Deller's voice was unique but his style, copied but never surpassed, became to a large extent the archetypal modern alto sound. As a vocal type, he was originally a high counter tenor, but later in his career he used the chest and middle register increasingly. Although Deller possessed a large voice, he was, as James Bowman remarked, first and foremost a miniaturist, loving most of all the delicate lute songs of the Elizabethans.

John Whitworth. Born 1921. Organ pupil, Ely Cathedral, choral scholar, King's College, Cambridge, lay vicar, Westminster Abbey until 1971. Studied vocal production privately with the tenor, Frank Titterton, then with Robert Poole. Whitworth uses both pharyngeal voice and upper chest register, but seemingly has little if any *upper* falsetto alone. The resulting tone is fuller than Deller's, much more trumpet-like, ringing through like an extremely high lyric tenor on occasion. His superb blend of head and chest makes him a low counter tenor of tremendous versatility. In early days he sang second counter tenor to Deller's first and the result was artistically satisfying, demonstrating the two English vocal types together. Whitworth uses vibrato very sparingly and judiciously. In tonal type and vocal production he to some extent foreshadowed Bowman, though Bowman uses more upper falsetto and thus has a far greater range upwards. Whitworth has been involved much in medieval music for which his range is especially suited, his voice covering so many varieties of contra-tenor parts.

Russell Oberlin. Born 1928 (U.S.A.). Studied voice at Juilliard School of Music, 1951. Tenor altino type, resulting in imperceptible register blending. His upper tone is extremely light, *not* like Deller's upper voice, but perhaps more resembling a mezzo soprano. The lower register is thinnish at the bottom, more substantial in mid-range. An extremely versatile, technically excellent singer, though his continuous use of vibrato often seems out of place in certain early works. The archetypal American counter tenor, he has sung as solo tenor. Is firm in his personal belief that his rare voice-type is the only true counter tenor, all other kinds being really 'male altos'. (He makes a clear distinction.) But he is generous in his praise of Deller, Esswood and Bowman, for example, though perhaps significantly not of Whitworth. It seems clear that Oberlin is a low counter tenor of the tenor altino type, there being no hint of *pure* pharyngeal production in his tone. Except for his decidedly modern technique, Oberlin, like Whitworth, fits well into the demands of medieval contra-tenor parts, though his lower 'tenor' finishes earlier and more thinly than Whitworth's 'baritone'.

Perceval Bridger. 1919–1970. Parish church boy chorister, then alto lay clerk at Exeter Cathedral, later St George's Chapel, Windsor Castle. Studied privately with E. Herbert Caesari. Owing to his tragically early death, and because he never made any solo gramophone records, he was never as well-known as the rest of the singers on this list. He may be heard in recordings of the Renaissance Singers after 1959 during their male soprano period. Bridger is included as a rarely met type of counter tenor. To me he never really seemed a 'counter tenor' at all but a soprano, though he definitely possessed all his faculties! Of all the names here, his career was perhaps most affected by the early reluctance of opera management to use altos for castrati parts, though he did appear in a few minor productions. He had a phenomenal upward range, including a comfortable top high C″, and he could sustain a far higher tessitura than the usual alto. His tone was roundish except for the highest notes, and very strong except for the lower notes. He used vibrato consistently and to the listener he seemed *only* to sing in upper falsetto: there appeared little pharyngeal. This despite Caesari being his singing teacher. The implication is that owing to Bridger's amazing upward range, the lower was incapable of much pharyngeal tonal development. His chest voice was light baritone or tenor. Another famous singing teacher wanted him to abandon his upper voice and to be trained (by him of course) as a tenor. Caesari would not hear of it. The result was this almost eunuchoid voice of incredible potential which sadly was under-exploited.

James Bowman. Born 1941. Chorister, Ely Cathedral, Choral Scholar, New College, Oxford. Alto lay vicar, Westminster Abbey for three years. To the listener, Bowman seems rather the Whitworth type of counter tenor, with an excellent blend of head and chest registers, but with a more developed pharyngeal capability *upwards*. In other words a low counter tenor with a good top. His rich sheer ringing power ensured his frequent engagement for opera, once opera management finally did the obvious and employed counter tenors. In fact one of his earliest first-rank engagements was in Britten's *Midsummer Night's Dream*, 1967. Bowman was a founder member of Munrow's famous Early Music Consort of London in which his direct trumpet-like tone matched the various instruments superbly. He uses vibrato only where the work demands it. He has been regarded as the leader of the second generation of counter tenors, and his influence has been great. A distinguished and exciting singer, he has performed every period of vocal music except the Romantic.

Paul Esswood. Born 1942. Studied voice with Gordon Clinton at Royal College of Music. Alto lay vicar, Westminster Abbey 1964–1971. The first College of Music-trained counter tenor of distinction. Esswood's style and tone recall Oberlin's upper voice, but without his extension downwards. Paul Esswood is a high counter tenor and seems to use only his head register. His technique suggests a gentle use of pharyngeal voice blending perfectly with the highly developed upper falsetto. He uses vibrato consistently. As with many subsequent college-trained counter tenors, it has been said that there is an element of effeminacy in the final resulting sound. This is not in any way to deprecate his virtuoso technique. Like Bowman, Esswood has appeared with distinction in many opera productions, for which his voice is highly suited. His range has also stood him in good stead for the high Bach cantata alto parts, many of which he has recorded in Germany.

Willard Cobb. Born 1929. Studied voice at Oberlin College Conservatoire, U.S.A. and Trinity College of Music, London. Like Perceval Bridger he is not extremely well-known, present in this list because of his distinctive style, and therefore useful reference as a vocal type. Like Russell Oberlin he is American, has sung and still sings as a solo tenor, but unlike Oberlin, Cobb's low counter tenor technique is somehow mid-Atlantic: the upper (pharyngeal) voice is very English. Both it and the lower tenor register are not at all effeminate.

René Jacobs. Born 1946. Studied singing with Devos (Brussels) and Frateur (Antwerp). The first modern Continental counter tenor (Jacobs is Belgian), he is included here especially because apart from Mark Deller, Jacobs seems most to have felt the influence of and affinity with Alfred Deller's style and voice type. At the same time, he has a very well matching tenor chest voice. He sings both as a high and low counter tenor and he has the thinnish, beautiful clear Deller sound in the upper falsetto, but no appreciable vibrato even in the pharyngeal areas. He has sung in North America and Asia as well as appearing widely throughout Europe. Besides concerts and early music, Jacobs has sung in productions of early opera. He has taught at Schola Cantorum Basiliensis and sung with Gustav Leonhardt.

Chapter 9

HAZARDS TO BE AWARE OF

THE SOLO COUNTER tenor is seldom a full-time soloist. Far fewer opportunities exist than for other voices for obvious reasons. There is the comparative narrowness of repertoire, and works made impossible because of modern pitch, and although the counter tenor should not be in competition with contraltos or tenors this is often the case. Even in those very works written for his voice this still happens today.

So, apart from a very exclusive, tiny band which includes James Bowman, Paul Esswood and regrettably few others, most British counter tenors are either currently cathedral lay clerks or in similar employ, members of small regular ensembles, or they supplement solo engagements in some other way to provide financial continuity.

It is essential that the demands of blend, especially in church music, do not result in a too unvaried tone in solo work. (Because he is in less regular demand as a soloist elsewhere, this danger is perhaps greatest to the counter tenor.) It should not be so if the singer varies his own style and approach from period to period, but choral directors are sometimes funny folk whose main aim is to make everybody, especially altos, sound identical in the interests of blend! There is a logic there, but the solo singer *must* be able to shake off the 'blend' voice when necessary.

Much argument could be entered into on this, but it is mentioned here as warning to younger men who rise through ecclesiastical backgrounds and not as full-time music students. Oddly enough, the same problem of unvaried tone also occurs for college voice students. They will tend to have continuous vibrato, which like many other 'serious' singers they will be powerless to turn off. This limits their stylistic effectiveness in medieval and Renaissance music, in fact well into the Baroque period. *Continuous* vibrato is a late nineteenth-century phenomenon in solo singing.

It is most unlikely too, that modern continuous vibrato was used in *ensemble* before that time. Early theorists on music who actually mention vibrato condemn it, both in connection with solo vocal, ensemble or instrumental music. It was an *ornament*, comparable to a mordent or trill or any other grace, and was expected to be used no more frequently than other ornamentation. Thurston Dart is firm about its modern misuse: (For 'fifty years ago' read seventy-six years. *The Interpretation of Music* first appeared in 1954.)

> The incessant vibrato which has so regrettably infected nine out of ten singers of the present day could not be obtained with the methods of breath control taught by the finest eighteenth and nineteenth century singing teachers. The evidence of early recordings shows that even fifty years ago it was used with the utmost care (though the tremolo seems to have been rather more common than it is today), and it is one of the greatest disfigurements of modern musical performance.

This problem so far affects the average solo counter tenor less than the average tenor or any other voice. But our concern is specifically with altos. This is all a plea that solo counter tenors watch for the dangers emanating from their singular situation. They should preserve integrity as soloists in their own right, should not under-sing their solo work because they are so used to singing in ensemble. They must not sound too bland and churchy, neither like a particular sort of lowish mezzo soprano.

There is another influence on the English and ultimately the European counter tenor, and that is the influence of the U.S.A. We have seen that the United States has developed its own solo counter tenors, but they are few in number. However accomplished, they tend to employ continuous vibrato and produce somewhat effeminate though seldom if ever woolly tone. There seems a tendency for those Americans who sing just in head voice on the English high counter-tenor pattern (but are encouraged to regard themselves as merely 'male altos'), to have been female trained and mostly in colleges of music (unless of course they have a church background). So they too invariably have an all-purpose, built-in vibrato and an effeminacy of technique, though I should add that they may be and often are very good technically.

It is of the utmost aesthetic importance that the English style is not swamped or changed for the worse by the tenor-altino influence. The indigenous product has integrity and an unbroken tradition. This is not to deny the possibility of revitalisation, but to stress that the indigenous is nearly always of merit, often greater merit. Also, no great help to the *spread* of counter-tenor singing and its general acceptance seems likely to come from too much United States influence.

For one thing the few counter tenors there do little work in comparison with ours, and ours need to do more. We might inherit more than we bargained for.

There is another reason. The reader may feel that I have perhaps overstressed the question of effeminacy, and suspect even in the present writer the presence of 'hang-ups' dismissed at the start of this book. This is not so. There is a far more serious point which I am approaching.

Oddly, there are *dangers* inherent in the very fact that there is over-all far less prejudice nowadays against the high male voice. Let us realise those dangers by considering the position of boy choristers in England.

Up to thirty years ago in this country, trained or untrained, boys sang like boys. In Britain there was a definite trained style which involved an obvious head tone and chest tone, and boys were encouraged to enjoy both. With the exception of the excellent Ernest Lough and the Romantic boy-soprano tradition at the Temple Church, the usual boy treble had little or no vibrato, and even if sometimes a little hooty, was always intensely boy-like! It was an indigenous style which people in many foreign countries found thrilling and also puzzling: *how* were those effortless high notes achieved, that strength and purity of tone, that maturity of sound? They would compare their admittedly musical but thinner, often scratchier boy soloists and boys' choirs, and wonder how the English could achieve such marvellous results.

We have seen how, in several instances over the centuries, the conservative element in English music ensured the preservation of a tradition others had allowed to weaken or alter. It is always assumed that our traditional English boy style is, like it or not, a peculiar phenomenon developed in this country alone. But there is the possibility that allowing for the Romantic patina of style which has affected all singers and instrumentalists, what modern European admirers heard was, like English discant, at least something of their *own* past!

One attractive hypothesis is that the English boy style is the glorious remains of a *European* style. Though there would have been variations of timbre owing to each country's distinctive language sound, Latin was the universal educated tongue. No doubt its pronunciation varied for the same reason, but Latin surely tended to control many of the possible movements away from the stylistic norm.

Let us examine the implications. Boys' voices had always had their parallel in men's, about one octave below. That their voices blend so well is no accident. The inherent harmonics of the lower voices are enhanced and strengthened first by the counter-tenor tone then by that of boy trebles. Indeed, very often in tenor-bass music or passages of larger works, particularly in a resonant building, one can almost hear non-existent alto or treble voices. This is the reason that counter tenors are so important to choral texture: their tone is high in harmonics; there is a lightness which does not, like the heavier contralto timbre, bear downwards upon the tenor, but raises, pointing and sharpening (tonally) the treble voices above.

It is surely no coincidence that the very greatest periods for counter tenors, namely the fifteenth, sixteenth and seventeenth centuries, are also known for a good part of that time for extremely high boys' voices, especially in England. In other words a conscious use of the full and extended male voice, as developed in counter tenor, tenor and bass was arguably seen to be present up one octave in the vocal range of the boy. The use of falsetto techniques was of course universal.

It is this highly developed head voice which has remained the English style, as it did – just – in alto singing. But with various changes of musical and vocal direction most Continental boys' choirs long ago developed a harder, more chesty tone. Add to this the various indigenous language sounds and we have today an often exciting but mostly unethereal European treble tone, sometimes even resembling a miniature tenor, and higher up, a miniature conventional Romantic female soprano! Just when this probable change took place would be the basis for an interesting study.

To add to this intriguing conjecture, as the *chest* based treble was surely the original sound produced by boys in the very earliest medieval music and before (see page 10) throughout Europe, including England, so it is tempting to assume that the gradual extension of men's vocal range throughout medieval times led universally to the *full* most beautiful flowering of boys' head-voice singing during the fifteenth and sixteenth centuries. This was not just in England. It was surely this sound which inspired the experiments which led to its preservation on the Continent in the castrato voice? Therefore the boys' head voice, used extensively and extremely high, must have been cultivated in Europe too.

David Wulstan is strongly against such an idea. Readers would be well advised to obtain his excellent paper 'Vocal Colour in English 16th Century Polyphony' for more study of this point. We merely underline that he makes out an extremely convincing case for the essential 'unevenness' of the spread of particular voice types throughout Europe for climatic, genetic, ethnic, sociological and, as a result of these, physiological reasons. He summarises a masterly exposition of several pages thus:

Genetical factors cannot be excluded from the forces which determine vocal colour. There is no reason to suppose, therefore, that

English singing should resemble that of any other nation in all respects. The faculty for falsetto singing (by adult male, boys' and women's voices), the paucity of 'true' tenor voices and the 'duller' tone production all may be cited as characteristic of English singing, and might have a genetical basis. Vocal quality would also be affected by the time at which boys' voices changed, and if Latin were superseded by the somewhat duller English language.

An intensive study of the whole question of pubertal voice change would surely bring out essential information which would affect tonal considerations. Wulstan's further comments on the timing and length of vocal puberty seem appropriate here:

Whatever the reasons for the timing of the 'breaking' period, its length is important. Many believe that singing must be stopped during this time, while others insist that regular singing without strain, rather than the disuse of the voice, is essential to the proper development of the changed voice. It has already been noted that the best alto singers report a gradual voice change; they also sang continuously through the breaking period. In many cases they were unaware that their singing voice had changed, for they had unconsciously altered their technique from soprano to alto; remarking only the loss of the top notes, they were subsequently surprised to find that they had, in addition, a bass voice. This curious compensation mechanism seems to be present in almost all voice changes, if to a less dramatic extent. However, although most breaking voices deepen fairly gradually, the phenomenon of the soprano apparently becoming a bass overnight is by no means unknown. Since the vocal fold must virtually double in length, such a spectacular breaking of the voice must represent the sudden disintegration of a compensating mechanism, rather than an instantaneous enlargement of the larynx. Current research into this mechanism may reveal that a facility for re-positioning the hyoid bone is a crucial factor, and that this control is essential for an easy command of falsetto.

Devotees of modern Continental boy tone are usually critical, even scornful of what they call the 'English cathedral hoot', though most will probably never have encountered that phenomenon. They dismiss all traditional English vocal production in boys, advocating a permanently hard, edgy, less heady quality as often heard abroad. John Whitworth says:

I suspect that the 'English hoot' may be put down in part to the training of English Cathedral Choristers in the nineteenth century by organists who were not singers.

English choirboys (until the advent of George Malcolm at Westminster Cathedral and Michael Howard at Ely Cathedral) were
made to produce sounds 'out of the back of their necks'; and when
their voices broke, few developed mature voices which could compete with their Continental counterparts.

The same muddy tone became admired by English organ
builders, producing the English 'octopod'.

While agreeing in essence with this view, it is important to reiterate
that the English 'hoot' was really a degeneration, or as Shakespeare
put it, 'a sea-change into something rich and strange', of a strong,
mature technique which existed before the nineteenth century. Malcolm and Howard trained their boys differently: the former to resemble not just the Continental, but to produce a tone thin, brilliant and
Spanish. Howard's boys always sounded 'English with guts'. I know
this from personal experience.

Actually, Michael Howard's famous boy tone was surely a reaction
against not 'the hoot' but the rather effete King's College, Cambridge
style of the time. The Ely sound was at least partly built on a foundation laid there by Sydney Campbell. Interestingly, it produced James
Bowman, also Nigel Perrin of the King's Singers, as well as attracting
as lay clerks Geoffrey Mitchell, Ian Harwood and Peter Giles, just to
name some counter tenors.

So, beginning in the 1950s cathedral choirs began to move away
from anything resembling 'hooty tone', that is those which had ever
really possessed it. For in fact, to qualify John Whitworth's comment
above, is it not possible that the real hoot as opposed to the rounded
cathedral sound was the result of nineteenth- and early twentieth-
century parish church choirmasters struggling to achieve a sonority
which only rolling aisles and fretted cathedral vaults could give? The
hoot was really a search for sonority in a dry acoustic.

There seems a distinct possibility that the development and affection for the English register-conscious sound might partly have come
about because our damp British climate has always been responsible
for coughs, colds, or phlegm, the singer's curse! English head tone
with its harmonic edge could have originated for this, but not solely
this reason, for the English style seems not to have been so widespread
in other parts of the British Isles unsophisticated musically.

Today in England, it is customary to admire a harder, yet still
undeniably *English*, tone. This is to the good, for having removed
much of the Romantic patina, we can now perform a much wider
range of music authentically. For naturally, there were types of music
not ideally served by the late nineteenth-century and earlier
twentieth-century version of the English sound. Our boys needed

some renewed decisiveness, a return to a brighter colour. This is what began at Westminster and Ely.

Most English choirs still train boys to sound like boys, retaining the fullness but banishing any hootiness. (Mature tone must not be confused with hooty tone.) But about twenty years ago, when many English choirs were experimenting tonally, there began a movement to train boys to sound like young girl sopranos, with vibrato and a weaker, less direct, less heady sound. The result was undeniably *musical*, but somehow stylistically ambiguous and, one suspected, less right for the English choir tradition. Those trebles did not resemble so much *boy* singers, but trained child sopranos, yet not at all like the Ernest Lough type which was securely based on the English tradition.

There is a vocal difference between boys and girls. Their voices emanate from apparently identical larynxes but the young male and female psyche differs. This has always resulted in an instinctively contrasting singing style and timbre for each. There is today a pressure for everything to be bi-sexual in the name of equal opportunity. Generally this could be healthy, but would this be so in the world of cathedral choirs? I think not, and for several reasons.

There is certainly growing pressure now to admit girls into choirs with boys. It could and even should be done it is said (nearly always by those to whom the tradition itself means little) because some of the choir or preparatory schools which supply cathedral choristers are going co-educational, like Wells Cathedral School for example. (Wells is a successful mixed specialist music school for the senior age group also.) 'We can't,' say some people, 'deny girls the *opportunity* any longer', quite forgetting or ignoring the fact that the purpose of the English cathedral choir tradition is not and never has been to provide social or even musical opportunities but to make a unique sound with a unique instrument to the glory of God. It is an aesthetic act of worship of the highest order, related to the monastic offices. A part of our *Opus Dei*. Such an objective is worlds away from considerations of sexual equality and women's rights.

'Girls can sound just the same as boys', is the fashionable phrase, and so a few can, and more than a few if the boys are trained differently, as unfortunately some are. Young women *can* be trained to sound excellent in early polyphonic music originally written for boys and sung today in secular concert performances – think of the superb Clerkes of Oxenford. At least one English parish church cathedral now has a mixed top line of boys and girls. Perhaps for the moment it works for them. Yet the latter must be a compromise and must eventually lead to problems.

Despite our liberal modern world the average boy still obstinately remains the staunch champion and instinctive embodiment of male virility. The boy chorister will sing like the proverbial angel if round him are other members of his peer group, clearly identified. He is seen to be among boy equals, and a member of an exclusive society. (This is his defence, *not* his motivation.)

The result of trebles performing music written exclusively for their voices over centuries is superb. It is also a source of already trained singers, future men for alto, tenor or bass. (Trained, that is, in the *style*.) There seems little to be gained *musically* by changing the situation. A mixed or exclusively young female top line, however good, is not the genuine article. A clever copy, seemingly identical in effect, can never be the real work of art, the real Chippendale chair, Michelangelo sculpture or the true medieval Gothic; in this case the clever copy, though well intentioned, may well end up by debilitating, then *destroying* the original aesthetic tradition – first the boys, and thereby those 'already trained' men.

All this might sound like a tirade, an obvious hobby horse, but there is a purpose to it. Some readers may know exactly why I mention girls in boys' choirs. I am anxious for the safety of a wonderful art form and concerned about its continued authenticity – likewise the countertenor tradition. For if the high adult male voice is trained to sound effeminate, however accomplished it might be musically, there will come a time when we are back to square one. If high counter tenors *sound* like mezzo sopranos, then why on earth should anybody engage a man when they could engage a woman singer? Particularly if the trend for authenticity fades, and more particularly if the choice is under social or moral pressure. Tradition is, in any case, not terribly fashionable just now, at least not when compared with 'equal opportunity'.

Far fetched? Reactionary? Ridiculous? Surely even the most 'liberal' reader of this book would accept that socio-politics and art make uneasy companions and such a mixture usually ends up with defeat or compromise for an existing art form caught in the crossfire. The more effeminate in character the high male voice, the more unlikely it is in the long run to survive as an art instrument.

Counter tenors must and can sound essentially *masculine*. They should sound like a man singing high, sometimes very high. They should not resemble in tone or style a low feminine voice. This is not to say that they should sound strained, just properly supported. Alto means high. It should sound it. Its character, its quality, its reason for existing, its musical literature before, say, the eighteenth century, and some after it; all these are concerned with a high male voice.

One of the problems so far with many college-trained counter tenors in England seems to be the lack of a good lower register. During their 'modern' training, they appear to be persuaded that not only is the head register all, but extending it downwards is not as useful as extending upwards. (We have already noted the number who are trained by women teachers and their students' frequent resemblance to the timbre of the average mezzo soprano.) A very real problem occurs when a counter tenor with a weak lower voice and no register change attempts, for example, a Purcell trio for A.T.B. He is swamped every bit as much as the old woolly altos were at times. This tempts the director of music to reassign the alto part to a high tenor, thinking at least that the audience will be able to hear it! Soon, editors, remembering Russell Oberlin and the tenor altino, are *specifying* tenor in new editions of old music, just as Sir John Stainer did when first presenting to the public the beautiful E minor Evening Service of Daniel Purcell. Stainer did it because most Victorian altos by his date presumably had not the vocal weight or suitable style to balance the tenor and bass. But that is past. (For Stainer's views on the alto question see the Appendix.)

Yet reassignment is happening again quite needlessly, given a good properly trained counter tenor. Unless a specialist high range voice, he should have the edge, resonance and pharyngeal strength to match a tenor and bass who *wish* to blend, however low the counter tenor part is written.

I give as an example a Purcell verse anthem, 'Give Sentence With Me', published in 1977 in *The Musical Times* with (1) an accompanying scholarly article and (2) an all revealing footnote at the end of the music itself. Eric Van Tassel writes:

(1) Our edition of 'Give Sentence', in prescribing a tenor for the highest solo part (originally in the alto-clef, in the contratenor partbook), implicitly enters a brief (with reservations) on one side of the haute-contre/countertenor controversy which has been much aired in recent years.

There are sound practical reasons for suspecting that the post-Restoration 'contratenor' soloist was often (though by no means always) not a falsettist but a high, light tenor – a *hautecontre*, or Rimski-Korsakov's *tenore altino*. And the considerations that led me to transcribe the contratenor solo part of this anthem for such a tenor were essentially practical ones. (1) The highest note in the part is 'G' (reached only five times, always in passages favourable to a tenor's un-false voice), while it goes as low as F sharp (bars 22–3) and E (bar 99) in context where a falsettist could easily be swamped. (2) The two upper solo parts – frequently paired in thirds in the Monteverdian manner – quite often reach a cadence by an approach in which, again, a falsettist would risk being swamped by his tenor partner (cf bars 15–16, 22–3, 28–9, 53–5, 98–9, 112–14,

*Or Alto: see the editorial notes on the back page.

Example 19 *Two extracts from* The Musical Times *(1977) version of Purcell's anthem, 'Give sentence with me, O God', demonstrate the reallocation of voice part from alto to tenor. Example A shows the normal tessitura of the counter-tenor part. Example B demonstrates an unusual depth for this part.* (By kind permission of The Musical Times.)

121–23/125–7). (3) The falsettist would surely be at risk where the alto-clef part goes below the tenor (see especially bars 26–7 and 92–4).

These tessituras are a not unusual feature in anthems of the period (parallels can be found elsewhere in Purcell, as also in Child, Humfrey, Blow, and others), and it is likely that a distinction was understood between high altos (falsettists, presumably), and low altos (*haute-contres* or something very like) – even though in most manuscripts both kinds of alto used the same notation.

(2) The highest solo part (top note G sharp) was probably sung by a high tenor, and the modern clef has been chosen accordingly. This part could be sung by a male alto if he can balance the middle voice (without forcing) in passages where the two parts cross.

For me to underline the fact that the head plus chest mechanism was used by all voices in Purcell's day would be enough to answer Higgenbottom and Van Tassel. Also note that no allowance has been made in their edition for (church) pitch variation since Purcell's time. The customary transposition today in seventeenth-century church music of about a tone upwards would lighten the effect, not that such a transposition is strictly necessary. The only point at which the alto part actually touches a low E is when in unison with the tenor (see Example B).

The reluctance of some to accept that counter tenors can possess enough tonal strength recurs from time to time like malaria. In Stainer's day perhaps it was understandable. Unfortunately, with the new young generation of 'mezzo' counter tenors, the Higgenbottom/Van Tassel view is also understandable, even if their apparent dismissal of older, stronger-trained voices is also very regrettable.

It is all very well those editors expecting rare tenor altini to be suddenly available in every cathedral or collegiate choir performing this music. It is at least as difficult to find this particular vocal type as in Purcell's time. What will probably happen in practice is that this alto verse part will be given to a normal tenor. Quite often, unfortunately, he will be thick-toned and possess conventional vibrato. The result will sound not at all authentic, but solid, opaque, and quite un-Purcellian.

As we have seen, this is hardly a new situation. Nigel Fortune's comments in notes accompanying an only semi-authentic sounding recording of Purcell's *King Arthur* are interesting. Writing in 1959, and calling attention to only one of the counter-tenor solos taken by the tenor (David Galliver) he says: '*I call, I call*, is difficult to cast: it is in the alto clef in the original, but the alto voice seems unsuitable for such bold sentiments, and it is sung in this performance by a tenor, even though the tessitura is a trifle high.' How this statement could have been made is a mystery when you consider that John Whitworth was in the cast (and he is given only a fraction of his due solo work). His particular timbre seems especially suited to bold sentiments and a virile low range.

Jeremy Noble, writing in the late 1950s in *The Musical Times* of the new Purcell Society edition of Purcell's scena 'In Guilty Night', was no more informed:

> It is a pity, though, that the editors decided to print the counter tenor part of Saul in the untransposed G clef, since few male altos carry the vocal weight for it, and fewer the dramatic weight; printed in a transposed G clef it might have attracted the attention of a high light tenor or two, and I can't help thinking that this was the kind of voice Purcell had in mind.

Here is a noted musicologist, apparently unable to hear the evidence round him, especially the voice of John Whitworth in this context, who shortly afterwards recorded the part of Saul for E.M.I. Noble's phrase 'decided to print the counter tenor part of Saul in the untransposed G clef' suggests that he was not thinking even of Oberlin – possibly of whom he had not then heard – but of a normal lyric tenor, who would perhaps find difficulty in this high part. Presumably, Mr Noble was advocating transposition downwards, perhaps of one tone, to make it easier for a tenor? He had little faith in the powers of the counter tenor.

It is surely about time that Bowman, Oberlin, Jacobs or some other counter tenor of today with a good low register recorded what could be the definitive performance of 'Saul and the Witch of Endor'. The Whitworth version is now unobtainable, and rather dated largely through considerations of the musical style of some of those round him. The Deller version, though not one of his best recordings, has many superb moments.

At the beginning of this book we suggested that despite progress much prejudice still existed, often disguised in spheres where it really mattered. This view may have been thought exaggerated by the reader, especially if that reader was familiar with Michael Tippett's remarks in the foreword of *A Singularity of Voice*:

> But Deller had to face extra problems and overcome peculiar sus-ceptibilities owing to the very nature of his voice. And again it is ironical to note that present day young people, hearing a lot of beat [music] where voices are high or low, quite irrespective of sex, and

generally accepting our permissive society where virility is no longer a he-man mythology, must find Deller's worries about his voice, as he talks of them in this book, quite outside their ken.

Such optimism seems premature. For not only is it the *music* the voices sing that is increasingly the point of division (and so these 'young people' would not accept the counter-tenor *repertoire*), but also there are modern teachers of classical voice production, writers, and singers who would most certainly not agree with Mr Tippett's view, or even with the desirability of the existence of the counter tenor.

Consider the following, written in 1963 by Elster Kay, an ex-choral scholar of King's College, Cambridge, no less, and at the time of publication at least, a teacher of voice in Cambridge. It occurs in his book *Bel Canto*. We have *never* read anything so vitriolic about a group of artists. It beats anything we've found yet in even the most uninformed literature on voice training. For sheer ignorance and prejudice what he says on altos and counter tenors can surely not be exceeded:

Falsetto. This type of tone is now known by cinematography to be created by pressing together the greater part of the free vibrating edges of the cords causing a node, so that only a small length is free to oscillate, combined with very low breath compression in the larynx. In legitimate singing it has no place except for the occasional production of comic effects such as the imitation by men of women's voices. It is used by yodellers whose technique consists of singing low notes in *voce piena* and then by allowing the laryngeal inlet to fly wide open suddenly thus minimizing laryngeal breath compression, to cause an instantaneous change of the mode of cord vibration, at the same time singing wide intervals, often of an octave, the upper note being in falsetto.

The sterile and emasculated quality of this type of tone is all too painfully familiar in England where it is to be heard in the form of so-called male altos in all church choirs, and frequently on the air in the form of again so-called 'counter-tenors'.

The male alto of medieval times was, like the male soprano, a castrato, not a falsettist. These men sang like women, that is, under full compression resulting in *voce piena* tone. The modern male alto is a baritone who perpetually sings an octave above his normal compass using falsetto tone. There have been recently before the public one or two male sopranos of the same falsetto kind: these are presumably tenors who sing an octave above their normal compass using falsetto tones. So far no professional success has attended the endeavours of any of these latter 'spuriosities'.

The vocalists (they are hardly to be described as singers), who nowadays are given the courtesy title of counter-tenors, are simply falsetto male altos who have the wit to develop a bright clear tone as contrasted with the dark, hooting tone of the traditional English cathedral alto. The excruciating monotony of the tone of these personages is due to their incomprehensibly obstinate refusal ever to use more than a single resonator adjustment. Their emasculated bleatings would be rendered the more curious if not the more agreeable were they to use all three resonator adjustments, which they perfectly well could. As it is we are faced with the painful choice of the screech of a night-jar, or the hoot of a sort of super-sonic owl. The most that can be said for this new kind of noise is that it is less disagreeable than the traditional kind. The medieval counter-tenor was a light tenor (*tenore bianco*) who, on passing above his *tessitura* (at F' or G'), immediately went into falsetto and by so doing was able to add five or six notes to his compass, singing up to G or A above the tenor high C. He was on his way to being a male falsetto soprano (not, of course, a castrato soprano). Such voices are rarely heard today, but they must exist in reasonable numbers. Handel and Purcell wrote for counter-tenor. The best example of writing for this voice in modern music is the part of the Astrologer in Rimski-Korsakov's opera *Le Coq d'Or*.

It should be noted that falsetto tone can be used through the middle and upper thirds of the natural baritone or tenor compass and there is no reason why women should not sing falsetto if they were so mentally deranged as to wish to do so. Happily they never seem to be so afflicted, although many women who are not trained singers but who have strong virile speaking voices, invariably and involuntarily break into falsetto when they sing.

Children before puberty are not falsettists, although in England, especially in cathedral choirs, they are usually trained to emit tone of a falsetto timbre, by singing in the low adjustment and under low air compression. It is perfectly possible to train a treble (that is a child soprano) to sing under full compression and to produce tone which is well on the way to *voce piena*. In England this is almost never done but in the Sistine choir a majority of the boys usually sing in this way. This type of training is possible in the case of children falsettists as distinct from adults because in the child the cordal nodes are fixed and will not open when laryngeal air pressure is increased.

(By permission of Dobson Books Ltd.)

Notice just how misguided an 'expert' can be! This long and remark-able quotation occurs near the end of this book so that the reader may be able to assess Mr Kay with physiological and historical knowledge. His view of falsetto technique inclines one to wonder if he lives in the same world as the rest of us, it is expressed in such especially odd statements. Could anybody describe Deller's vocalistic skills as excruciatingly monotonous?

Before we leave the book *Bel Canto*, it might be interesting to note its date once again – 1963. Deller still at his peak, Whitworth, Oberlin, Wynne, Burgess, Bridger, Pearmain, Mitchell and soon M. Deller and Brett, all turning in good performances which give the lie to Mr Kay's views.

If the Bowman-Esswood generation had taken Mr Kay seriously then there could surely have been no more counter tenors for a while. Perhaps those of his persuasion were hoping for this very thing. If so they were disappointed.

There was perhaps at least a little more excuse for *The Times* music critic, the late H. C. Colles (*Essays and Lectures*, Oxford, 1945), writing before the modern renaissance was really under way in the person of Deller, but only little excuse for a musically educated man who could write: 'Handel must have chuckled to himself over our Cathedral Altos squawking in falsetto, but if that was the sort of thing the English liked, they should have it. As a matter of fact he began his 'Ode for Queen Anne's Birthday' with a recitative in which the male alto was invited to do his worst, and he probably did.'

Frederick Hodgson has commented of the H. C. Colles remarks: 'This can be seen to contain nothing but prejudice when it is remembered that Handel soon made friends with English singers, among them such celebrated altos as Hughes, Powell and Barrow, who sang frequently for Handel, and who, by their great reputations, did anything but 'squawk in falsetto'. (Incidentally, Hodgson's memoirs, *Singing in the Choir*, soon to be published by Dobson, will prove fascinating reading. He began as an alto in about 1930, and can be said to belong to and reflect the views of the Romantic school.)

The truth is that the counter tenor/alto voice was increasingly scorned by the prejudiced when the voice was in decline during the later nineteenth century and near oblivion in the first half of the twentieth. Sometimes of course, gentle fun has been made of counter tenors. Any worthwhile endeavour can withstand genuine fun at its expense. Think of the mirth that the figure of the coloratura soprano has evoked at times. It does not matter. There have been so many truly great singers of this type. Who cares for those who cannot appreciate them? And there *is* a funny side of every human activity.

Old Sir Frederick Bridge, late Organist Emeritus of Westminster Abbey (and known affectionately as 'Westminster Bridge'), told the story of the dreadful old alto performing a recitative in Purcell's anthem *Thy Word is a Lantern*. The scene was the Chapel Royal. 'I suppose,' writes Bridge of the aged alto, 'with his cracked and comical voice, he somewhat annoyed an old Peer who sat immediately behind the choir and was rather given to thinking aloud. When the singer had finished his sentence, 'The ungodly have laid a snare for me,' the old Peer ejaculated, loudly enough to be heard by the choir, 'I wish to Heaven they'd caught you!'

There is a difference between fun and malicious wit, however. In Deller's early days on the concert platform, as we have seen, he encountered so called 'wit' from those who should have known better, fellow musicians, leaders of orchestras for the most part. One instance has already been described, earlier. On another occasion, Deller had just left the concert platform in Liverpool, when yet another orchestra leader said to him: 'If I got up to sing like that in public my mother would disown me.' *Mother?* Interesting.

The Times music critic writing in about 1960 was equally pre-judiced. He was discussing the vogue of using counter tenors for solo alto parts in *Messiah*, and the re-allocation of certain arias to different voices from those previously expected, the intention being to return to authenticity. *The Times* critic starts off well enough:

Handel hardly ever played '*The* Messiah' twice alike. [My italics.] Everything depended on what singers he had available and since taste in singing was changing during the middle years of the century enough to enable him to modify in the oratorios the conventions that he observed in his Italian operas, *we are not obliged, if we do not like the hooting of counter tenors and falsetti* [my italics], to make our performances as top-heavy with high voices as was fashionable in Handel's youth.

He is entitled to his preferences but prejudice surfaces in the most surprising ways and it is not often acknowledged by its perpetrators. As late as 1968, in his book *A Guide to Good Singing and Speaking*, Julian Gardiner, after describing the male alto voice coolly admits, by way of admiring the female chest voice as used in folk, pop and light music, that he derives great pleasure from training and listening to it, and:

That is more than I can say about counter tenors! Maybe it is prejudice, but I am not alone in this. It is a deep seated instinct and runs parallel to our attitude towards transvestism on stage. A man masquerading as a woman is completely unacceptable except in broad farce. In contrast, the woman transvestist can be a delight to both eye and ear. Her long and honourable lineage takes in Cherubino, Quinquin, Oscar and Prince Orlofsky . . . to say nothing of the glamorous principal boys of English pantomime. In the same way, if she uses it correctly, her chest voice does nothing to detract from and probably emphasises her sexual charms.

I wonder whether a woman would agree with Mr Gardiner's male point of view? The truth is that such views are entirely subjective and probably depend on which sex is watching the stage. Mr Gardiner has merely had the courage to come out into the open, acknowledged his prejudice and explained his feelings. Objectively it still remains unreasonable; art should be above all this!

I must report a most humorous twist at this point. Julian Gardiner's book, in the 1968 edition before me, has on the back of the jacket an extensive blurb for *A Singularity of Voice*, Alfred Deller's biography! (The first edition was also published by Cassell.) Such poetic justice; a humorist must have been lurking at Cassell's.

The vestry joker cannot really compete with his cheery: 'Hullo gentlemen and altos!' or 'Morning, ladies!' (This addressed to the alto section.) A suitable four letter word reply has often been a happy response. Anything less ladylike cannot be imagined.

Chapter 10

ALL'S WELL THAT ENDS WELL?

I MENTIONED at the start of this book that in the 1950s it was an unrewarding search seeking any reference to the counter-tenor voice in books on technique, and an utterly vain one hoping for reference to modern singers of this type.

One would have thought that by the early 1960s the purely historical role at least of the counter tenor would be quite clear, but no less a musical writer than Percy M. Young could make two odd errors in his book *The Choral Tradition* (Hutchinson) in *1962*, namely that Byrd's Mass for Three Voices was scored for *contralto*, tenor and bass (in text) and *soprano*, alto and bass (index of principal works section). Both are of course quite wrong! In fact Mr Young almost consistently uses the word contralto instead of alto in his quoted musical examples of early music. This is completely ambiguous. That example must have been a rare phenomenon in 1962.

The Deller entry in *Great Singers* by Kurt Pahlen (W. H. Allen, 1973) reads:

> Alfred Deller is a counter tenor, a rare class akin to the coloratura soprano among women's voices. But since the repertoire for this voice is extremely limited, it has necessitated the rediscovery of long-forgotten works or the performance of modern compositions which have sometimes offered rewarding tasks for Deller, for example Orff's *Carmina Burana*, and Britten's *Midsummer Night's Dream*.

The situation has improved a little, but only a little in the ultra-conservative world of the vocal textbook. There is nearly always at least reference to be found to the counter tenor although some are damning, and some damning with faint praise. I myself have never read anything very enthusiastic. Medical books on laryngology sometimes rather put the professors of voice to shame.

In Chapter Five, 'The Phenomenal Voice', in *Music and the Brain*, published in 1977, A. S. Khambata contributes a wealth of information and ideas on human vocal possibilities. He suggests that the counter-tenor voice is peculiarly English (which admittedly in modern times it has tended to be), and goes on with somewhat grudging praise:

This rather specialised category of male voice is perhaps a by-blow of the original castrati soprani and contralti, but it has lingered on through . . . Cathedral singing in this country . . . [He mentions Deller as the catalyst to the new movement] . . . The speaking and so-called normal singing voice of this breed of singer is generally of a baritone colour, the particular characteristic of the counter tenor voice being a well-developed falsetto which is extended downwards into the chest register.

Khambata goes on to say that in his opinion the counter tenor is best heard in a medium-sized concert hall. He considers it too small for the larger spaces of a conventional opera house, but he is not over familiar with the vocal tone of solo counter tenors: 'The use of the falsetto in such a manner tends to produce characteristic hooting qualities in the voice, but there are notable exceptions, particularly that admirable singer James Bowman.'

Other than the odd arguable point (the English counter tenor is not a 'modern derivative' of castrati or Italian falsetti contralti, but an ancient voice type, as we have seen) even the slightly qualified enthusiasm in an important book is refreshing after the vitriolic views of Elster Kay. There is a cool look in the amusingly named *The Voice and Its Disorders* by Margaret Greene, 1972 (but first published by Pitman, 1957). A medical textbook, it has a chapter on abnormal mutation (alarming as a title!) in which occurs the following paragraph, describing the counter-tenor family:

Natural tenor singers are occasionally found having a freak vocal range, able to sing with facility in the falsetto register. The peculiar thin and silvery voice of the counter tenor always has a certain vogue. The fluty, rather haunting quality of voice is due to reinforcement of a limited range of overtones in contrast to the deep baritone or bass voice which is enriched by a wide range of harmonics. Alfred Deller has popularised counter-tenor singing in our time. The voice of the male falsetto singer is rather richer in harmonics than that of the boy by reason of the larger adult resonators.

Perhaps we should at least find comfort in the fact that before 1943 and Deller, the paragraph quoted would have not just been a little condescending, but scornful or pertubed according to the view of the writer on its particular form of medico-psychological disorder!

The cautious admission by the modern medical world that the falsetto production of the highest male voice is an artistic instrument seems now to be in an exact parallel with that of the music colleges, those institutions which train most other singers and instrumentalists so ably.

There is apparent official blessing from the important colleges, demonstrated by the presence of an alto/counter-tenor division in their singing examinations at various levels; there is other welcome evidence too – that of the presence of a specialist teacher of counter-tenor singing on certain college staffs. All this is gratifying and surely pleases the pioneers. The recognition they had fought for seems to be here.

In practice, there may still be some cause for concern. First, there are many different and quite legitimate views on all voice production. With many teachers for each 'conventional' voice class, soprano, mezzo, contralto, tenor, baritone, bass, a balance is undoubtedly achieved. Teacher A may not be right for student A, but is better for student B. Teacher B is clearly right for student A and so on. It is just as much a matter of personality and chemistry as vocal considerations.

Teachers of singing, usually themselves singers of a particular denomination, usually teach pupils of that denomination, but also, quite reasonably, other voices too. So all in all, the situation over what can be called 'conventional' voice divisions is healthy. There is a plethora of choice and room for manoeuvre.

Because few traditional voice teachers yet know anything much of training the counter-tenor type of voice (some do not wish to know), many would leave its teaching to perhaps the one man on the staff who does. It is only too clear at times from aural evidence that others, while knowing little of this particular subject, but because they are competent voice teachers otherwise, take on the young counter tenor, often with unfortunate results. This is by no means confined to colleges of music. The trouble seems to be that counter tenors are sometimes taken to be an odd variety of contralto, and too often trained as such.

The counter tenor must be seen, essentially, first as an *historical* voice. It cannot be measured by and should not be trained according to the same post-Romantic criteria as modern voice types, in much the same way as gamba tone and technique cannot be evaluated by the same criteria as those of the cello. Until there is a modern repertoire approaching in size its historical one, and the counter tenor is written for without question just like any other modern vocal range, it will stand to some extent apart.

An eighteenth-century castrato returning today would probably meet much musical criticism from certain reactionary quarters, and this would likely be first from ignorance, secondly from tonal unfamiliarity, thirdly from jealously of his incredible technique! Yet this voice type produced some of the greatest singers the world has ever seen.

We are not suggesting that the present situation is parallel for counter tenors, but there is some affinity. Despite the very real and much welcomed advances there still seems some way to go before vigilance can be relaxed to prevent young counter tenors from being turned into male contraltos in the modern sense, with anachronistic style and sound.

We decided to find out what the music colleges could tell us, so wrote explaining the reasons for the enquiry, enclosing a questionnaire and sent it to seven of them – five in London, one in the provinces and one in Scotland. All seven colleges replied to David Mallinder's letter. They were the Royal Academy, the Royal College, Guildhall, Trinity School of Music, London, the Royal Northern and Royal Scottish. Some were obviously keen to help while some gave perfunctory answers, in one case not returning the questionnaire but sending instead a curt letter. Even these perfunctory replies were of use, since they gave an insight into the attitude towards counter tenors at these colleges. Naturally, those colleges which had specialist counter-tenor teachers were more helpful, and seemed to take pride in the fact. Four of the seven colleges had specialists.

The present counter-tenor teachers at these four colleges had been there for between three and twenty-three years, an average of eight-and-a-half years. All four provided the name of their present teachers. In one case the teacher quoted is not known to be a singer at all, but a conductor. Perhaps he has hidden talent as a teacher of voice production?

In the case of colleges without specialists, the 'normal' singing teachers taught the counter tenors. It was slightly worrying that in one, counter tenors were being trained by contraltos. This is not to question their ability as teachers and their previous status as singers, but to express concern at the possible tone and style of counter tenors trained by them.

John Whitworth tells me that when he was on the staff of another well-known music college he was not allowed to teach counter-tenor students there but had to keep to his general musicianship area. The counter tenors, instead of reaping the benefit of a distinguished singer of their own type, were trained by a woman!

Numbers of counter tenors training at any of the colleges were very low – ranging from none to six students – and the numbers showed no definite trend upwards or downwards but fluctuated. Likewise, in open diploma examinations, only about one per cent of the entries were counter tenors, although the pass rate, where given, was usually one hundred per cent.

In view of the low numbers of counter-tenor students, no teacher had more students than he or she could handle.

The question relating to the popularity of counter-tenor students with the singing staff: 'Do any of your singing tutors refuse to teach counter tenors', produced amusing answers, usually of the 'We don't ask' variety. Only one college (Royal Northern) definitely stated that the women teachers objected to teaching counter tenors. Strangely, the Royal Northern made no mention of the connection with Deller, or of the Deller memorial plan to establish a scholarship there for early music students with special reference to the counter-tenor voice.

Four of the seven colleges named well-known counter tenors trained by them: not surprisingly those four colleges which had specialist courses for counter tenors, or who ran a course integral with one in early music.

It would appear from the examination results that the counter-tenor student tends to be of a much higher standard than the other voices, or at least he takes himself that much more seriously, in view of the very small but very successful numbers.

So there seems some cause for optimism. One further point. We may rejoice with those students lucky enough to be taken by the single specialist counter-tenor teacher on the college staff. But he is a singer himself. His voice and style are of a particular type. What of those who come to him for training and vocal development? If voice, ideas and/or temperament are not compatible then there is a problem just as bad as that met by other counter-tenor students. If all is well there is likely to be just the one teacher; and his students will all be in danger of sounding alike. The answer is surely that, ideally, counter-tenor teachers of different style should be employed part-time on college staffs.

Despite the presence of a few counter-tenor teachers in colleges of music, there is no reason to assume that one is always present on the panel at singing examinations – especially open diplomas – at which counter-tenor candidates are being heard. In view of the many marked misunderstandings about the qualities and essential characteristics of this voice, this presence will be necessary for some years yet. During the viva voce questions at one such examination, a candidate was asked by one of the three examiners, a lady, what he called his voice. 'Counter tenor', he replied, puzzled.

'Counter tenors were high tenors,' she replied authoritatively. '*You are a male alto.*' His careful reactions to that were not enough to fail him, thank goodness. Hearing of that incident helped to convince the author of the need for the present book.

The question asked at the outset of this book was specific: 'Counter tenor – the mythical voice?' Was counter tenor merely a term, never a voice as such? If so, because 'counter tenor' was so much argued over, perhaps the term was best dropped, letting altos be altos, tenors be tenors, and the devil take the hindmost! For some might still say in exasperation that the term caused more trouble than it was worth. But why should it be abandoned? There is no longer any problem. The question has thus been answered.

To conclude, the counter tenor began life as the contra-tenor *part*. The earliest medieval times it could be and often was much lower in range. It could be sung also by what we would now call baritone or tenor voices. As time passed and music developed, the contra-tenor, still sung by various types of voice where applicable, developed too, extending and gradually rising in pitch after leaving behind its lower half as the bass of what grew into our 'modern' vocal system. When contra or counter tenor became a recognisable and exclusively high voice part, sung by specialists, it divided further, first into two equal parts, then into low and high divisions. Much solo music was composed for both, sacred and secular.

The lower, the 'low' counter tenor, was sung either by 'baritones' with an extended pharyngeal or middle falsetto head register (like Whitworth), or unusually high 'tenors' (like Oberlin). The latter were and are extremely rare. The upper, or 'high' counter tenor, was sung by specialist falsettists, 'baritones' (like Deller) or 'tenors' (like Jacobs) using their pharyngeal and upper falsetto head registers extended high and expertly to the top of the treble stave. A tenor altino with good pharyngeal and upper falsetto might also fit here, but he was still more a rarity.

Falsettists were always in the majority and their varied timbres the norm. The tenor altino can certainly claim to be a counter tenor, but he is one of a family. He is not alone. Let us assume for the moment that Russell Oberlin has been correct all along, and that his voice type is exclusively the historic counter tenor, all others developed from middle and upper falsetto being male altos, and a different species. That this should seem unlikely, as it probably does at this stage, does not matter. There are initially at least one or two points in favour of Oberlin's view. You will have already considered them in the light of the arguments which form the bulk of this book.

Suppose he is right. Solo counter tenors have been renascent since 1943. There are many excellent singers who are constantly before the musical public, broadcasting and recording. Music colleges, though not exactly overflowing with potential counter tenors, do number them among their full-time students. Yet there seems little sign of young tenor altini in their ranks, even from the United States from where one would expect most to come. Oberlin himself teaches in a New York college. If *he* cannot find them, who can?

His recent broadcast talk (in December 1980 – though a repeat) over B.B.C. Radio was ostensibly on problems of performing Handel's solo arias. It was in reality a reiteration of his usual counter tenor/alto point of view and a plea for more, as he puts it, 'natural counter tenors' to come forward. They must be hiding in music colleges, he claimed, unaware of their vocal potential, content to sing as ordinary tenors. This is possible but unlikely. Any vocal student glimpsing a rare opportunity to stand out from the very competitive herd, to specialise in earlier music and ultimately make much money with his rare voice type, would be insane to ignore the chance! For Oberlin is quite right: the tenor altino can perform much of the *standard* Romantic and modern lyric tenor repertoire too.

One of Oberlin's other claims – and I would obviously agree with this – is that counter tenors exclusively should be engaged for lower castrati parts. A young tenor altino trained for this could surely be successful. (Yet in a radio broadcast a few years back, Oberlin stated categorically that the voice he called male alto was the closest modern equivalent to castrato. Of course he was making another point.) Certainly when opera managements do use counter tenors, tenor altini are not cast. Where are they all, these tenor altini – who were presumably not only the exclusive performers of music of this range for several centuries as soloists, but also formed the 'alto' voices in choirs over the whole of Europe? The truth is that the bulk of the counter-tenor population must always have been the developed falsettists.

Since the completion of the manuscript of this work, the sixth edition of the prestigious *Grove's Dictionary of Music and Musicians* has been published. It was with some excitement, even trepidation, that I opened the relevant articles to my own subject. Perhaps what I was about to read would pre-empt much of my own thesis, albeit on a tiny scale. No, the counter-tenor entry is both smaller and lower in profile than in the fifth edition. It is, I thought, essentially an exercise in 'fencemanship', which is fair enough; but when one compares the length of the article with others of similar importance it is sadly wanting in detail.

The same writer, Owen Jander, is responsible for a similarly sized entry on the French *haute-contre* voice. As I have already implied, I myself regard the haute-contre as identical to the low counter tenor and Italian contralto tenor, with a vocal production based on either the pharyngeal or the tenor altino. Owen Jander would seem only partly to agree. The reader is invited to make up his own mind. The various arguments put forth over recent years, notably in *The Musical Times* (see Bibliography) exactly parallel those applied to the counter-tenor question. There can be little doubt that we are considering not an additional high male voice but the French manifestation of the same counter-tenor family. Certainly the term *haute-contre* was derived in the late fifteenth or early sixteenth century from contra tenor altus.

I was gratified to read the articles on individual important counter-tenor singers. Progress continues to be made.

Though legitimately also one of the counter-tenor family, the mellow alto of the Romantic period with its non-ringing tone but excellent blending qualities, perhaps for modern usage, might be better termed 'alto' (possibly also the rare Bridger type of extra high 'Spanish'-falsettist) leaving the classical, harder-edged ringing-toned singer the term 'counter tenor'. The nomenclature fits today's situation in the same way as calling a high bass a baritone helps understanding.

Alfred Deller has used the analogy of trumpet and bugle, for the counter tenor could be said to resemble the trumpet family. It is a particularly happy analogy. There are or were, by name, Clarino and Clarions, valved and valveless, slide and keyed trumpets; there are B flat, C and D, even bass trumpets, cornets of brass (do not forget the wooden variety) and bugles. Charles Claggat invented a double trumpet in the eighteenth century, which could play in both B and E flat. Some trumpets are familiar, some not, but all are varieties of trumpet. Ironically, it is the 'natural' trumpet, the simplest, without valves, which is most limited in range and ability. It has the use of a single fundamental and from this, one harmonic series. So it follows that, by definition, the 'unnatural' or if you like the 'acquired' or 'developed' most sophisticated forms of the trumpet are the most useful and versatile. From them can come the most subtleties. One man's definition of *natural* could be undeveloped.

Perhaps there is here a lesson for students of the counter tenor, and indeed all voices. There is little of value in art which has not been achieved by hard work and involved both heart-searching and drudgery before its satisfactory completion and legitimate candidature for the definition of Art.

The counter tenor is not mythical or extinct. It is a voice family and not a rare one. But its employment and development still are rare compared to other vocal ranges, as is its cultivation as high art.

Appendix A
THE COUNTER TENOR AND THE PARISH CHOIR

Counter tenors must have been present in parish churches well before the mid-nineteenth century. As has been described, there were a few influential parish churches which enjoyed the services of professional singers in medieval times. This all ended at the Reformation and if not then most certainly at the Commonwealth. Thereafter existed a very ad hoc arrangement of mixed gallery choirs in all but cathedrals and collegiate foundations.

Cathedral music, naturally enough, has always needed counter tenors, but when the Oxford Movement of the mid-nineteenth century brought surpliced choirs into most parish chancels, they must have required them too. The quality of those who came forward we can only guess. Were there enough, or were they augmented by boys? Altos disenchanted with the later nineteenth-century choral society must have flocked to parish choirs, but this would hardly have provided enough voices for the many new large church choruses.

Despite the resurgence of interest in the counter-tenor voice and the more esoteric branches of choral music, at the humbler levels of the parish choir the alto shortage still exists.

Choirmen are normally unpaid, and are singing for fun. Their singing training is limited to the weekly choir practice and their aspirations run along fairly conventional lines. To most people, tenor and bass are the men's voices, with anything higher left to ladies, boys or girls. Compound this with a choirmaster or mistress with a similar outlook, and the potential counter tenor is still-born.

Let us not blame the choirmaster overmuch. Most have to accept the choir voices they get, and with good grace. Also, though he does his best, he is often more organist than choirmaster and runs the choir as well as he is able. These days he may not even be a trained organist but the local piano teacher, and have no knowledge of voice-training other than that which he has picked up on the way. It is unlikely that he will have started his choir from scratch, and will have to use the singers that he has inherited from his predecessor. They may be men and boys, but today are most likely to be a mixture of boys and girls, men and women.

However friendly, efficient or desirable from a parish and social point of view, a mixed choir is not a good training ground for young counter tenors, for reasons often other than musical. If the alto line is being sung by women, the young counter tenor may find singing in their company embarrassing – he is seen to be singing a 'woman's' part! The ladies, in their turn, may mother him showing him the ropes, and this will embarrass him even more. In addition the girls singing the treble part will think that a lad singing with the ladies is 'funny'. Trivial and childish though this may be, it is still off-putting even thirty-seven years after Deller's concert debut.

For a boy or group of boys asked to sing alto without adult help, the problems are still great. Numerically, the group would be small and quite apart from having to read the alto line (no mean task for amateurs), the volume produced might not be sufficient to be heard. Again, remember what J. Varley Roberts had to say about boy altos even when they do produce adequate tone for the choral balance.

In a mixed choir it is more likely that the hopeful counter tenor will be asked to sing with contraltos. If the boy, in growing, attempts as he matures to obtain a more brilliant 'counter tenor' tone, the ladies may well resent the eclipsing or discomfiting of their own voices, since a counter tenor on full bore will make their own tone seem pallid in the case of the usual run of parish contraltos (usually second sopranos). *Trained* contraltos find that a counter tenor in their midst presents problems of blend. His lighter, more agile tone makes their voices feel and sound an octave below, thus affecting choral blend and balance. The young counter tenor himself, singing with contraltos, will find invariably that he develops a less masculine style.

Ideally, to encourage young altos, the choirmaster should himself be an enthusiast for this voice and be seen to regard it as of great importance in his choir. It will help if he has a man singing counter tenor who is also popular enough to encourage youngsters just starting. Or the choirmaster may know a counter tenor (from a cathedral, if he is lucky) who would occasionally sing in, or demonstrate to his choir, encourage his own brood suggesting possibilities for future breaking voices. He may even be able to arrange a 'master class' at a moderate fee for his young altos, and it would be a fillip for them to sing out of their parish church environment, perhaps even at the cathedral song school.

Separate parts-practices at choir rehearsal are not uncommon, and provide the counter tenors with opportunities to make mistakes in comparative privacy, away from the main body of the choir. To enlist the help of a cathedral counter tenor or a singing teacher who under-stands this particular voice would be a bonus at these sessions and well worth a fee.

If the church is situated near a cathedral or similar establishment which employs a professional male choir, visits to services can give valuable assistance, especially when it is known that music containing counter-tenor solos will be sung. It goes without saying that whether convenient to a cathedral or not, the aspiring counter tenor should learn from a wide selection of gramophone records, and also record himself often on a tape machine with *well amplified* play-back facilities. To listen to oneself on a 'tinny tranny' is a waste of time and can be utterly misleading. Quite clearly, once the voice has settled the sooner the young alto can obtain singing lessons from a suitable teacher, the better.

The music sung by the parish choir needs to be chosen with some care if the choirmaster wishes to train, not ruin the voices of young counter tenors. Hymns and Anglican chants seldom pose any difficulty as the range of the alto parts is quite limited. Settings of the canticles are usually all right, being written for the most part for counter tenors, but newer Eucharist settings and anthems can be more troublesome. A Romantic repertoire presents more obvious difficulty to the *adult* alto than to the young beginner, for the late adolescent can usually sing any number of high alto notes.

The young man in his early twenties who has decided to train himself as a counter tenor may not find this. The danger is that real youngsters do not develop enough vocal weight for the true counter-tenor range if they are forever singing what amount to mezzo-soprano parts in music often written for women.

The Tudor composers, used to counterpoint (where every voice part has its own identity) seldom wrote above B flat for the counter tenor, although expertise was and still is needed to sing these parts. The simpler Tudor anthems, in what amounts almost to block har-mony, seldom contain difficult voice parts. The composers of the Restoration period, as we have seen, wrote a great deal for alto, either in solo or ensemble. Although written for the virtuosi of the day, some of these anthems are singable by a well-trained parish choir and provide opportunity for exposed singing after *careful* preparation.

When performing music written for one specific voice part (for example solo sections in anthems) it is a mistake to allot another voice type to them except in exceptional circumstances. It is a common temptation experienced by choirmasters to allocate trebles to solo alto parts. Although this may often be done through apparent expediency, it will not encourage the counter tenors to improve their own tone, volume or technique. It will merely cause resentment. If the choir-master regards his 'parts' as highly as he regards his top line, he will surely take time and trouble to develop them so that they can give a satisfactory performance.

In defence of choirmasters who do reassign, it is only fair to add that they may not at the time possess singers capable of such performance. So they must either swap the parts or forgo the anthem. If forced to switch voices, they should proclaim that it is a stop-gap measure for this particular occasion, certainly not a desirable situation.

Certain music publishers and editors have been guilty of changing the composer's intentions with respect to voice parts allocated; this is particularly true of foreign editions of pre-Romantic works. It is not uncommon for a piece originally written for alto and tenor to be re-allocated to tenor 1 and tenor 2. This occurs very often because the editor expects a mixed choir. Any musician should be able to decide from the date of the composition and a little simple research whether the part allocation is authentic or not. He should not hesitate to change them back to what he considers correct.

However difficult it may now be for the young counter tenor in a mixed choir, things are surely better than twenty-five years ago. People are not so *surprised* at the high male voice. I remember how, even as Alfred Deller, John Whitworth and others were becoming widely known in the early 1950s, I was involved as a very adolescent alto in a Royal School of Church Music Festival in Ealing, London. The choirs, a very mixed gathering indeed, were required to process, robed, along the street to the church from the hall. I was walking with two men amongst a bevy of girl and women 'altos'. A friend told me later that after a decent gap had come a huge pride of tenors, in which the friend himself had been included. One had asked him: 'Those chaps ahead – what are *they*? They should be back with the men.'

'They are altos', the friend replied, 'from our choir.'

The man had laughed disbelievingly: 'What! Do they still have *those* in your church?'

Appendix B
DEFINING THE COUNTER TENOR

Several entries of different date and differing conclusion from musical encyclopaedias or works of reference are given here. They have been chosen for their particular relevance to the present book. Readers are asked to study them in the light of the material they have just read. The differing conclusions perhaps suggest why a work such as that here presented was necessary. I have not included the *Grove* article as it is too long and rather odd in places (I refer to the Fifth edition).

Example B is surprising in places, considering that Barrett was himself an alto singer of repute. William Alexander Barrett was music critic of *The Morning Post* from 1867 until his death in 1891, and edited *The Monthly Musical Record* and *The Musical Times*. He wrote various erudite books on music. *Example D* mentions alti naturali and castrati in 1924! Professor Alessandro Moreschi, the last Sistine Chapel castrato, died that year. *Example E* is notable less for its conclusions than its emphasis and enthusiasm for the true male alto – an unusual reversal! Otherwise its thesis is muddled. *Example H* is interesting in that, although it gives the best set of definitions in the collection, it appears to be muddled about the high and low counter-tenor question, confusing *low* counter tenor with counter tenor bassus. Is it wrong? Remembering the thesis on Elford (page 113) surely Westrup and Harrison's statement could stand. The low counter tenor could be the bassus with the head register extension. Think of Purcell's high bass (baritone) parts.

A. Harwood's Dictionary, 1782.
Alto signifies the Upper or Counter Tenor, and is commonly met with
    in Musick of several parts.
Counter Tenor (in Musick) one of the middle Parts, so called because it
    is as it were opposed to the tenor.
No entry under Falsetto

B. Dictionary of Musical Terms, Stainer and Barrett. Revised edition, 1898.

Alto voice. Called also counter-tenor, when used by men, and counter-alto or contralto, when used by women. It is the deepest tone of voice among women and boys, to whom it may be said to be natural, and it is called the highest voice among men for lack of a better term to describe it. Properly speaking, the tenor voice is the highest man's voice, the alto or counter-tenor voice being entirely an artificial production, and simply a development of the *falsetto*. The register usually written for this voice lies between tenor G and treble C,

As the best notes of the alto voice are within the octave from B flat, those notes are most generally employed, for the higher notes are harsh and discordant, and the lower of small musical quality, and therefore ineffective. The alto voice in man is mostly formed upon an indifferent bass voice, and there is always a break between the chest and the head voice; this break varies between C and E and the careful union of the chest and head qualities of

voice, and the judicious employment of the '*mezza voce*' are characteristic of every good alto singer. The alto voice is almost peculiar to English singers, not one of the Continental nations possessing the capability of producing the quality or of appreciating it when produced; the consequence is, that there is no music written for this voice by any but English composers, and the majority of writers of the present day forming their style upon the foreign model, neglect and ignore the voice, disregarding its claim to usefulness, in places and at times, when and where female voices are unavailable. The value of the voice, its flexibility, sympathetic quality, and harmonious power, when carefully cultivated, are well displayed in cathedral music, and glee singing: a great number of melodious compositions by the most noted English writers, depend upon the alto voice for their proper effect. Many of the songs in Handel's oratorios were assigned to this voice, which are now, in consequence of the heightened pitch at present employed, sung by females: for instance, the part of Solomon in the oratorio of that name; of Barak and Sisera in the oratorio of 'Deborah'; and of Daniel in 'Belshazzar'; are each given to an alto voice. As this practice is of quite recent growth, it is but reasonable to conclude that Handel intended the music of the wisest king, and that of the two brave warriors to be sung by men altos, rather than by women, for the sake of appearance, if no more powerful reason. The fact before alluded to, of the non-recognition of the voice by foreigners, has given an advantage to English musical literature not enjoyed by any other people, in the cultivation and sole possession of the Glee and the Anthem.

As many of the principal effects are obtained in these two species of composition through the medium of the alto voice, if only for the sake of the performance of the many noble specimens of art in these two styles, the alto voice will always be cultivated in England until such time as the Glee and Anthem cease to exist. The cultivation of the Part-song has almost superseded the use of the alto voice in modern music, for the upper part in this class of composition is given to tenor voices, and the difficulty in producing the notes of the higher register so far influences the character of the music written, that many of the part-songs for male voices are of a bold, boisterous style, entirely different to that of the glee, which by reason of the peculiarity of the alto voice is of a more quiet character, depending in a great measure for its effect upon delicate and expressive singing. Many composers of eminence have completely ignored the alto voice, whether male or female, a quantity of music for Church use being written for treble, tenor, and bass, as by Cherubini and others.

In quality and power of expression the female alto voice is peculiar, and unlike any other voice. Its character is grave, tender, spiritual, and moving, and is admirably adapted to express emotions of dignity, grandeur, and piety. The male alto being an artificial voice, its usefulness is of limited duration, for when the singer is past fifty years of age the voice becomes harsh, reedy, nasal, and the break is painfully apparent.

C. **Dictionary of Music** (translated from the German), Dr Hugo Riemann, Augener and Co., 1902–8.

Alto, (1) *Alto voice* (Ital. *Contr'alto* [*Alto*], French, *Haute-contre*; in the Latin designation of the voices *Altus*, *Vox alta*, or *Contratenor*), the lower of women's and boys' voices, chiefly in chest register. In the time of complicated mensural music – which could not be performed by boys because it took years to learn the rules – the high parts (*A*. and Discant, *i.e.* soprano) were sung by men with falsetto voices (*Alti naturali*), or indeed by *evirati*, as women were not allowed to sing in the churches (*'mulier taceat in ecclesia'*); for this reason the discant and alto parts of that period have only a very moderate compass upwards, and on the other hand a greater one downwards. The normal compass of the genuine alto voice extends from A, in a deep A. (contralto) from F (exceptionally E, D) to E'', F'' (but in voices of specially wide compass higher still). Viewed historically, the alto part was the one last introduced by composers; for over the normal men's part which took the *Cantus firmus* (tenor), a higher one was first placed, to which was given the name of *Discant*. Afterwards a third lower voice was placed under the tenor, which at once served as a foundation (harmonic support, basis) and, if the tenor descended, as a middle filling-up voice. Finally, this third voice separated into two: the bass became definitely the support of the harmony, while the contra-tenor or alto (*altus*), as a fourth voice, was interpolated between tenor and discant.

Counter Tenor: Male Alto voice (see Alto)

D. Black's Dictionary of Music and Musicians, 1924.

Alto: The highest male voice or counter tenor, extended to include the falsetto tenor register sung by alti naturali or castrati. The term is less properly applied to low voices of boys and contralto voices of women.

Counter tenor voice: Alto

Falsetto: The third and uppermost register of male or female voices, such as that of the male counter tenor; so called because it was thought to be unnatural. Falsetto singers were employed at an early date in the Sistine Chapel choir, displaced by the voce devirato, and again restored.

E. A Dictionary of Church Music, G. W. Stubbings, London, The Epworth Press, 1949.

Alto: The next higher vocal part to the tenor, which was originally the principal melody. In modern vocal part choir music the principal part is in the treble or the third above the tenor, and the alto part is that immediately below the melody.

The alto voices are those singing the alto part in a male choir. In a mixed choir of men and women the alto part is sung by women's voices, usually called contralto. The musical effect of an alto part sung by men is strikingly different from the same part sung by women: the male alto voice sounds higher than the tenor, the women's contralto voice sounds lower than the treble.

Counter tenor: A high tenor voice which sings the alto part of English church music for male choirs. The counter tenor voice has the same character as that of the tenor, and thereby differs from the true male alto or falsetto voice.

Falsetto: The true English male alto voice produced normally by baritone or bass singers by the utilisation of the head register. By careful training this head register can be merged into the normal 'chest' register without a perceptible break.

F. The Concise Oxford Dictionary of Music, 1952.

Alto: A type of male falsetto chiefly cultivated in Britain, where church music and the glee provide for its use. In the performance of the choruses of oratorios, etc., it has been gradually superseded by the women's contralto voice (also sometimes, but inaccurately called 'alto').

No entry under counter tenor.

G. Man and His Music, Alec Harman and Anthony Milner, 1959.

Counter tenor (or Male Alto) voice: a falsetto development of a normal tenor or bass voice.

H. Collins Music Encyclopaedia, Westrup and Harrison, 1959.

(Extensively revised in 1976, but with no change to the following entries, now called *Collins Encyclopaedia of Music*.)

Alto 1. Lit. 'high' L. The highest adult male voice, now employed mainly in church choirs and male-voice choirs. The range of the voice is roughly two octaves from though the lower notes lack resonance. The upper part of the compass is made possible by the cultivation of the falsetto voice. In seventeenth-century England the alto (also known as counter tenor) was popular as a solo voice.

Counter Tenor: The highest male voice (also known as alto), produced by using the head register. English composers of the late seventeenth century frequently wrote solos for this voice which demand not only a mastery of expression but also a brilliant ringing tone.

Contra Tenor: In fourteenth and early fifteenth century music the name for a part with roughly the same range as a tenor, which it often crosses. In the course of the fifteenth century a distinction developed between contra tenor altus (high contra tenor) and contra tenor bassus (low contra tenor) with a prevailing range respectively above and below the tenor. Those terms were subsequently reduced to altus (alto) and bassus (bass).

(By kind permission of Collins, Ltd.)

I. Harvard Dictionary of Music, 2nd Edition, 1969. Willi Apel.

Contra tenor. abbr. Contra. In compositions of fourteenth and early fifteenth century name for a third voice part added to the basic voice texture of discant (superius) and tenor. It has about the same range as the tenor with which it frequently crosses so that the lowest note may fall now to the tenor now to the contra. Its contour is usually much less melodic than that of the other two parts to which it is added for harmonic completeness. With the establishment about 1450 (Ockegham, Obrecht) of four part writing and the consequent separation of ranges the contra tenor split in two parts: the contra tenor altus (high contra) or simply alto and contra tenor bassus (low contra) or simply bassus. This process explains the name alto (high) for a part that from a modern point of view can hardly be considered 'high' as well as the use for the term counter tenor for the male alto.

J. The International Cyclopaedia of Music and Musicians, 10th Edition, 1975 (orig. 1938). Dodd Mead and Co. N.Y.

Counter tenor: High tenor, usually falsetto, the highest male voice.

Alto or Contralto: The lowest of the three types of female or boys' voices (the other two being mezzo-soprano and soprano) with a normal range from A or for deep voices below middle C up to E, and eleventh above the same note.

The term is also used for a male voice of like range of the natural falsetto or castrato type . . .

Appendix C
THE COUNTER TENOR AS AN ARTISTIC PHENOMENON

Despite its original development as a European voice, how very *English* the counter tenor is. I refer to a characteristic not only musical, an artistic quality which is discernible in other forms of expression.

Some years ago, Nicholas Pevsner published a book called *The Englishness of English Art*, based on his Reith Lectures for B.B.C. radio. In this book he expounded a very believable thesis, that there was in English art a peculiar and unique quality. Perhaps his main point concerned our love of *line*, sinuous, sensuous, flowing and ever present.

It has pervaded our architecture (think of English cathedrals in terms of extreme length, never of extreme height); painting and drawing (a preoccupation with line pervades even tonal areas of pure painting, for example Gainsborough's almost *crosshatched* solid colour areas, and just think of Blake); language (the flowing subtleties of English prose and poetry); music (the idiosyncratic vocal lines of, for example, a Tallis motet with the accent on an *individual* journey, sometimes leading to strange semitonal clashes and that marvellous flourish, the 'English' cadence).

The second characteristic is idiosyncrasy, a refusal to be bound by rationality, the peculiar phenomenon which has given rise for example to Edward Lear, Lewis Carroll, Rowland Emmett, the Goons, Hoffnung and 'Monty Python's Flying Circus' – a surrealist world. It is this which spawned the English eccentric and the legend of mad dogs and Englishmen. Our brilliance in the invention of team games and sports – the majority were devised by the English – is surely essentially an escape into an unreal world.

The third characteristic is tradition and conservatism. The composer Dunstable led Europe in the fifteenth century primarily because he and the other English composers were part of a *conservative* tradition. While other European composers were desperately looking for the new, Dunstable was able to point the way as a result of the English independent line (yes, line!) which had valued discant and developed those strange dissonances we now call thirds and sixths.

It is my contention that the alto or counter-tenor voice fulfils all these English characteristics and that is why, after a glorious heyday, a reluctant fading, it survived banishment to a semi-anonymous place in the cathedral and parish church choir stall; and why there is more English music existing for more English counter tenors.

All voices sing a single line, but the sound of the high male voice is *ultra*-linear – if not always thin, then essentially lithe. It is decidedly otherworldly, inhabiting a strange unreal world somewhere in the head, indefinably more than falsetto. It is eccentric and irrational: men do not normally sing as high as women, therefore who but the English would favour over many centuries a purely natural voice which does? The counter tenor is itself the result of English conservatism. Its continued existence stems from English reluctance to embrace the new or recognise when the game is up, the battle lost!

Despite eighteenth-century high fashion, the English quietly preferred the natural homegrown product to the foreign artificial castrati who were vocally superior. Despite the introduction of contralti during the eighteenth century it was a long slow process to freeze the counter tenor from the concert platform, and when it was accomplished it was not permanent.

His retreat to the church from whence he came is very English too. English music and musicians have been bound up traditionally with the church, to the fury and no doubt despair of many an agnostic or atheist. Perhaps the victory of the counter tenor against the odds is very English too!

DISCOGRAPHY

In cases where a record set is recommended, an alternative single record is also suggested.

1. Individual Artists

(Exclusively from those featured in Chapter 8)

Alfred Deller   (a) *The English Renaissance*: 3 record set
(solo work interspersed with
Deller Consort items.)
    Harmonia Mundi HM 260

                    (b) *Alfred Deller Recital*:
Campian, and Handel's *Sosarme*
    L'Oiseau – Lyre OLS 109

                    (c) *A Midsummer Night's Dream*: 3 record set,
opera by Benjamin Britten
    Decca SET 338–40

(see complete discography in *A Singularity of Voice*)

John Whitworth   (a) *Sound the Trumpet*
from 'Come Ye Sons of Art',
Purcell
(with Deller)
    L'oiseau – Lyre OLS 102

                    (b) *The Fairy Queen*,
Purcell
    L'Oiseau – Lyre OLS 121–3

Russell Oberlin   Only *Messiah* is available in the United
Kingdom
(see section 7)

James Bowman   (a) *Stabat Mater & Nisi Dominus*,
Vivaldi
L'Oiseau – Lyre DSLO 506
(b) *Te Deum in D*,
Purcell
(with Charles Brett plus the Choir of St
John's College, Cambridge)
Argo ZRG 724

Paul Esswood   (a) *Bach Cantatas* (almost complete set)
(with the following boys' choirs:
Tölzer Knäbenchor
Hanover Knäbenchor
Vienna Boys' Choir)
Telefunken Series EX 6
(b) *L'Incoronizione di Poppea*: 5 record set,
opera by Monteverdi
HD 6–35247

René Jacobs   (a) *Italian Baroque Recital*
Telefunken AW 6 42226
(b) *German Church Cantatas and Arias*
Accent ACC 7912

2. The Counter Tenor in Mixed Ensemble (small)
Deller Consort (Alfred & Mark Deller) *Morley*. Harmonia Mundi:
HM 241

Purcell Consort of Voices (Grayston Burgess & John Whitworth)
Music of the Early Renaissance. Turnabout TVS 34058

3. Male Ensemble (small)
Pro Cantione Antiqua (Paul Esswood, Kevin Smith, Timothy Penrose) (8–9–10 voices) *Spanish Church Music of the Renaissance* 3 record set. Telefunken FK 6 35371

Pro Cantione Antiqua (Paul Esswood, Keith Davis, Geoffrey Mitchell) (9 voices) *Lamentations,* Tallis; *Mass for Three Voices*, Byrd. Archiv 2533113

The King's Singers (Nigel Perrin & Alistair Hume) (6 voices) *A Concert Collection*. HMV CSD 3766

Canterbury Clerkes (Peter Giles) (3 voices) *Canterbury Clerkes Shal Syng*. Wealden WS 193

4. Choral, Boys and Men

Choir of King's College, Cambridge (dir. Boris Ord) *Festival of Lessons and Carols* (No 3). Argo ZRG 5190

Choir of King's College, Cambridge (dir. David Willcocks) *Requiem*, Fauré. E.M.I. ASD 2358

Canterbury Cathedral Choir (dir. Allan Wicks) *Bridge Through Time*, Peter Phillips & modern composers. Grosvenor GRS 1030

Choir of Christ Church, Oxford (dir. Simon Preston) *Mass for 4 Voices, Mass for 5 Voices,* Byrd. Argo ZRG 858

5. Choral, Mixed Voices with Counter Tenors

The Clerkes of Oxenford (dir. David Wulstan) *Tudor Church Music*, Tallis. Classics for Pleasure CFP 40069

6. Choral, with Male Sopranos (falsetti) and counter tenors.

Renaissance Singers (dir. Mirchael Howard). (At present all records are deleted but are occasionally obtainable secondhand. Seek Argo RG186.)

7. A Single Major Work Recorded by Several Counter Tenors

Messiah Handel

Bowman	(3 record set) HMV SLS 845 (Willcocks)
Esswood	(3 record set) HMV SLS 774 (Mackerras)
Oberlin	(3 record set) CBS M25–603 (Bernstein)
Brett	(3 record set) CBS 79336 (Malgoire)
Deller	(deleted 78rpm records of two arias; not available at present [Feb 1981] 'He was Despised' HMV B 10682 'O Thou That Tellest' HMV C 4222)

The Fairy Queen Purcell

Whitworth	(3 record set) L'Oiseau-Lyre OLS 121–3 (Lewis)
Deller	(3 record set) Harmonia Mundi HM 231 (Deller)
Bowman	(2 record set) (shortened version) Decca SET 499–500 Britten
Deller	(3 record set) (Not at present available in the U.K. but perhaps in the future it may be.) Vanguard (Deller)

8. Contrasting Types of Boys' Tone
St John's College, Cambs. See section 1.
Various Knäbenchors. See section 1.
King's College, Cambs. See section 4.
Canterbury Cathedral. See section 4.
Christ Church Cathedral, Oxford. See section 4.

(a) Watch out for secondhand (or reissued) copies of: Choir of Westminster Cathedral (dir. George Malcolm) (1959) *Tenebrae*, Victoria. Decca Eclipse ECS 747

(b) Andrew Lyle – Boy Soprano (1962) Abbey LPB 707

(c) Master Ernest Lough – Boy Soprano (1927) *Hear My Prayer* & other solos, Mendelssohn. Pearl Records GEMM 211

(d) Watch out for secondhand (or reissued) copy of: Ely Choristers & Renaissance Singers (J. Whitworth & dir. M. Howard) *Music for the Feast of Christmas*. Decca Eclipse ECS 660

(e) Escolania de Música Monserrat *Missa de Batalia*, *Misa de Gloria*, Joan Cererols. Deutsche Harmonia Mundi 06599714

(f) Regensburger Domspatzen *A Christmas Concert*. Deutsche Grammophon 2536 410

(g) 11 English Cathedral & Collegiate Choirs *40 Christmas Carols*. Abbey LPB 820

9. Famous Choir Once Having Male Soprani and Alti but Now Mixed
Choir of the Sistine Chapel (dir. Bartolucci) *Palestrina etc*. Acanta DC 21841

10. Modern Large British Choral Society (no counter tenors)
Huddersfield Choral Society (cond. M. Sargent) *Highlights from 'Messiah'*. Classics for Pleasure CFP 40020

Compiled with the help of *The Long Player* and *Forward's Classical Music*, Canterbury.

BIBLIOGRAPHY

Articles, Papers or Monographs:

Ardran & Wulstan, 'The Alto or Counter tenor voice', *Music and Letters*, 1967.

Baldwin, O. & Wilson, T., 'Alfred Deller, John Freeman and Mr Pate', *Music and Letters*, 1 (1969), 103.

Cyr, Mary, ★ 'On Performing 18th Century Haute-contre Roles', *The Musical Times*, 1977.

Hodgson, Frederick, 'The Countertenor', *The Musical Times*, 1965.

Hodgson, Frederick, 'The Contemporary Alto', *The Musical Times*, 1965.

Hough, John, 'The Historical Significance of the Counter Tenor', *Proceedings of the Royal Musical Assoc.*, 1937.

Jennings, Paul, 'Voice Beyond Compare', *Observer* Colour Magazine, 1971.

Johnson, David, 'The 18th Century Glee', *The Musical Times*, 1979.

Mendel, Arthur, 'Pitch in the 16th & 17th Centuries', *Musical Quarterly*, July 1948.

Mendel, Arthur, 'Pitch in Western Music Since 1500' a re-examination, *Acta Musicologica 50*, 1978.

Monk, Dr W. H., 'The Cultivation of Church Music', *Proceedings of the Royal Musical Assoc.*, VIII, 5/12/1881.

Prendergast, Dr A. H., 'The Man's Alto in English Music', *Zeitschrift der Internationalen Musikgesellschaft*, 1900.

Rose, Dr Bernard, 'Vocal Pitch in 16th and 17th Century Music', *Royal School of Church Music Journal*, 1965.

Sadie, Stanley, 'Concert Life in 18th Century England', *Proceedings of the Royal Musical Assoc.*, 1959.

Scholes, Percy, 'The Decline of the Male Alto', *Mirror of Music*, 1947.

Stubbs, G. Edward, 'The Adult Male Alto', Gray. N.Y. (Novello), 1908.

Tassel, Eric Van, 'Two Purcell Discoveries', *The Musical Times*, May, 1977.

Tatnell, Roland, 'Falsetto Practice: A Brief Study', *The Consort*, 1965.

Ward, Stuart Humphrey, 'The Male Alto in Church Music', *The Musical Times*, Oct., 1956.

Whitworth, John, 'The Countertenor Voice & its solo Repertoire in England', *Royal School of Church Music Journal*, 1965.

Wright, B. Forsyte, 'The Alto & Counter tenor Voices', *The Musical Times*, Nov., 1959.

Wulstan, David, 'Vocal Colour in English 16th Century Polyphony', *P.M.M.S. Journal*, 1980.

Anonymous, 'Men of the High "C"'s', *Newsweek*, 10 January 1972.

Zaslaw, Neal, ★'The Enigma of the Haute-contre', *The Musical Times*, 1974.

★ Both these articles had ensuing correspondence which should also be referred to. See also *Grove's Dictionary of Music and Musicians*, 5th and 6th editions.

Books

Behnke, Kate Emil, *The Technique of Singing*, Williams & Norgate, 1945.

Bridge, Sir F., *A Westminster Pilgrim*, Novello/Hutchinson, 1919.

Bumpus, John S., *A History of English Cathedral Music*, T. Werner Laurie, 1890.

Burney, Dr Charles, *The Handel Commemoration Festival, 1784*, London, 1785.

Butler, Charles, *The Principles of Musick*, London, 1636.

★Caesari, E. Herbert, *The Voice of the Mind*, Hale, 1951.

Critchley & Henson (Ed.), *Music and the Brain*, Heinemann, 1977.

Cummings, W. H., *Henry Purcell*, Sampson Low & Marston, 1881.

Dart, Thurston, *The Interpretation of Music*, Hutchinson, 1975 (4th ed.).

Dent, Edward J., *The Rise of Romantic Opera*, Cambridge University Press, 1976.

Donnington, Robert, *The Interpretation of Early Music*, Faber, 1975 edition.

Fellowes, E. H., *English Cathedral Music*, Methuen, 1941 (enlarged edition).

Fellowes, E. H., *English Madrigal Composers*, Oxford University Press, 1919.

Fiske, Roger, *English Theatre Music in the 18th Century*, Oxford University Press, 1973.

★Frisell, Anthony, *The Tenor Voice*, Bruce Humphries, Boston, 1964.

*Frisell, Anthony, *The Baritone Voice*, Crescendo Pub. Co., Boston, 1973.

Gardiner, Julian, *A Guide to Good Singing and Speech*, Cassell, 1968.

Greene, Margaret, *The Voice and its Disorders*, Pitman, 1957. Reprinted, 1972.

Hardwick, Michael & Mollie, *A Singularity of Voice*, Cassell, 1966. 1st ed. with Ardran & Wulstan appendix.

Hardwick, M. & M., *Alfred Deller: A Singularity of Voice*, Proteus, 1980. 2nd ed. expanded, but without appendix.

Harrison, Frank Ll., *Music in Medieval Britain*, Routledge & Kegan Paul, 1958.

Hawkins, Sir John, *A History of the Science of Music*, London, 1776.

*Hewlett, Arthur, *Thinking Afresh About the Voice*, Ernest George White Society, 1970. 2nd ed. 1973.

Holland, A. K., *Henry Purcell*, Penguin Books, 1933.

Kay, Elster, *Bel Canto*, Dobson, 1963.

Knapp, J. Merrill, *Selected List of Music for Men's Voices*, Princeton University Press, 1952.

Lysons, Rev D., *The History of the Meetings of the Three Choirs*, Gloucester, 1812.

Pahlen, Kurt, *Great Singers*, W. H. Allen, 1973.

*Palmer, E. Davidson, *A Manual of Voice Training*, Galliard.

Parrish & Ohl, *Masterpieces of Music before 1750*, Faber, 1952.

Percy (Ed.), *Northumberland Household Book*, London, 1770.

Pevsner, Nicholas, *The Englishness of English Art*, B.B.C., 1955 (The Architectural Press).

Pine, Edward, *The Westminster Abbey Singers*, Dobson, 1953.

Punt, Norman A., *The Singer's and Actor's Throat*, Heinemann.

*Reid, Cornelius, *The Free Voice*, Joseph Patelson Music House. Reprinted 1974.

Roberts, J. Varley, *A Practical Method of Training Choristers*, Oxford University Press, 1898 (1914 edition).

Robertson & Stevens, *The Pelican History of Music* Vol 1, Penguin Books, 1960. Rep. 1974.

Robertson & Stevens, *The Pelican History of Music* Vol 2, Penguin Books, 1963.

Stanley, D., *The Science of Voice*, Carl Fischer Inc. N.Y.

Steane, J. B., *The Grand Tradition*, Duckworth, 1974.

Stevens, John, *Music & Poetry in the Early Tudor Court*, Cambridge University Press, 1979.

Walker, Ernest, *A History of Music in England*, Oxford University Press, 1952 ed.

Westrup, J. A., *Henry Purcell*, Dent, 1937. Reprinted 1947.

*White, Ernest G., *The Voice Beautiful*, Dent, 3rd edition, 1931.

Young, Percy M., *Handel*, Dent, 1947. Reprinted 1948.
Young, Percy M., *A History of British Music*, Benn, 1973.
Young, Percy M., *The Choral Tradition*, Hutchinson, 1962.

★ Asterisked titles are recommended for the counter tenor vocal student.

INDEX